Wanderings In Corsica

Its History And Its Heroes
Vol. II

by

Ferdinand Gregorovius

Wanderings In Corsica
Its History And Its Heroes
Vol. II
by Ferdinand Gregorovius

ISBN: 978-93-68093-33-6

Published by

DOUBLE 9 BOOKS

2/13-B, Ansari Road
Daryaganj, New Delhi – 110002
info@double9books.com
www.double9books.com
Tel. 011-40042856

ABOUT THE AUTHOR

Ferdinand Gregorovius was a German historian, born on January 19, 1821, in Nidzica, Poland, and is best known for his work on the medieval history of Rome. Gregorovius developed a deep interest in the city of Rome and its historical significance, dedicating much of his career to exploring its medieval past. His most renowned work, History of the City of Rome in the Middle Ages, is a comprehensive study that spans several volumes and provides a detailed examination of the city's political, cultural, and religious developments during the medieval period. Gregorovius's scholarship is characterized by a thorough analysis of primary sources and a keen understanding of the historical forces that shaped Rome's evolution. His works also include studies on key figures in Roman history, such as Lucrezia Borgia: Daughter of Pope Alexander VI, which highlights his interest in the intricate lives of historical personalities. Throughout his career, Gregorovius was recognized for his intellectual rigor and contributions to historical research. He passed away on May 1, 1891, in Munich, Germany, leaving behind a legacy of important historical writings that continue to influence the study of medieval Rome and its role in European history.

CONTENTS

BOOK VIII
WANDERINGS IN CORSICA

BOOK IX
WANDERINGS IN CORSICA

BOOK VI

CHAPTER I
TO ISOLA ROSSA THROUGH NEBBIO

Crossing from Bastia the hills which form the continuation of the Serra of Cape Corso, you reach the district of Nebbio, on the other side of the island. The excellent road first ascends Monte Bello for about a league. To the left, you look down upon the plain of Biguglia and Furiani, and the large inlet into which the river Bevinco flows. On gaining the ridge, the sea becomes visible on both sides. The road now descends towards the western shore—the eastern has vanished, and the enchanting panorama of the Gulf of San Fiorenzo suddenly unfolds itself to the eye. A shore of low, reddish rocks, almost without vegetation, and singularly zigzagged, encircles the deep blue basin. The sight is grand, strange, and southern.

On the declivity of the mountain stands the gloomy village of Barbiguano; the road passes it through groves of chestnuts and olives. This road was made by Count Marbœuf, and it was here that Bernadotte worked among the other labourers. The *conducteur* of the Diligence pointed out to me that its vast curves describe an *M*.

We were now approaching the beautiful Gulf of San Fiorenzo, which lay within its silent, monotonous, red margin, smiling the "unnumbered smile" that Æschylus speaks of, from the countless waves and wavelets that crisped its lustrous surface. And from a valley watered by a winding brook smiled gaily back to it thousands on thousands of laurel-roses or oleanders, whose red blossoms clothed its slopes far and wide. In our northern homes the brook is glad when it can clothe its margin with alder and willow; here, in the beautiful south, it decks itself with the gorgeous oleander.

The region is almost entirely uncultivated. I saw frequently, here and there, forsaken or half-ruined houses, picturesque objects in the landscape, for they were covered over and over with ivy, whose festoons obscured the very doors and windows. In such little ivy houses must the elves dwell, and titter, and twinkle their roguish eyes when a sunbeam or the moonlight steals in through the lattice of creepers to see what knavery the little wights are about. The history of those who once lived there was perhaps bloody and cruel; the Barbary Corsairs may have expelled them, or the murderous wars with Genoa, or the Vendetta.

Old Genoese towers are seen at intervals along the coast.

The country becomes more and more picturesque in the neighbourhood of San Fiorenzo. To the right stretched now the full expanse of the gulf— to the left, sweeping round it in a wide semicircle, towered far in the background the amphitheatre of the hills. They are the proud hills of Col di Tenda, at the foot of which the Romans were once defeated by the Corsicans. They encircle the little province of Nebbio—the district around the Gulf of San Fiorenzo, towards which alone the amphitheatre of mountains opens. It is a hilly province of great aridity, but rich in wine, in fruit, in olives, and chestnuts. Since the earliest times, Nebbio has been considered as a natural stronghold, and all invaders of the island, from the Romans to the French, have sought to force an entrance, and to effect a firm footing at this point—a circumstance which has made it the theatre of innumerable conflicts.

Nebbio, as at present divided, contains four cantons or pieves—San Fiorenzo, Oletta, Murato, and Santo Pietro di Tenda. San Fiorenzo is the principal place.

We reached the little town, which consists of but few houses, and has only five hundred and eighty inhabitants, at mid-day. It has a magnificent situation on one of the finest gulfs of Corsica. The only large valley of Nebbio—the valley of Aliso—traversed by a stream of the same name, lies before the town. The Aliso flows lazily through a marsh that poisons the whole region with malaria. On its margin stood a solitary fan-palm, giving, in the sultry glare of noon, a tropical character to the whole landscape. Some women and children lay idling round a cistern, their metal water-pitchers beside them—a group that harmonized admirably with the palm.

The Corsican strand on the gulfs is, throughout, idyllic; its pictures have a half Homeric, half Old Testament character.

In a quarter of an hour I had walked over the town. A little fort, which, with its cupola-crowned tower, looks more like a Turkish mosque than a castle, protects the harbour, in which a few fishing-boats lay at anchor. The situation of San Fiorenzo is so singularly advantageous—the gulf, one of the finest in the Mediterranean, holds out such tempting commercial facilities, that one cannot but be astonished at the prevailing desolation. Napoleon, in Antommarchi's memoirs, mentions the place in these terms: "San Fiorenzo has one of the finest situations I have ever seen. It lies most favourably for commerce; it touches France, borders on Italy; its landing-places are safe and convenient; its roads can accommodate large fleets. I should have built there a large and beautiful city, which would have become a metropolis."

According to Ptolemy, the old city of Cersunum must have stood in the neighbourhood of the gulf. The considerable town of Nebbio lay here in the Middle Ages, and its ruins are still visible half a mile from the present San Fiorenzo. On an eminence rises still the old Cathedral of the Bishops of Nebbio, very much dilapidated, but still imposing. It exhibits the style of the Pisan Basilica, and was probably built in the eleventh or twelfth century. The church was dedicated to Santa Maria dell' Assunta. Beside it stand the ruins of the bishop's residence. The bishops who lived here were no less warlike than the most turbulent of the Corsican seigniors. They gave themselves the title of Counts of Nebbio, and it is related that they appeared in the popular assembly of the Terra del Commune with their swords by their side; and that when they read mass, they had always a pair of loaded pistols lying on the altar. The city fell into decay like Accia and Sagone, two other considerable cities and bishoprics of Corsica. At the present day many Roman coins are found in that quarter, and many urns have been dug out of Roman tombs there.

The more modern town of San Fiorenzo was one of the first places which gave its adherence to the Bank of Genoa, in consequence of which the city enjoyed many rights and privileges. The Bank sent over a Castellano and a Podestà yearly, who conducted affairs along with four consuls. In later wars, the Castle of San Fiorenzo was frequently of importance.

The fresh-caught fish with which our table was here supplied, were excellent. Scarcely had we despatched them when we resumed our journey. The road now for some distance leaves the shore, and ascends a range of hills which sometimes shut out the view of the sea. This coast country continues mountainous and barren into the province of Balagna, and as far as Isola Rossa. The Plutonic forces have scattered large fragments of rock on every side. They cover the declivities in gigantic blocks or shattered into debris; slate, limestone, granite, are everywhere visible.

The olive and the chestnut are no longer so abundant; but the wild olive-shrub (oleastro) covers the hills, with the arbutus, rosemary, myrtle, and erica. All this shrubbery had suffered from the sun; the reddish brown tinge of the twigs, the gray of the olive-bushes, and the weather-worn stones, gave the region, as far as the eye reached, a melancholy tone. The glimmering of the heated air is the only motion in this desert stillness; not a bird sings, only the grasshopper chirps. Sometimes you see a flock of black goats lying under an olive-tree, or scouring over the rocks, seized with the panic-terror.

From time to time we passed little lonely wayside taverns, where the mules of the *diligenza* were changed, or we stopped where a spring filled a stone trough, at which man and beast were equally glad to slake their thirst.

I saw in some places little fields of grain—barley and rye. The grain had been already cut down, and was being threshed upon the field. The arrangement for this is very simple. In the middle of the field is a little round threshing-floor, built of stone, and upon this the Corsican throws down his sheaves, and has them trodden out by oxen, which drag a heavy stone behind them. I observed that, contrary to the scriptural injunction, the ox was always muzzled. Innumerable threshing-floors of this description were scattered over the fields, yet no village was in sight. Near the threshing-floors stood little barns, four square erections of stone, with flat roofs. The circular threshing-floors, and these little gray houses, dotting the fields far and wide, had a most singular appearance; they seemed the dwellings of gnomes. The Corsican laughs when you tell him how the husbandman of the north swings the flail with his own arms; such galley-slave toil he would submit to at no price.

During the whole journey I saw no wheeled vehicle but our own. Now and again a Corsican met us on horseback; his double-barrel slung behind him, and his parasol over his head.

At length, after crossing the little river Ostriconi, we again approached the shore. The coast has frequently only an elevation of a hundred feet; then it again shoots upwards in the steepest and rudest forms. The mountains grow more and more imposing as you approach Isola Rossa. They are the romantic summits of Balagna—the Promised Land of the Corsicans, for it literally flows with honey and oil. Some of the mountains wore snow-caps, and glittered with crystalline splendour.

Yonder lies Isola Rossa before us on the strand! yonder the two gray towers of the Pisans! yonder the blood-red islet-cliffs that give the town its name! What an exquisite little idyl of the sea-shore and the sunset! Silent mountains bending over a silent sea, gray olives holding out to the pilgrim their branches of peace, a hospitable smoke ascending from the hearths—verily, I swear that I am come to the enchanted shore of the Lotus-eaters.

CHAPTER II
STRAND-IDYL OF ISOLA ROSSA

— —"Of which fruit what man soe'er
Once tasted, no desire felt he to come
With tidings back, or seek his country more.
But rather wish'd to feed on lotus still
With the Lotophagi, and to renounce
All thoughts of home." —*Odyssey*.

A large rural esplanade lies at the entrance of the little town, enclosed however within its walls, which look like the walls of gardens. In the centre of the esplanade rises a square fountain of granite, surmounted by a marble bust of Paoli. It had been placed there two months previously. Paoli is the founder of Isola Rossa. He founded it in the year 1758, when the war with the Genoese was at its hottest, and the Republic was in possession of the neighbouring fortified town of Algajola. He said at the time: "I have erected the gallows on which I shall hang Algajola." The Genoese came with their gun-boats to hinder the operations, but the new town rose under their hail of balls; and Isola Rossa has now 1860 inhabitants, and is important as the emporium and principal seaport of the oil-abounding Balagna.

I found some children playing round the fountain; among them, a beautiful boy of six, with the darkest curling hair, and large, dark, impressive eyes. The child was lovely as an angel. "Do you know, children," I asked, "who that man is there on the fountain?" "Yes, we know," said they, "it is Pasquale Paoli." The children asked me what country I came from; and when I told them to guess, they guessed all the countries, and at last Egypt, but they knew nothing of Germany. Since then, they follow me wherever I go; I cannot get rid of them. They sing me songs, and bring me coral-dust, and painted shells from the shore. I find them everywhere; and they bring their companions to see me, so that, like the Piper of Hameln,[A] I draw crowds of children after me, and they accompany me even into the sea. Earth-shaking Neptune is friendly, and the blue-footed Nereids approve, and the dolphins play close by, among the crystal waves.

This is a place where one may well be a child among children. The sense of remoteness and seclusion one has here, on the shore and in the woods, soothes and strengthens. The little town lies still as a dream. The little flat-roofed houses with their green jalousies, the two snow-white towers of the little church—everything has a miniature look, and an air of privacy and retirement. In the sea stand the three red cliffs; an ancient tower keeps watch over them, and tells in the silent evening old stories of the Saracens; swifts and blue wild pigeons circle round it. I ascended these rocks in the evening; they are connected with the land by a dike. A grotto difficult of access, and open to the sea, penetrates on one side the rugged cliff. Not far off a new mole is being built; French workmen were occupied in elevating huge cubical masses of cemented stone by machinery, and then launching them into the waves.

The evening landscape is very beautiful, from the Red Islands. To the right, the sea and the whole peninsula of Cape Corso veiled in haze; to the left, running out into the gulf, a red tongue of land; in the foreground the little city, fishing-skiffs, and one or two sailing-vessels in the harbour. In the background three glorious hills—Monte di Santa Angiola, Santa Susanna, and the rugged Monte Feliceto; on their slopes olive-groves and numerous black villages. Here and there glow the fires of the goat-herds.

Nowhere can people lead a more patriarchal and peaceable life than do the inhabitants of Isola Rossa. The land yields its produce, and the sea too. They have enough. In the evening they sit and gossip on the mole, or they angle in the still water, or wander in the olive-groves and orange-gardens. Through the day the fisherman prepares his nets, and the handicraftsman sits plying his work under the mulberry-tree before his door. Here should be no lack of song and guitar. I had made myself at home in a little coffeehouse. The young hostess could sing beautifully; at my wish a little company assembled in the evening, and I had twanging of guitars and charming Corsican songs to my heart's content.

The children who followed me sang me songs too, the Marseillaise, the Girondist's March, and Bertram's Parting, the last with new words in honour of the President of France, the refrain always closing with *Vive Louis Napoléon!* Little Camillo could sing the Marseillaise best.

We looked for shells on the beach. There are as many of them as you can desire opposite the little nunnery which stands in the garden by the sea, and in which the Sisters of the Madonna alle Grazie live. The Madonna-

Sisters have an enchanting view of sea and hill from their villa; and perhaps some of them have dreams of their lost romance of life and love, when the golden sickle of the moon is shining so beautifully above Monte Reparata as it is now. The strand is, as far as you can see, snow-white, broidered with coral-dust and the most exquisite shells. Little Camillo was indefatigable in picking up what he thought would please me. He was fondest, however, of the little living *leppere*—mussels which suck themselves fast to stones. These he brought out of the water, and forthwith consumed with great gusto, wondering that I would not share his feast. In the evening we bathed together, and swam through the phosphorescent waves amid a million sparks.

Beautiful child-world! It is good sometimes when its voices begin again to speak. The people of Isola Rossa will not let me leave them. They have taken it into their heads that I am a rich baron, and propose that I should buy an estate beside them. To lose one's-self here might be worth while.

"Yes, the Vendetta is our ruin!" said a citizen of the Red Islands to me. "Do you see the little mercato, our market-hall yonder, with its white pillars? Last year a citizen was walking up and down there; suddenly a shot was fired, and the man fell dead! In broad daylight Massoni had come into the town, had put a bullet into the breast of his foe yonder in the mercato, and away he was again into the hills; and that all in broad daylight!"

There is the house where Paoli was surprised, when the famous Dumouriez made his plot to capture him. And here landed, for the last time, Theodore von Neuhoff, King of the Corsicans, only to put out again to sea—for he had dreamed his dream of royalty to an end.

I went one day with an Alsatian of the tenth regiment, which is at present distributed over Corsica, to Monte Santa Reparata, and the paese of the same name. It is difficult to paint in words the picture of such a Corsican village among the hills. The reader will come nearest to it if he imagines rows of blackish towers, divided longitudinally so as properly to be only half towers, and furnished with windows, doors, and loop-holes. The houses are constructed of granite stones, often totally undressed, generally only covered with a coating of clay, from which sometimes plants grow. Very narrow and steep stairs of stone lead up to the door. The mountain Corsicans probably inhabited the same sort of dwellings in the times of the Etruscans and Carthaginians. I found everywhere poverty and a want of cleanliness; swine housing with the human inmates in cavernous little rooms, into which the light fell through the door. These poor people live high up on the mountains, in an ocean of air and light, and yet their abodes are those of troglodytes. I saw a pale young woman issue from one of these dens with a child in her arms, and asked her if she had ever felt herself well, since she lived constantly in the dark. She stared at me, and laughed.

In another house, I found a mother putting her three children to bed. All three stood naked on the clay floor, and looked sickly and wasted. The beds on which the poor things slept were very wretched little nests. These stout-hearted mountaineers are nurtured in poverty and misery. They are at once huntsmen, herdsmen, and husbandmen. Their sole wealth is the olive, the oil of which they sell in the towns. But not every one is rich in olives. Here, therefore, life is rendered miserable, not by the evils of civilisation, but by those of a primitive condition on which no advance has been made.

I went into the church, the black façade of which attracted me. The white spire is new. The steeples of the Corsican churches are not pointed, but end in a belfry, with a pierced, curving roof. The interior of the church had a gallery and a great altar, a singularly uncouth affair of whitened stone, with most extravagant decorations. Above the altar stood the inscription in Latin: "Holy Reparata, pray for thy people;" *populus*—it sounds antique and democratic. Some rude attempts at painting were meant to adorn the walls, and there were niches with half-projecting columns on each side, their capitals Corinthian, or entirely fanciful. An interdict lies at present on the Church of the Holy Reparata, and there is no mass read in it. On the death of their priest, the people refused to accept of the successor sent by the Bishop of Ajaccio. They split into two parties, and the feud became bloody. The interdict which was in consequence laid upon the church, has not yet settled the dispute.

I passed through the narrow and dirty lanes of the village to the edge of the valley, from which there is an extensive view of the range of hills enclosing the Balagna. Many brown villages lie along the circle of the hills, and many olive-woods. The arid rocks contrast powerfully with the green of the gardens and groves. The Corsican who guided me to this point, stuttered, and had erysipelas in his face; I believe he was half-witted. I made him name to me the villages in the dale of the Balagna. He told me, in a thick gurgling tone of voice, a great deal that I only half understood, but I understood very well what he meant when he pointed to more than one place, and gurgled:

Ammazzato, ammazzato col colpo di fucile,—he was showing me the spots among the rocks where human blood had been shed. I shuddered, and left his disagreeable company as speedily as possible. I returned through the paese of Oggilione, descending by narrow shepherds' paths through olive-groves. Armed Corsicans came riding up on little horses, which clambered nimbly from rock to rock. Evening fell, and the desolate Monte Feliceto lay bathed in softest colours; a bell among the hills tinkled the Ave Maria, and a goat-herd on a slope blew his horn. All this harmonized beautifully; and by the time I reached Isola Rossa, my mood was once more idyllic.

The contrasts here are frightfully abrupt—child-life, shepherd-life, and blood-red murder.

CHAPTER III
VITTORIA MALASPINA

"Ed il modo ancor m'offende." —*Francesca di Rimini.*

I had become acquainted in Bastia with a gentleman of Balagna, Signor Mutius Malaspina. He is a descendant of the Tuscan Malaspinas, who governed Corsica in the eleventh century. Through his wife he became connected with the Paoli family, for Vittoria Malaspina was a great-granddaughter of Hyacinth Paoli, and descended from the renowned Clemens. Her father, Giovanni Pietri, Councillor of State, is one of the most meritorious public men in Corsica, and universally beloved.

Signor Malaspina had offered me hospitality in his house at Monticello, a paese in the hills a few miles above Isola Rossa, and I had gladly consented to be a guest in a house where Pasquale had once lived, and from which he has dated so many of his letters. Malaspina gave me a letter to present at his house, which, he said, I should not fail to find open, even though he himself might not have yet returned.

I had accordingly come to Isola Rossa with the intention of going up to Monticello, and spending some days there. I learned, however, on my journey, what I had been totally ignorant of, and what Malaspina had concealed from me—the fearful misfortune, namely, which, less than three years previously, had there befallen his family; so that I now did not know which to be most astonished at, the unparalleled nature of the catastrophe, or the character of the Corsican, who, notwithstanding what had happened, offered hospitality to an unknown stranger. I could no longer prevail upon myself to accept of it in a house where it had been murdered, but I went up to Monticello, to honour misfortune with human sympathy.

The house of the Malaspina family lies at the entrance of the paese, on the plateau of a rock hung with verdure; it is a large old mansion of the earliest times, stern, strong, and castle-like. Dark cypresses mourn round its terraces. Even from a distance they announce to the wanderer the tragedy that was enacted beside them. A neglected little esplanade lies at the entrance of the house. There is a little chapel on it encircled by young plane-trees; it covers the family burial-vault.

Passing under the arched doorway of the mansion, I ascended a narrow and gloomy stone staircase, and looked round for the inhabitants. The house seemed utterly forsaken and desolate. I walked through large dreary rooms, which the genius of comfort had deserted. At length I found the housekeeper, an old lady in mourning, and along with her, a girl eight years old, the youngest daughter. It cost me a great deal of trouble to gain any approach to a welcome from the ancient dame, but she gradually laid aside her distrust.

I put no questions. But the little Felicina asked me of her own accord to come and see her mother's room, and in her innocence said a great deal more than enough.

The old Marcantonia sat down beside me, and told me the story; and what she related I shall faithfully repeat, withholding only the unhappy man's surname, and the name of his native city.

"In the summer of 1849, a great many Italians fled their country, and came over to Corsica. There was one among them whom the authorities were going to send back, but Signor Pietri, who is kind to everybody, so managed matters that he was allowed to stay, and he took him into his own house in Isola Rossa. The stranger—his name was Giustiniano, stayed a month with Signor Pietri down there in Isola Rossa, and as at the end of that time the Signor had to go to Ajaccio to the council, Signor Mutius and Signora Vittoria brought Giustiniano up here. He had every kind of enjoyment with us that he could desire, horses and hunting, a good table, and plenty of company. The Italian was very pleasant and very affable, but he was melancholy, because he had to live in a foreign country. Every one liked the Signora Vittoria, and most of all, the poor; she was an angel."

"Was she beautiful?"

"She had a delicate complexion, still blacker hair than Felicina, and wonderfully beautiful hands and feet. She was large and full. The Italian, instead of finding himself happy in our house, where he enjoyed the most kind and friendly treatment possible, grew more melancholy every day. He began to speak little and to eat little, and looked as pale as death. He wandered about for hours among the hills, and often sat as if oppressed with some great grief, without saying a word."

"Did he never make any disclosure of his love to the Signora?"

"He once followed her into her room, but she made him instantly quit it, and told the servant to say nothing of the affair to her master. Some days before the 20th of December — it is almost three years ago now — Giustiniano began to look so wretched, that we believed he would become seriously ill. We talked of his going to Bastia, for the sake of the change, and he himself had expressed a wish to do so. There were three days during which he did not eat a morsel. One morning, when I brought him his coffee as usual, I found his door locked. I came again after a while, and called him by name. He opened the door. I was terrified to see how he looked. I asked him, 'Signor, what ails you?' He laid his hand on my shoulder, as I now lay mine on yours, and said to me: 'Ah! Marcantonietta, if you knew how sore my heart is!' He did not say another word. I saw a pistol lying on his table, and powder in a paper, and bullets. He had made Felicina's elder sister fetch them for him from the bottega, the evening before. He now said he was going back to Bastia, to take ship there for another country. He took farewell of us all, and rode away down towards Isola Rossa. It was the 20th of December. On the morning of that day, the Signora Vittoria had said to me: 'I had a bad dream last night; I thought my sick *compare* (godmother, gossip) was dying. I will go and see her to-day, and take a cordial with me.' For that was her way. She often visited sick people, and took them wine, oil, or fruits."

Here Marcantonia wept bitterly.

"Signor Malaspina had gone off to Speloncato; I was out, there was nobody in the house but the sick Madamigella Matilde — she was a relative of the Signora — the youngest children, and a maid-servant. It was the afternoon. As I was returning home, I heard a shot. I thought there were huntsmen in the hills, or that some one was blasting rocks. But soon after, I heard a second shot, and it seemed to come from the house. I was trembling in every limb when I entered the house; and, in terrible anxiety, I asked the girl, where is the Signora? She was trembling too, and she said: 'Ah, *Dio mio!* She is up stairs in her room changing her dress, for she is going to see the sick woman.' Run, I said, and see after her."

"The girl came rushing down stairs again as pale as a corpse. 'Something must have happened,' said she, 'for the Signora's door is standing wide open, and everything in the room is tumbled up and down, and the stranger's door is locked.' I ran up with the girl, and Felicina and her sister — it was frightful to see my poor Signora's room — the Italian's door was fastened.

We knocked, we called, at last we tore the door off its hinges—there, Signor, we saw before us!—but I shall tell you no more."

No, not a word more, Marcantonia! I rose, thrilled and shocked, and went out. The little Felicina and the housekeeper followed me. They led me to the little chapel. The child and the old woman kneeled down before the altar, and prayed. I took a myrtle twig from the altar, and threw it on the spot beneath which Vittoria lies buried. And sadly I wandered down towards Isola Rossa.

One can hardly grasp in thought the enormity of such a deed, much less prevail on one's-self to talk of it. Giustiniano had suddenly returned after leaving Monticello, and secretly gone up stairs; his room, and that of Vittoria, were on the same flat, separated by a passage. Giustiniano rushed in on her, armed with a pistol and a dagger. He wrestled fearfully with the powerful woman. He threw her on the floor, he dragged her into his room;—she was already dying, pierced with his dagger-thrusts. Her beautiful hair was found strewed about the floor, and the room all disordered with the struggle. Giustiniano threw the unhappy lady on his bed—he shot her with a pistol through the temples—he took her rings from her fingers, and put them on his own—then he lay down by her side, and blew out his brains.

So they were found by old Marcantonia, and poor little Felicina, then a child of five; weeping, she cried: "That is my mother's blood"—a fearful sight, a horrid catastrophe, to be impressed for life on a child's soul. The people of Monticello wanted to tear Giustiniano limb from limb. Malaspina, who had returned without the least misgiving from Speloncato, prevented this. The body was interred among the rocks of Mount Monticello. Vittoria was thirty-six years old, and the mother of six children. Giustiniano had scarcely reached his twenty-fifth year.

I found Mutius Malaspina a plain and unpretending man, with iron features and an iron composure. I should have refrained from telling the tragic story here, were it not that it is already in every one's mouth, and even published in a little book printed in Bastia, which contains also sonnets on Vittoria. The memory of Vittoria Malaspina will endure while the island lasts. When centuries have passed, the melancholy fate of the noble woman, which I learned from the mouth of a member of the family in the house itself, will have become a popular tradition. Even when I was at Monticello, I could see how quickly real events, in the mouths of the people, began to assume something of the mythical. The same old housekeeper informed me, that the ghost of poor Vittoria had appeared to a sick woman in the paese. And soon the report will spread, too, that her murderer rises nightly from his tomb among the rocks, pale and restless as when in life, and glides towards the house where he perpetrated the dreadful deed.

Disposed to take a very gloomy view of human nature, I descended the hills, musing on the narrow boundary at which love, the noblest of all passions, becomes a criminal and terrific madness, if it passes it by a hair's-breadth. How closely in the human soul the divine borders on the devilish! and how comes it that the same feeling supplies the material for both? I saw neither the hills nor the serene sea; I cursed all Corsica, and wished I had never set foot on its bloody soil. Suddenly the beautiful child Camillo came leaping to my side. The little fellow had followed me over stock and stone up the hills. He now came towards me, holding out a handful of bramble-berries that he had plucked, and with bright friendly eyes asked me to take some. The sight of the innocent child brought back my good humour. It seemed as if he had thrown himself in my way, to show me how beautiful and innocent man leaves the hands of Nature. Camillo ran along by my side, bounding from stone to stone, till all at once he said: "I am tired; I want to sit a little." He sat down on a fragment of rock. I thought I had never seen a more beautiful child. When I said this to his elder brother, he answered: "Yes, everybody likes Camilluccio; in the procession of Corpus Domini he was an angel, and had a snow-white robe on, and a great palm-branch in his hand." I looked with delight upon the boy as he sat upon the rock, gazing silently from his large eyes, the beautiful raven curls hanging wild about his face. His little dress was torn; for his parents were poor. All at once he began unasked to sing the Marseillaise:—

"Allons enfans de la patrie...

Contre nous de la tyrannie

L'étendard sanglant est levé."

It was strange to hear the Marseillaise from the mouth of so lovely a child, and to see the grave face with which he sang. But how historical this bloody song sounds in the mouth of a Corsican boy! As little Camillo sang—"Tyranny has raised its bloody flag against us!" I thought, Poor child! Heaven guard you, and grant that you do not fall some day yet from the bullet of the Vendetta, nor wander as avenger in the hills.

As we approached Isola Rossa, we were alarmed by a red glow, as of flame, in the little town. I hastened on, believing fire had broken out. It proved to be a bonfire. The children, girls and boys, had kindled a huge bonfire on the Paoli Place, had joined hands and were dancing round about it in a ring, laughing and singing. They sang numberless little couplets of their own composition, some of which I still remember:—

Amo un presidente,	I love a president—
Sta in letto senza dente.	He lies in bed, and has no teeth.
Amo un ufficiale,	I love an officer—
Sta in letto senza male.	He lies in bed, and nothing ails him.
Amo un pastore,	I love a herdsman—
Sta in letto senza amore.	He lies in bed, and has nothing to love.
Amo un cameriere,	I love a valet—
Sta in letto senza bere.	He lies in bed, and has nothing to drink.

The youngsters seemed to have an exhaustless store of these little verses, and kept singing and swinging round the fire as if they would never stop. The melody was charming, *naïve*, childlike. I was so pleased with this extemporized child's festival, that in honour of it I improvised one or two couplets myself, whereupon the little folks burst into such uproarious shouts of merriment, as made all Isola Rossa ring again.

On the following day, I drove in a *char-à-banc* to Calvi. Little Camillo was standing beside the vehicle as I stepped into it, and said sorrowfully: *Non me piace che tu ci abbandoni*—I'm not pleased that you're going to leave us. The wanderer fills his note-book with sketches of mountain, stream, and town, records deeds honourable and vile, why not for once preserve the picture of a beautiful child? When long years have elapsed, the face still returns upon our inward vision, and haunts the memory like a lovely song.

CHAPTER IV
FROM ISOLA ROSSA TO CALVI

My vetturino was not long in informing me that I had the honour of travelling in an extraordinary vehicle. "For," said he, "in this same *char-à-banc* I drove last year the three great bandits—Arrighi, Massoni, and Xaver. They came up to me as I was driving along, all armed to the teeth, and ordered me to take them to Calvi. I did so without saying a word, and after that they let me turn back unharmed. Now they are all dead."

The road from Isola Rossa to Calvi keeps constantly by the coast. The ruins of many villages, destroyed by the Saracens, are visible on the hills. Above Monticello lie the ruins of a castle which belonged to the famous Giudice della Rocca, the lieutenant of the Pisans. This righteous judge of his people still lives in the memory of the Corsicans. He was just, they tell, even towards the brutes. One day he heard an unusual bleating among the lambs of a flock in the Balagna; he asked the shepherd what ailed them, and the man confessed that they were bleating for hunger, as the milk had been taken from their dams. Giudice thereupon ordered that the sheep should henceforth not be milked till the lambs were satisfied.

The first town I passed was Algajola, a seaport of considerable antiquity, but with only two hundred inhabitants. Lying in ruins, as the bombs of the English left it sixty years ago, it bears mournful and striking testimony to the present state of Corsica. Even the inhabited houses resemble black ruins. A friendly old man, whom the wars of Napoleon had at one time taken as far as Berlin, showed me what was remarkable in Algajola, pointing out to me a great heap of stones as the *Palazzo della Communità*. In the time of the Genoese, Algajola was the central point of the Balagna; and as it was so situated that the inhabitants of every village in the province could travel to it and return home the same day, the Genoese fortified it, and raised it to a residency of one of their lieutenants of the island.

But the most notable thing about the little town is its story of two faithful lovers, Chiarina and Tamante. The French had condemned Tamante to death; but his true-love armed herself, and with the aid of her friends rescued him from execution. The noble deeds that spring from faithful love are everywhere honoured by the people, and become immortal in their traditions; the story of Chiarina and Tamante is popular over the whole of Italy, and I have found it selling as a cheap pamphlet in the streets of Rome.

On the shore near Algajola there is a quarry of singularly beautiful blue granite. I saw a pillar there which would do honour to an Indian or Egyptian temple. It is sixty feet in length, and twelve feet in diameter. It has been lying for years neglected on the field, exposed to the injuries of the weather, and noticed at most by the passing traveller, or the eagle that alights on it. Originally intended for a monument to Napoleon in Ajaccio, it was never removed from the quarry, as the necessary sum could not be raised for its transport. It will probably now be conveyed to Paris. The enormous block which supports the Vendôme pillar in Paris is also of this same exquisite granite of Algajola. With what just pride, therefore, may the Corsican stand before that pillar of Austerlitz, and tell the French: "My country produced both the great man up yonder, and the glorious granite on which he stands."

By and bye I reached Lumio, a high-lying village, whose black-brown, tower-like houses it had been at a distance totally impossible to distinguish from the rocks. Green jalousies marked here and there the house of a man of some means. Descendants of the ancient seigniors still live in all these villages; and men of the proudest names, and endless pedigree, live in the gloomy paeses of Corsica among the common people, and mix in their society. Nowhere in the world, perhaps, is so much democratic equality in social life to be found as in this island, where distinctions of rank are hardly ever visible, and the peasant conducts himself before the noble with the upright bearing of an independent man, as I have often myself seen. Above Calvi, in this region, lives Peter Napoleon, Lucian's son—at the time I was in Corsica the only Bonaparte resident on the native island of the family. The Balagnese are fond of him; they say he is a good hunter, associates freely with the shepherds, and has not forgotten that his forefathers belonged to the Corsicans. The election of Louis Napoleon of course filled the Corsican people with pride and exultation. I found the portrait of this man everywhere throughout the island, and heard his energy praised as Corsican energy. Men of more insight, however, did not allow their patriotism to carry them so far; and I heard Corsicans express the opinion that the Napoleons were tyrants, and the *last* oppressors of liberty.

Lumio has many orange-orchards, and such an astonishing quantity of cactus-hedges as I found nowhere else, except at Calvi. The cactus has here the size and stem of a tree. The view of the valley and gulf of Calvi from the mountains of Lumio is very beautiful. Calvi lies on a tongue of land at the foot of the hills of Calenzana. With its dark flat houses, two cupolas rising high above them, and the walls of the fort, which stands at the extreme end of the little peninsula, it has a striking resemblance to a Moorish city.

Calvi is the leading town of the smallest of the arrondissements of Corsica. This arrondissement contains six cantons, thirty-four communes, and about 25,000 inhabitants, and extends over almost the entire north-west of the island, mountains and coast. Not one half of it is under cultivation, for the whole district of coast from Galeria lies completely waste. The Balagna alone is well cultivated, and it has also the larger proportion of the population.

The little city of Calvi, containing at present about 1680 inhabitants, owes its origin to Giovaninello, lord of Nebbio, the bitter enemy of Giudice della Rocca, and an adherent of Genoa. The town, therefore, became subject to Genoa, and it remained constantly true to the Republic. Like the Bonifazians, the Calvese were allowed important privileges. In the time of Filippini, Calvi contained four hundred hearths; and he terms it one of the principal cities of Corsica for two reasons—its antiquity, and the handsomeness of the houses, as he adds, "in comparison with those of the interior." The Bank of Genoa, he says, built the fortress; and, according to some, its erection cost 1850 scudi.

Calvi lies on the tongue of land which terminates one of the ranges of hills that encircle the extensive basin round the gulf. These hills are bare, and consist of granite and porphyry. They form an imposing amphitheatre. Olives and vines thrive on their slopes, and their base is covered with yew, and shrubbery of myrtle, albatro, and tinus, the blossoms of which supply the bees with honey. From this arises the bitterness of the Corsican honey, to which allusion is made by Ovid and Virgil. Calenzana particularly abounds in honey. A stream flows through the valley of these hills, and forms in the neighbourhood of Calvi a marsh, the exhalations of which are dangerous. This marsh has the name of *La Vigna del Vescovo*—the Bishop's Vineyard— and its origin is connected with one of those significant popular traditions which so much amuse the traveller in Corsica.

CHAPTER V
CALVI AND ITS MEN

The miasma of the marsh made the Borgo of Calvi—the little suburb—unhealthy. More salubrious is the air of the fortress above, which encloses the city proper. I ascended to this old Genoese citadel—the strongest fortification in Corsica next to Bonifazio. Above the gate, I read these words—*Civitas Calvis semper fidelis*. Calvi was unfailingly true to the Genoese. Fidelity is always beautiful when it is not slavish, and Calvi was in fact a Genoese colony. The proverbial fidelity of Calvi, as expressed in the motto over its gate, has become in more than one sense historical. When the republican General, Casabianca, after the heroic defence of Calvi against the English, was obliged to capitulate in the year 1794, one of the stipulations of surrender was, that the old inscription above mentioned should remain untouched. This condition was honourably fulfilled, as the inscription itself still testifies.

There is only one point in regard to which Genoa and the "ever-faithful" Calvi are at feud. For the Calvese affirm that Columbus was a fellow-countryman of theirs. They say that his family, admittedly Genoese, had at an early period settled in Calvi. A very earnest contest was in fact for some time maintained about this question of birth, as formerly the seven cities disputed about the cradle of Homer. It is affirmed that Genoa suppressed the family register of the Colombos of Calvi, and changed the name of one of the streets of the town, the Colombo Street, into the street *Del Filo*. I find it also recorded that inhabitants of Calvi were the first Corsicans who sailed to America. I am informed further, that the name Colombo still exists in Calvi. Corsican authors even of the present day claim the great discoverer as their fellow-countryman; and Napoleon, during his residence in Elba, proposed instituting historical researches in regard to this point. We shall forbear attempting to settle it; Columbus in his will calls himself a native Genoese. The world might become envious if it were established that fate had bestowed upon the little Corsica the man who was greater even than Napoleon.

Valiant men enough do honour to Calvi; and when we look at this little town within the fortress, and see that it is nothing but the heap of black and shattered ruins to which the bombs of the English reduced it, we read in its chronicle of desolation the history of departed heroes. Very strange is the aspect of a city, which, shattered by a bombardment almost a century ago, remains still at the present day in ruins. The clock of time seems here in Corsica to have stood still. An iron hand has maintained its grasp upon the past—upon the old popular customs—the dirges of the Etruscans, the family feuds of the Middle Ages, the barbarism of the Vendetta, the ancient, simple modes of life, and the ancient heroism; and as the people live in cities that have become gray in ruin, they live socially, in a state that, for the cultivated nations, is hoary tradition.

In the principal church of Calvi, whose Moorish cupola is pierced by the balls of the English, they show the tomb of a family that bears the dearest, the most precious of all names—the name Libertà—Freedom! It is the old heroic family of the Baglioni which has this title. In the year 1400, when certain aristocrats in Calvi had made themselves tyrants of the town, and were on the point of putting the city into the hands of the Arragonese, a young man named Baglioni arose, and suddenly, with his friends, attacked the two tyrants in the citadel, as once Pelopidas fell upon the tyrants of Thebes, put them to the sword, and called the people to freedom. From that call—Libertà! Libertà!—came the surname which his grateful fellow-citizens immediately gave him, and which his family has ever since borne. The three heroic brothers, Piero, Antonio, and Bartolommeo Libertà, were descendants of Baglioni. They had emigrated to Marseilles. This city was in the hands of the League, and, though left alone, continued to defy Henry IV. after he had entered Paris, and received the submission of the House of Guise. Casaux, the consul of the League, was the tyrant of Marseilles; he had determined to surrender the town to the Spanish fleet, which was commanded by the celebrated Andreas Doria. Piero Libertà, with his brothers and other bold men of Marseilles, conspired to rescue the city. Piero collected them in his house, and, when they had matured their plan, they proceeded daringly to its instant execution. They burst into the citadel of Marseilles, and, with his own hand, Piero Libertà sent a lance through the throat of the consul Casaux. When he had either slain or disarmed all the guards, he shut the doors of the castle, and, with the bloody sword in his hand, he ran through the city, shouting, "Libertà! Libertà!" The people rose at his call, ran to arms, stormed the towers and fortifications of Marseilles, and freed the city. Immediately the Duke of Guise took possession of Marseilles in the name of Henry IV., and he dated from the Camp of Rosny, the 6th March 1596, a memorial eulogizing Piero Libertà. He made him supreme judge of Marseilles, captain of the Porta Reale, governor of *Nostra Donna della Guardia*, and heaped upon him other honours besides. This happened at the same time that another Corsican, Alfonso Ornano, the son of Sampiero, won Lyons for the King of France, on which occasion Henry IV. called out: "Now am I king."

Piero Libertà died not many years after the deliverance of Marseilles. The town buried him in state, and placed his statue in the City Hall. These words were engraven on the pedestal of the statue: *Petro Libertæ Libertatis assertori, heroi, malorum averrunco, pacis civiumque restauratori, &c.*

The reproductive power that characterizes the Corsican families is truly remarkable. Any one who has directed attention to the history of this nation will have found, that almost universally the abilities of the father descend to the son and the son's sons.

It is not with a light heart that I now pass from the tomb of the family of Libertà, to that field of Calenzana, where lie graves of Schiavitù—of Slavery. They are the graves of five hundred brave Germans, sons of my fatherland, who were bought and sold, and who fell there at Calenzana.

I have told how it was in the history of the Corsicans. The Emperor Charles VI. had sold a corps of German auxiliaries to the Genoese, and the Genoese despatched them to Corsica. On the 2d of February 1732, the Corsicans under their general, Ceccaldi, attacked the German troops at Calenzana; these latter were commanded by Camillo Doria and Des Devins. After a fearful struggle the imperial troops were beaten, and five hundred Germans lay dead on the field of Calenzana. The Corsicans buried the strangers who had come to fight against the liberties of their country, on the beautiful mountain-slope between Calvi and Calenzana. Beneath a foreign soil rest there the bones of my unhappy countrymen. Rocks of dark, blood-tinged porphyry stand near. Myrtles and flowering herbs crown the graves. And still every year at the Festival of All-Souls, the clergy of Calenzana visit these graves of their foes—*Camposanto dei Tedeschi*, as people call the field of Calenzana; and sprinkle with consecrated water the ground where the poor mercenaries fell. Such is the vengeance the Corsican takes upon the foes who come to assassinate his independence! I feel as if on me—one of the few Germans who have ever stood upon the graves of the mercenaries of Calenzana, and probably the only German who has thus made public mention of them—devolved the duty of thanking, in the name of my country, the noble Corsican people for their generous sympathy and wide-hearted humanity.

The Corsicans gave my countrymen a grave; I will write their epitaph:—

We came, five hundred luckless mercenaries,
Sold by the Emperor to Genoa,
To crush the freedom of the Corsicans—
We came, and paid the penalty in blood;
We expiate the crime in foreign graves.
Call us not guilty, give us tender pity,
The foeman's soil a pitying shelter lends.
Despise not, wanderer, children of a time
So dark; ye who now live, wipe off the stain!

Those were in truth dark times when our fathers were sold like a brutish herd, and sent to Corsica, it might be, or to America. But Pasquale Paoli arose here—in the other hemisphere Washington; and beyond the Rhine, the rights of man became clamorous. The reproach of these old times was wiped away, and with the rest of it, the reproach of Calenzana; for the children of those who lie here in slavish graves fought for wife and child and the independence of their country, fought for European freedom, and vanquished the Corsican despot.

The sun is setting; it throws its splendours on the gulf, and the rocky hills of Calenzana are all a-glow. How magical is this southern haze of distance, and how delicate the tones of the colouring! All transition has a profound effect upon the human soul. On the boundary line where the transition is made from Being to non-existence, or from non-existence to Being, lies the fairest and deepest poesy of life. It is not otherwise in history. Its most wonderful phenomena invariably occur on the boundary where two different periods of culture touch, and pass the one into the other; as in Nature, the seasons of the year and the times of the day exhibit the most glorious phenomena when they are merging into one another. I believe it is the same with the history of the individual. Here too, the transitions from one period to another, from one phase of culture to another, are full of enchantment, and more fruitful than all other periods, for it is in them alone that the germs of poetry and productive power are developed.

There is a world-forsaken loneliness about Calvi which is almost fabulous. No movement on the still mirror of the gulf—no ship on all those miles of sea—no bird cleaving the air—the black tower rising yonder on the snow-white strand like a dark shape in a dream. But here sits an eagle, a magnificent creature, resting with a grave majesty—now he takes flight, and with mighty strokes of his pinions makes for the hills. He is satiated with blood.—There I have started a fox, the first I have met with in Corsica, where these animals attain an astonishing size, and, like wolves, commit depredations among the sheep. He was sitting much at his ease upon the shore, apparently enjoying the rose-red of the waves, and quite lost in the contemplation of nature, for he was in such a brown study that I got within five paces of him. Suddenly Master Reynard jumped up, and as the strand was narrow I had the pleasure of stopping his way, and making him lose his composure for a minute or two. Hereupon he doubled cunningly, turned the enemy's flank, and ran merrily away into the hills. He is very well off in Corsica, where the beasts make him their king, as there are no wolves.

After dark, I stepped into a boat, and rowed about in the gulf. What a glorious night-picture! The sky of Italy set with sparkling stars—a magic transparency in the atmosphere—away at the extremity of the headland a flashing beacon—lights in the castle of Calvi—one or two sleeping ships on the water—herdsmen's fires on the dark hills above—the waves phosphorescing round the boat, and the drops sparkling as they fall from the oars—in the deep stillness the sounds of a mandoline borne from the shore.

CHAPTER VI
A MUSICAL FESTIVAL

The poetry of this evening was not yet exhausted. I had scarcely fallen asleep in my little locanda, when the twanging of citherns, and the sounds of voices singing in parts, awakened me. They played and sang for at least an hour before the house. It was meant for a young girl who was one of its inmates. They sang first a serenade, then Voceros or dirges. Singular, that a young girl should be serenaded with dirges; and the proper serenade itself with which they commenced was as mournful as a Vocero. It is impossible to tell how overpoweringly touching is the solemn melancholy of this music in the stillness of the night; the tones are so wailing, so monotonous, and long drawn out. The first voice sang solo, then the second joined, and the third, and at last the whole band. They sang *in recitativo*, as they sing in Italy the ritornello. In the ritornello too, sentiments not meant to be melancholy are sung in an almost plaintive strain; but when this in itself melancholy kind of music is applied to the Vocero, the whole soul is thrilled with sadness. I had heard night-singing in other parts of Corsica, but none of such a powerful and solemn character as this; I shall never forget the dirges of that night in Calvi. Often yet I hear their echo; and one word particularly, *speranza*, becomes frequently audible to me in the plaintive tones in which it was sung.

In the morning I wandered accidentally into the shop of an old shoemaker, who proved to be the cithern-player of the previous night. At my request he readily brought out his instrument. The Corsican *cetera* has sixteen sides; it has almost the form of the mandoline; but is larger, and has the sounding-board not quite round, but somewhat flattened. The strings are struck with a little, flat, pointed ram's-horn. I found here, therefore, the universal experience confirmed, that shoemakers as a class are thoughtful, musical, and poetical. This Hans Sachs of Calvi readily got an assemblage of the best singers together. Shoes and lasts were thrown into a corner, and the little company collected in a room behind the shop, the window of which looked out upon the gulf through a profusion of flowers and creeping plants; the singers drew their seats together, their leader took his cithern, and opened in rich full tones. But let me mention who the singers were. There was first of all the old shoemaker as *maestro*; then there was his young apprentice, who learnt from him music and boot-making; then a well-dressed young man of the legal profession; and finally a silver-haired old man of seventy-four. Old as he was, he sang right heartily, though not perhaps with all the vigour of his youth; as the notes of the Corsican Voceros are very long, the amiable old fellow sometimes lost breath.

Now commenced a really beautiful concert. They sang whatever I wanted, serenades and voceradi or laments, but generally laments, because the originality and beauty of these charmed me most. One among the many Voceros was upon the death of a soldier. The story was this. A young man from the mountains has left his father, mother, and sister, and gone to serve on the Continent. After many years he returns home an officer. He ascends to his paese; none of his relations recognise him. He confides the secret to his sister only, to her unspeakable joy. He bids his father and mother, to whom he has not made himself known, prepare for to-morrow a meal as sumptuous as they can—he will pay them for it. In the evening he takes his gun, and goes out to shoot. He has left a knapsack heavy with gold in his chamber. His father discovers this, and determines to murder the stranger that same night. The horrid deed is consummated. When morning has come, and noon has come, but still not her brother, his sister inquires after the stranger; in the anguish of her heart she tells her parents that he is her brother. They rush into the room, father, mother, and sister, and——there he lies in his blood! Now follows the Lamento of the sister. The story is true; the popular ballads of the Corsicans invariably deal with real events. The shoemaker narrated the circumstances in most dramatic style, and the silver-haired old man assisted him with the liveliest gestures; then the first snatched up his cithern, and they sang the lamento.

These friendly minstrels, whom I told that I would translate their songs into my native tongue, and that I would not forget them and the hours I had spent with them, entreated me to stay yet this other evening in Calvi, and they would spend the whole night in singing to me; but if I was resolved on leaving, then I must go to Zilia, which, they said, had the best singers in Corsica. "Ah!" said the shoemaker, "the best of them all is dead. He sang as mellow as any bird, but he went to the hills and became a bandit, and the country-people protected him long from the officers, because he sang so beautifully; but they caught him at last, and he lost his head in Corte."

Thus Calvi became an oasis of song to me in these quiet, thinly-inhabited regions. I found it interesting, therefore, to remember that two of the best Corsican poets had been natives of Calvi—Giovanni Baptista Agnese, a writer of religious poetry born in the year 1611, and Vincenzo Giubega, who died in the year 1800, at the age of thirty-nine, as judge in Ajaccio. Giubega is not unjustly termed the Anacreon of Corsica. I have read some beautiful love-poems and sonnets of his, characterized by much grace and feeling.

Few of his songs survive; he burned most of them before his death. As Sophocles says that memory is the queen of things, and because the muse of poetry herself is a daughter of Mnemosyne, I shall mention here another once world-renowned Corsican of Calvi—Giulio Giudi, in the year 1581 the wonder of Padua on account of his unfortunate memory. He could repeat 36,000 names after once hearing them. People called him *Giudi della gran memoria*. But he produced nothing; his memory had killed all his creative faculty. Pico von Mirandola, who lived before him, produced, but he died young. It is with the precious gift of memory as with all other gifts—they are a curse of the gods, when they give too much.

I have already mentioned the name of Salvatore Viale. This author, a native of Bastia, is the most productive poet the island can yet boast of. One of his works is a comic poem called *La Dinomachia*, in the vein of the *Secchia Rapita* of Tassoni; and he has translated Anacreon, and part of Byron. Byron in Corsica, therefore!—Viale has earned the gratitude of his country by an unwearied scientific activity, and his illustrations of the manners and customs of the Corsicans are highly meritorious. Corsica has also a translator of Horace—Giuseppe Ottaviano Savelli, a friend of Alfieri, of whom I have already spoken. I could name many more Corsican poets, as, for example, Biadelli of Bastia, who died in the year 1822, a writer of songs. But their poems will never attain more than a Corsican celebrity. The most beautiful poetry of Corsica is her popular poetry, and Grief is the greatest Corsican poet.

CHAPTER VII
THE CORSICAN DIRGES

In order to understand the Corsican dirges, we must consider them in their relation to the existent usages in connexion with death—usages which date from a remote antiquity. Among a people with whom death assumes, more than anywhere else, the character of a destroying angel, whose bloody form is almost constantly before their eyes, it is natural to expect that the dead should have a more striking cultus than elsewhere. There is something mysterious and impressive in the circumstance, that the finest poetry of the Corsicans is the poetry of death, and that they hardly ever compose or sing except in the frenzy of grief. Most of these strange flowers of their popular poetry have their root in blood.

When a death has occurred, the relatives standing round the bed repeat the prayers of the rosary; they then raise a loud wail (*grido*). The corpse is now laid upon a table standing by the wall, called the *tola*. The head, on which a cap is placed, rests on a pillow. To preserve the natural appearance of the features, the head is bound with a cloth or fillet, supporting the chin, and fastened beneath the cap. If it is a young girl, she lies in a white shroud, and on her head is a wreath of flowers; if it is a grown-up female, she usually wears a coloured dress; that of aged women is black. A male corpse lies in a shroud and Phrygian cap, resembling thus the Etruscan dead, as they may be seen, surrounded with mourners, in representations contained in the Etrurian Museum of the Vatican.

The friends watch and wail beside the tola often throughout the whole night; and fire is always kept burning. But the principal lament occurs early on the morning of the funeral, when the body is laid in the coffin, and before the Brothers of Death come to lift the bier. The friends and relatives come from the neighbouring villages to the funeral. This assemblage is called the *corteo*, cortege, or procession, or the *scirrata*—a word which looks like the German *schaar*, though the origin cannot be accurately ascertained. A woman, always the poetess of the dirge which she sings, leads a chorus of wailing females. They say, therefore, in Corsica—*andare alla scirrata*, when the women go in procession to the house where the dead body lies; if it is the body of a man who has been killed, they say: *andare alla gridata*—to go to the wailing, or, more strictly, the howling. When the women of the chorus enter the house, they greet the widow, mother, or sister of the dead, as the case may be, keeping head bended towards head for about half a minute. Then a woman of the family invites the assembled females to begin the lament. They form a circle, the *cerchio* or *caracollo*, about the tola, and move round the dead body howling, breaking the circle, and again closing it, always with loud lamentation and gestures of the wildest grief.

This pantomime is not the same in all parts of the country. In some places it has become altogether obsolete, in others it has a milder form; among the mountains, far in the interior, particularly in Niolo, such usages exist in all their old pagan force, and resemble the death-dances of Sardinia. Their dramatic animation and ecstatic fury shock and horrify the spectator. They are all women who dance, wail, and sing. Like Mænads, the hair dishevelled and flying about the breast, eyes darting fire, their black mantles waving, they sway to and fro and round the tola, shriek, strike their hands together, beat their breasts, tear their hair, weep, sob, throw themselves on the bier, besprinkle themselves with dust; then the lament ceases, and these women sit silent, like a sisterhood of sibyls, on the floor of the chamber of death, breathing deeply, and calming themselves. There is a fearful contrast between this wild death-dance, with its shrieks and howling, and the corpse lying in the midst of it rigid and still, and yet ruling all the while the frantic orgies. Among the mountains, the wailers tear their faces till the blood flows, because, according to ancient heathen belief, blood is acceptable to the dead, and appeases the shade. This is called *raspa* or *scalfitto*.

There is a demoniac wildness about these wailing women, which reaches a frightful pitch when their dance and lament concern a murdered man. Then they become the very Furies themselves, the snaky-haired avengers of murder, as Æschylus has painted them. Their loose hair, howling, singing revenge, circling in their horrid dance, the effect of their chant on the murderer who hears it is frequently so overpowering, that, seized with shuddering horror and agony of conscience, he betrays himself. I have read of a murderer who, disguised in the cowled capote of the Brothers of Death, had the hardihood to hold one of the tapers by the bier of him whom he had helped to assassinate; and who, when he heard the dirge begin to shriek for vengeance, trembled so violently that the taper fell from his hand. In criminal trials, affirmations on the part of witnesses that the accused has been seen to tremble during the lament, are received as condemnatory proof. Yes! there is many a man in this island like the Orestes of Æschylus, of whom the prophetess might say—

"On the navel-stone behold a man

With crime polluted to the altar clinging,
And in his bloody hand he held a sword
Dripping with recent murder;

And, stretch'd before him, an unearthly host
Of strangest women, on the sacred seats
Sleeping—not women, but a Gorgon brood,
And worse than Gorgons, or the ravenous crew
That filched the feast of Phineus (such I've seen
In painted terror); but these are wingless, black,
Incarnate horrors."[B]

The silence of the grave now reigns in the chamber. Nothing is heard but the deep breathing of those weird women cowering on the floor, wrapped in their mantles, the head sunk upon the breast, expressing the deepest grief in the manner customary among the ancient Greeks, whose artists represent those overwhelmed with sorrow as covering the head and concealing the face. Nature herself has given the human being only two ways of indicating extreme suffering—the irrepressible outburst of feeling in the loud cry in which the whole vital energy seems to concentrate itself, and the profound silence in which the vital energies sink into stupor. Suddenly one of the women springs out of the cowering circle, and, like an inspired seeress, begins the song upon the dead. She chants it *in recitativo*, strophe after strophe, ending each with a wo! wo! wo! which the chorus of wailers repeat, as in the Greek tragedy. The woman who thus sings and leads the chorus, has also composed the dirge, or has improvised it as she sang. In Sardinia, it is usually the youngest girl who leads. As a general rule, these songs of revenge or of eulogy, in which the praise of the dead is mingled with complaint for his loss, or with calls for vengeance on his murderers, are improvised on the spot.

How strangely contradictory to the culture of our time the state of things in a country where we can still witness scenes like these, which seem separated from our present European civilisation by a gulf of three thousand years!

Let the reader imagine, then, the corpse upon the tola, the women crouching round it on the ground; a young girl rises, and, her countenance flaming with enthusiasm, improvises, like a Miriam or a Sappho, verses of the most surpassing grace, and full of the boldest images; exhaustlessly her wrapt soul pours forth the rhythmic stream of dithyrambs, which express melodiously all that is deepest and highest in human sorrow. The chorus wails at the close of each strophe, Deh! deh! deh! I know not whether anywhere in the world a picture could be found, which combines the repulsive with the beautiful in a manner so profoundly poetical and significant as such a scene, where a maiden sings before a bier what her pure young soul has that moment been inspired with, while a chorus of Furies howl the accompaniment; or where a girl, with flaming eye and glowing cheek, rises like an Erinnys over her murdered brother who lies armed upon the tola, and imprecates vengeance in verses whose fierce and bloody language no male lips could utter more relentlessly. In this country, where the position of woman is low and menial, it is nevertheless woman that sits in judgment, and summons the criminal before the tribunal of her plaint. Thus, too, the chorus of the maid-servants, in the Libation-bearers of Æschylus, sings—

 ——"Son, the strong-jaw'd funeral fire

 Burns not the mind in the smoky pyre;

 Sleeps, but not forgets the dead

 To show betimes his anger dread.

 For the dead the living moan,

 That the murderer may be known.

 They who mourn for parent slain

 Shall not pour the wail in vain.

 Bright disclosure shall not lack

 Who through darkness hunts the track."[C]

Some of these seeresses, who may be compared to the Germanic Velleda, become celebrated for their inspired singing; as Mariola delle Piazzole, a leader of the dirge-choruses, whose improvisations were everywhere in request; and Clorinda Franceschi of Casinca. In Sardinia, the women of the chorus are called *Piagnoni* or *prefiche*; in Corsica, *vecoratrici* or *ballatrici*. It is not always a practised leader of choruses who sings; in many cases it is some relative of the deceased—the mother, the wife, very frequently the sister. For the grief-burdened heart relieves itself in plaints that are eloquent without art, and renders the thoughts poetical, and the language elevated, even though the improvisatrice may be gifted with no special poetic talent. Moreover, the dirges have a standing form; and long before a death occurs, the Corsican woman has familiarized herself with the popular laments, which pass from mouth to mouth as other songs do with us. A cast of gloom is thus diffused over the whole life of the people here. When the Corsicans are sitting together, and begin to sing, they choose very frequently a Lamento, as if they wished to practise for that lament which, perhaps, each of them will yet sing in earnest over the tola of a brother, a husband, or a child.

The pantomimic dance that accompanies the lament is called in Corsica the *ballata* (*ballo funebre*); *ballatare sopra un cadavere*, is to dance over a corpse. The wailing is termed *vocerare*, the dirge *Vocero, Compito,* or *Ballata.* In Sardinia these obsequies are called *Titio* or *Attito.* This word is said to be derived from the cry of grief *ahi! ahi! ahi!* with which the leader of the chorus concludes each strophe, and which the wailers repeat. The corresponding cry with the Latins was *atat,* and in the Greek tragedies we find *otototoi;* among the Germans the vehement cry of suffering is frequently *ahtatata,* as any one may remark who notices what he ejaculates when he has burnt his fingers, and is dancing a *ballata* with the pain.[D]

When the Brothers of Death have arrived before the house to take away the bier, a loud wail is again raised, and the funeral procession now accompanies the deceased with laments to the church, where he receives consecration, and from the church again with wail and song to the churchyard. The obsequies are closed with a meal called the *convito* or *conforto;* a repast called the *veglia* has previously been given those who watched by the corpse, and each Brother of Death receives a cake. The *conforto* is given to the relations and friends of the deceased, either in his own house or in that of a kinsman, and it is customary to invite the guests with a pressing vehemency. It honours the departed if the repast be on as munificent a scale as possible; and if he has been respected during his life, it is observable in the number of the guests. Great expense is frequently lavished on this funeral banquet (*banchetto*), and bread and meats are distributed through the houses of the village. Black is the Corsican mourning colour; frequently the beard is allowed to remain for a long time uncut. When the anniversary of the funeral comes round, the banquet is sometimes repeated.

Such is the Corsican cultus of the dead, as it is preserved at the present day in the interior and the southern parts of the island. It is remarkable as a remnant of primitive paganism subsisting in the midst of our modern Christendom, and in combination with Christian usages. How old this *ballata* may be, and when and how it was brought into the country, are questions difficult to answer, and I shall not here venture upon their discussion.

The expressions of grief over beloved dead are everywhere the same — the weeping and lamenting, the copious and eloquent allusion to what they were in life, and to the affection that was felt for them. Passionate emotion finds vent in lively, forcible, and dramatic indications of grief. But the restraining power of culture, which regulates even the emotional part of our nature, checks those over whom it has established its sway, and refuses to the feelings all expression by extravagant gesture. It is not so in a primitive state of society, or among children. Neither is it so among the common people, so called, who represent, in the midst of our civilisation, the epic period of human development. If we wish to convince ourselves that the epic men, heroes, chiefs, and kings, demeaned themselves as passionately in giving expression to their grief, as the Corsicans of the present time in their *ballata*, we must read the songs of Firdusi, Homer, and the Bible. Esau cries aloud and weeps for the stolen blessing; Jacob rends his clothes for Joseph; Job rends his garments, and tears his hair, and falls to the earth, and his friends do the same, lifting up their voice and weeping, and each rends his garment and sprinkles dust upon his head towards heaven. David rends his garments for Saul and Jonathan, and afflicts himself, and weeps, and laments; he does the same for Absalom: "the king wept, and had his head covered, and he went barefoot."

Still more passionate and unbridled are the outbursts of grief with the men of Homer. Achilles laments for Patroclus, with both hands he strews black dust upon his head—

"Then, stretch'd in ashes, at the vast extent
Of his whole length he lay, disordering wild
With his own hands, and rending off his hair.
The maidens, captured by himself in war
And by Patroclus, shrieking from the tent
Ran forth, and hemm'd the glorious chief around;
All smote their bosoms, and all, fainting, fell."

When Hector falls, Hecuba tears her hair, and Priam piteously mourns and laments; and afterwards he says to Achilles, when he is begging of him a couch whereon to rest himself, that he has constantly sighed and groaned, full of endless sorrow, "rolling myself upon the earth in the court." So, in Firdusi, the hero Rustem tears his hair for his son Sohrab, roars for grief, and weeps blood; Sohrab's mother throws fire upon her head, rends her clothes, swoons continually, fills the hall with dust, weeps day and night, and dies in a year. The expression of the emotion is here in gigantic proportion, as the forms of the heroes themselves are colossal.

In the Nibelungenlied, the greatest tragedy of the Vendetta, the expression of passionate grief is no less colossal. Chrimhild raises her wail of sorrow over the dead Siegfrid,—blood gushes from her throat, she weeps blood above his corpse, and all the women help her with their lamentations.

In almost all the instances alluded to, we find the passion of sorrow pouring itself forth lyrically in the dirge. No loftier utterance of this kind is to be found than the lament of David for Saul and Jonathan. For the sake of the Corsican dirges, let us quote it here—

> The beauty of Israel is slain upon thy high places:
> How are the mighty fallen!
>
> Tell it not in Gath,—publish it not in the streets of Askelon;
> Lest the daughters of the Philistines rejoice,
> Lest the daughters of the uncircumcised triumph.
>
> Ye mountains of Gilboa, let there be no dew,
> Neither let there be rain, upon you, nor fields of offerings:
> For there the shield of the mighty is vilely cast away,
> The shield of Saul, as though he had not been anointed with oil.
>
> From the blood of the slain,—from the fat of the mighty,
> The bow of Jonathan turned not back,
> And the sword of Saul returned not empty.
>
> Saul and Jonathan were lovely and pleasant in their lives,
> And in their death they were not divided:
> They were swifter than eagles,—they were stronger than lions.
>
> Ye daughters of Israel, weep over Saul,
> Who clothed you in scarlet, with other delights,
> Who put on ornaments of gold upon your apparel.
>
> How are the mighty fallen in the midst of the battle!
> O Jonathan, thou wast slain in thine high places.
>
> I am distressed for thee, my brother Jonathan:
> Very pleasant hast thou been unto me:
> Thy love to me was wonderful,—passing the love of women.
> How are the mighty fallen,—and the weapons of war perished!

The lament around the dead body of Hector, in the last canto of the Iliad, is thoroughly dramatic, and completely resembles a *ballata* over the tola. Let us hear this vocero too.

(Andromache takes up the lament.)

My hero! thou hast fall'n in prime of life,
Me leaving here a widow, and the fruit
Of our ill-fated loves—a helpless child,
Whom grown to manhood I despair to see.
For, ere that season, from her topmost height
Precipitated shall this city fall,
Since thou hast perish'd, once her sure defence,
Faithful protector of her spotless wives
And all their little ones. Those wives shall soon
In Grecian barks capacious hence be borne,
And I among the rest. But thou, my child!
Shalt either share my fate, ordain'd to drudge
Beneath some tyrant in a distant clime,
Or, seizing thy weak hand, some furious Greek
Shall headlong hurl thee from the tower of Troy
To a sad death—whose brother, it may chance,
Whose father or whose son brave Hector slew,
For he made many a Grecian bite the ground.
Thy father, boy, bore never into fight
A milky mind, and for that self-same cause
Is now bewail'd in ev'ry house of Troy.
Sorrow unutterable thou hast caused
Thy parents, Hector! but to me hast left
Largest bequest of misery, to whom,
Dying, thou neither didst thy arms extend
Forth from thy bed, nor gav'st me precious word,
To be remember'd day and night with tears.
So spake she weeping, whom her maidens all
With sighs accompanied.

(Hecuba takes up the lament.)

Hector! far dearest of my sons to me,
Thee living must the gods have also loved,
Whose kindness even in the bands of death
Attends thee; for what son soe'er of ours

Achilles seized besides, to Samos, him,
Or Imbrus, or the dreaded Lemnian coast,
Far o'er the barren deep, for sale he sent;
But thee, poor victim of his ruthless spear,
Oft, at his wheels, around Patroclus' tomb
He dragg'd as he would waken into life
His friend whom thou hadst slain—yet still he slept.
But thou, the freshness of a fragrant flower
New-gather'd hold'st, and more resemblest far
Some youth whom Phœbus with his gentle shafts
Hath pierced at home, than one in battle slain.
So spake the queen, exciting in all hearts
Sorrow immeasurable.

(*Helen takes up the lament.*)
Hector! far dearest of my brothers here!
Me godlike Paris to the shores of Troy
Seduced, and made me partner of his bed,
But, O that I had perish'd first at home!
For this, since stolen from my native land
I wander'd hither, is the twentieth year,
Yet never heard I once hard speech from thee,
Or taunt morose: but if it ever chanced
That male or female of thy father's house
Blamed me, and even if herself the queen
(For in the king, whate'er befell, I found
Always a father)—thou hast interposed
Thy gentle temper and thy gentle speech
To soothe them; therefore, with a breaking heart
Thee and my wretched self at once I mourn,
For other friend within the ample bounds
Of Ilium have I none, nor hope to hear
Kind word again, with horror view'd by all.
So spake she weeping, and the countless throng
With groans replied.[E]

The Pelasgians, Greeks, Phœnicians, the Egyptians more especially, the ancient tribes of Italy, the Etruscans, the Romans, all lamented their dead with song and loud wailing; this is not less true of the Celts (*e.g.* the Irish) and the ancient Germans. Usages of this kind exist among the uncivilised tribes of America and Africa at the present day; and are to be found in other Italian countries besides Corsica and Sardinia, particularly in the Neapolitan territory.

Peter Cyrnæus finds the Corsican cultus of the dead very similar to that prevalent among the ancient Romans. Those who are acquainted with ancient Roman customs, will agree with the Corsican historian. They had the wailing women, called, as they are at the present day in Sardinia, *præficæ*, and they had the dirges (*næniæ*).[F] In connexion with the funeral obsequies of Germanicus, Tacitus speaks of the ceremonies, the songs in praise of the deceased, the weeping and wailing and exciting to violent grief, as ancient Roman usages. In the laws of the twelve tables, the *ballata* was called *lessus*, and punished as barbarous. The laws of Solon forbade it in these terms— "The women shall not scratch their cheeks, neither shall the *lessus* be held at burials; the women shall not tear the face."

The funeral-banquet is also an ancient pagan custom. Three sources may be assigned as its origin: the necessity of refreshment after the exhaustion induced by the ceremonies observed; the honour shown to the deceased by a last festive meal, of which he is in a certain sense the giver; and the religious and mystic symbolism involved in the partaking of food—an act which denotes the return from the sphere of death to that of life, and indicates that the mourners now once more have their share in the common every-day world. Among the Phœnicians, Pelasgians, Egyptians, and Etruscans, this meal consisted chiefly in beans and eggs. These two kinds of food are, according to the ancient Oriental and Pythagorean mysticism, symbols of the active and passive forces of vitality and productivity. At the present time, beans and eggs are eaten in many parts of Sardinia on occasion of the funeral repast; I have not heard, however, that this occurs in Corsica. The Roman name for the funeral feast was Silicernium.[G] The Trojans who have attended as mourners the obsequies of Hector, also return to a stately banquet in the house of Priam.

The Corsican Voceros or dirges, some specimens of which I shall now give, are all composed in the Corsican dialect of the Italian. The Trochaic measure usually prevails in them, though it is frequently transgressed. Triple rhymes are general; but here also departures from the rule occur. This measure, and the monotony of the rhymes, have a profoundly melancholy effect, and it would be difficult to find a rhythm more suitable as an expression of grief. The Voceros themselves are of two classes: the wild, terrific chant of revenge, and the milder lament for the loss of a departed friend. These songs throw much light upon the Corsican character. They show how vengeful and hot-blooded the temperament of the Corsican is, and how strong his passions. It is frightful to think that these ballads are almost all composed by women, since woman is destined to give expression to the gentler emotions of the soul, and to soften the rude vigour of the masculine nature. Throughout the entire range of popular poetry, I know of no instance in which the horrible and frightful pervade the material of the ballad to the same extent, and we observe here the strange power of poetry in general, which can throw around even what is in itself appalling a softening tinge of melancholy beauty. For the Corsican poetry may on the other hand, and does frequently, become the vehicle of tenderest emotion and the most delicate sentiment. In the Voceros is to be found the imagery of Homer, of the Psalms, and of the Song of Solomon. Altogether artless, they bear the stamp of improvisations which admit of being indefinitely lengthened in the same strain; and because they are improvisations, they are alive with the inspiration of the moment of overflowing feeling. The inexpressible innocence and touching simplicity of many Voceros transport us from our every-day life into the world of children, of shepherds, or of the patriarchs. No poetic genius can invent these utterances of nature. Beautiful songs, like tears wept by a noble sorrow, are sometimes called pearls—I call the Voceros blood-red Corsican corals.[H]

THE VOCERO, OR CORSICAN DIRGE

E come i gru van cantando lor lai.—*Dante.*

VOCERO ON CHILINA OF CARCHETO D'OREZZA

(*The Mother sings.*)
Ah! already they sing the Ave,
And I still hang weeping here—
All the women are come to see thee
Dress'd for death upon thy bier;
Mother's darling, my Chilina,
More than jewels bright and dear!

Whiter wast thou than the hill-snow,
Than the rice more pure and fine;
Now thy body is on the tola,

And thy soul where angels shine;
Ah, Chilina! why this cruel
Haste to leave me, daughter mine?

O Chilina! thou didst keep me
Like a lady of the land;
Bringing water, splitting firewood,
Still it was my daughter's hand;
Now has death her wings unfolded,
Lonely and bereaved I stand.

Where are now the nimble fingers,
Moving finely, moving fast,
As she spun upon the spindle,
Or the knots and meshes cast?—
Death, the sudden thief, he snatch'd her,
As he stole on tiptoe past.

How, Chilina, couldst thou leave us,
Go to yonder darksome place,
Where no firelight and no sunlight
Cheers the cold, the narrow space?
Ah, Chili! mine eyes will seek thee,
And they will not find thy face!

All so soon to be forsaken—
How could I such woe foresee?
Ah! thy sister Annadea,
She will meet thee joyfully—
She will beam with brighter glory
When she clasps her own Chili.

Thou wilt go no more to Ave,
Thou wilt go to mass no more;
My Chilina, mother's darling,
This is grief that wounds me sore—
That I now must live so lonely,
Who so blithely lived before.

(*A girl, one of her playmates, enters, and takes up the dirge.*)
Now arise, arise Chilina!
We have come to fetch the bride;
Hark the bells! thy horse is waiting,
To Carcheto thou must ride,
There to stand before the altar
With the bridegroom by thy side.

—Thou movest not, thou speakest not,
She will not ope her eyes;
Thy little hands are bound, Chili,
Thy little feet are bound, Chili;
Sisters, she fain would go with us,
Loose her, and let her rise.

(*One of the women takes up the dirge.*)
Hush, O hush thee, Magdalena!
Something I would ask the child;
Sooner, haply, than her mother,
She will give me answer mild.
At her head the wailing mother
Sobs and shrieks in grief so wild.

VOCERO ON THE DEATH OF CÆSARIO AND CAPPATO [I]

Jesus, Joseph, and Marie,
And the holy sacrament,
All in blessed companie,
Help me now with my lament.
It shall ring from hill to shore—
The two heroes are no more!

Ye may walk the world all over,
Ye may search through every state,
But the good Cæsario's mate
All your quest will not discover.
He could well and wisely speak,
Bend the strong, and win the weak.

Like a dog the base Mastini
Cowardly revenge did take;
Stealthily crept within brake,
Hounded on by the Mastini.
There he waited for his foe,
There he dealt the dastard blow.

Pauses now with carbine ready,
Sees approach Chiucchinu;
When he has him full in view,
Takes a certain aim and steady;
And he sees him earthward stagger,
As if struck through with a dagger.

Cappato in wrath up-started,
Fierce as lion from his lair;
At Tangone's throat he darted,
Who for life doth make his prayer.
Dearly must he rue the day,
That he mingled in the fray.

Paolo stayed when these departed;—
In the covert of the wood
He will tarry, steadfast-hearted,
He will bear a name of blood;
He will sweep down on the plain,
He will cover it with slain.

Patience till the winter's snow
Be dissolved from off the land;
Then shall sudden vengeance flow
From the mountains to the strand!
Spreading, catching, far and near,
Like the fiery flame's career.

Stab the richest and the noblest,
Stab a dozen—'tis too few;
That were hardly worthy vengeance

For the boots of Chiucchinu.
Vengeance too must pity show
For the hapless Cappato.

So concludes my lamentation,
I have now no more to say.
Wo upon you in the day
Of your coming desolation!
Take good heed, that may avail;
But if not, the mourners wail.

VOCERO OF A MAIDEN UPON THE DEATH OF HER TWO BROTH- ERS WHO WERE SLAIN IN ONE DAY

(*Mixed dialect of either side of the mountains.*)
(*The sister sings.*)
Oh! the bearing proud of Piero,
Oh! the boasting of Orazio—
They had made the land a desert
Betwixt here and San Brancazio,
Satiated with our heart's blood
Are Michele and Orazio.

Death, O death, how black and dreadful—
How remorseless is thy sway!
From a home once full thou'st taken,
Save the nest-egg, all away;
Is it fit that I, an orphan,
Here as head of house should stay?

I alone, amongst all women,
By this hearth my place maintain'd;
Over five strong, gallant brothers,
I the right to rule obtain'd:
Past and gone that sweet dominion,
Lost the prize that I had gain'd!

I will put on the faldetta,

Black my garment as their pall;
For no more one ray of gladness
On this lonely heart can fall:
Which has lost five noble brothers,
Father, mother—seven in all.

I will send at once to Asco,
Blackest pine-black I will crave,
Black as raven's wing the raiment
That from henceforth I will have;
While my life ebbs back and forwards
Like the rain-flood in their grave.

See ye not the ceaseless fountains
From these clouded eyes that well,
O'er the two beloved brothers
That in one hour bravely fell?
Two deaths are at once proclaimed
By the tolling of one bell.

Thou my crown of gold so ruddy—
Thou my ring of precious stone;
O Pierù! my former gladness—
O Orà! my present moan!
In the Chapel of Tallanu,
Like you two there is not one.

And to you, too, Rev'rend Curate,
Bitter words I needs must say;
For the love my kin still show'd you,
Thanklessly you now repay;
Three years since we number'd seven—
You have borne them all away.

Only to the first street's ending
Will I follow in your train—
Follow, blinded by my weeping—
Weeping, get me home again,

This the saddest, last procession
Of the five dear brothers slain.

VOCERO OF A HERDSMAN'S WIFE OF TALAVO, ON HER HUSBAND

On the beach his corpse is lying
Where the two old cork-trees spread;
O Francesco! faithful herdsman!
Fearful 'tis to see thee dead!
How shall I, by thee forsaken,
Gloomy forest-pathways tread?

I will tear away the branches
From yon spreading Palo-tree—
Leathern bags and caps shall no more
From its boughs suspended be;
And the sheep-dog he most valued,
With his ears clipp'd, all shall see.

Wo! wo! wo! my heart is breaking,
Let your wailing fill the air;
O my brothers! O my sisters!
Such a stroke is hard to bear.
From the house the head is taken,
God has doom'd me to despair.

(*After the burial is over, the shepherdess returns to her cabin, and describes*
the ceremony to her friends and relations.)
On the bier I saw them lay him,
Towards Prunelli carry slow;
There, in dumb but heartfelt mourning.
Flocks and cattle bleat and low—
E'en the kids between the hurdles
Bah, bah, bah! their loss to show.

In the Church of Blessed Mary,
In the holy churchyard ground,
Chants and prays the rev'rend Father,

With attendant priests around;
Loud as at a noble's burial,
Peals the sad and solemn sound.

When the funeral was over,
Oh, how hastily each rose!
Straight an open grave discov'ring,
My Francesco to enclose;
Borne on by a rush of people.
Towards that grave the coffin goes.

Oh! but what their cruel purpose!
Oh! the thought is endless wo;
I looked down, in hopes the sunlight
Through some grave-wall chink might flow;
But I saw then my husband lower'd
Into darkness—lower'd slow.

VOCERO ON THE DEATH OF ROMANA, THE DAUGHTER OF DARI-OLA DANESI OF ZUANI

(*The Mother sings.*)
See, she lies now on the tola,
She, my child of sixteen years.
Darling daughter! her short life-lease
Has been fraught with pain and tears,
Now her snowy festal garment—
Her transparent veil she wears.

In that snowy festal garment
Far away she now must go,
For the Lord of all forbids her
Longer to remain below.
They who wear an angel's semblance,
Early to the angels go.

Where, belov'd, are now the roses
On thy chisell'd cheeks and lips?—
All the blossoms of thy beauty

Death with icy fingers strips;
Seems the change on which I'm gazing,
Like a sudden sun-eclipse.

Oh! amongst the band of maidens
Thou wert fairest of the fair;
To the rose all flowers are subject,
With the moon no stars compare;
Other charms with thine contrasted,
Show'd thy beauty still more rare.

When the youths from yonder village
To thy presence would aspire,
Straight they seem'd like pine-wood torches
Kindled at a glowing fire.
Thou to all wert mild and courteous,
But not one might venture nigher.

In the church each eye was straining
To espy thee as we pass'd;
All, from first to last, kept gazing,
But thine eyes were downward cast.
Service ended, thou wouldst pray me,
"Let us hurry homeward fast."

Oh how highly wert thou valued,
Honour'd both by great and small;
Taught and train'd by Heavenly teaching,
Wise with wisdom best of all!
From the world thy spirit screening,
Prayer and praise its special call.

Who can ever soothe my anguish?
Oh, my glory and my pride!
Since the Lord has bid thee leave me,
Call'd thee with Him to abide;
Wherefore does not His compassion
Bid my agony subside!

Yet in heaven thou'rt resting sweetly,
From all burdens smiling free;
If too bright for earth thy beauty,
As all own'd who look'd on thee —
How much brighter, thro' its presence,
Henceforth Paradise will be!

But for me the earth will only
Seem a place of wo and tears,
And each day of hopeless longing
Lengthen to a thousand years;
While I ask of thee, my daughter,
From each stranger that appears.

Death, why did'st thou from my bosom
Such a loving daughter tear?
Wherefore, in a nest now empty,
Leave me lonely to despair?
When I miss her care and tendance,
How shall I life's burden bear?

Lonely 'midst my kindred standing,
Helpless with my neighbours by;
Who will wipe away the pain-drops
When I lay me down to die?
Who will give the drink I thirst for
When the fever rages high?

Oh! thou fondly cherish'd daughter,
Think upon my wretched case,
When grown old, by all forsaken;
Far from help or friendly face,
Never knowing peace or comfort,
Even for a moment's space.

If, like thee, I were permitted
From this cold world to depart,
Having seen thy early fading —

Hope and glory of my heart!
I should find thee up in heaven,
And live with thee where thou art.

Therefore pray our dear Lord Jesus,
Till He calls me ceaseless pray!
For my only hope I cannot
Live on thus from day to day—
Cannot end these vain lamentings—
Cannot weep my tears away!

VOCERO OF A GIRL FOR HER FATHER

I came forth from Calanca
At the twelfth hour of the night,
And everywhere I sought him,
I sought him by torchlight,—
And when I found my father,
'Twas his corpse that met my sight.

(Another girl enters, seeking a relative, also slain.)
Ye who would find Matteju,
Go farther up the steep;
The dead here is my father,
And I must stay to weep.

Take apron, trowel, hammer,
My father, and come away,
For you must work at the chapel
Of San Marcello to-day;
But they had slain my father,
And my brother wounded lay.

Oh, scissors to cut my long locks,
Make haste and bring to me!
Let me staunch with my hair those gashes
Where the blood is running free—
For the red drops on my fingers
Are a fearful sight to see.

I will dye me a mandilè,
In his blood I will dye it red;
And when I have time to be merry,
I will deck with it my head.[J]

Now I bear him to Calanca—
To the Church of the Holy Cross,
Still crying, O speak, my father!
Still wailing for my loss—
For they have crucified him,
Like Christ upon the cross.

TEXT OF THE PRECEDING VOCERO

Eo partu dalle Calanche
Circa quattr' ore di notte:
Mi ne falgu cu la teda
A circà per tutte l'orte,
Per truvallu lu mio vabu:
Ma li avianu datu morte.

Cullatevene più in su,
Chi truvarete a Matteju;
Perchè questu è lu mio vabu,
E l'aghiu da pienghie eju.
Via, pigliatemi u scuzzale
La cazzola e lu martellu.
Nun ci vulete andà, vabu,
A travaglià a San Marcellu?
Tombu m'hann lu miò vabu,
E feritu u miò fratellu.

Or circatemi e trisore,
E qui prestu ne venite:
Vogliu toudemi i capelli
Per tuppalli le ferite;
Chi di lu sangue di vabu
N'achiu carcu le miò dite.

Di lu vostru sangue, o vabu,
Bogliu tinghiemi un mandile;
Lu mi vogliu mette a collu
Quandu avrachiu oziu di ride.

Eo collu per le Calanche
Falgu per la Santa Croce,
Sempre chiamand uvi, vabu:
Rispunditemi una voce.
Mi l'hanu crucifissatu
Cume Ghesù Cristu in croce.

I have added the original text of this vocero, to give the reader some idea of the Corsican dialect, and enable him to compare it, if he is interested in such matters, with the Italian spoken on the Continent. I find a great resemblance between the dialect of Corsica and that used by the lower orders in Rome, particularly in Trastevere.[K] All the Italian popular dialects, however, have a tendency to drop or mutilate the infinitive endings, *are* and *ire*, and to substitute *r* for *l*. The Corsican says *soretra* for *sorella*. Philologists have pronounced the Corsican one of the purest of the Italian dialects, and Tommaseo especially has much to say in its praise in his collection of Tuscan, Corsican, and Greek popular songs—which contains also, though in a defective form, a number of Corsican dirges, with elucidations. In this book he calls the Corsican dialect "a powerful language, and of all the dialects of the Italian tongue, one of the most thoroughly Italian." It seems to me to be genuine gold compared with the *patois* of the Piedmontese and Lombards, and the dialects of Parma and Bologna. Even from the single specimen communicated, the reader will see that the language of the Corsicans, though no doubt one of the lower forms of Italian, is soft and graceful.

BOOK VII
WANDERINGS IN CORSICA

CHAPTER I
TO CORTE THROUGH BALAGNA

I gave up the thought of a journey which I had at one time intended to make along the coast from Calvi to Sagone, where the large gulfs of Porto and Sagone, and those of Galeria and Girolata run into the country. The region is for the most part uncultivated, and the roads are frightful.

I travelled through the glorious valley of Balagna by the Diligenza which runs between Calvi and Corte. As I have already mentioned, this large, beautiful, and well-cultivated district receives the name of the Garden of Corsica. Lofty mountains enclose it, snow-capped summits like Mount Tolo, and the mighty Grosso—heights of the finest forms, and that would enchant the landscape painter. Great numbers of villages are seen upon the slopes, San Reparato, Muro, Belgodere, Costa, Speloncata, Feliceto, Nessa, Occhiatana—all formerly seats of noble families and Caporali, and full of memories of old times. The Malaspinas once ruled here, the Tuscan margraves of Massa and the Lunigian marches, a race of powerful seigniors, whom Dante celebrates in the *Divine Comedy*. When he finds Currado Malaspina in purgatory, we have the following verses:—

"Oh, never have I seen thy land, I said;

But where throughout all Europe may be found

The spot to which thy glory hath not spread?

The fame that o'er this house such lustre throws

Makes both its nobles and the land renowned:

E'en he who ne'er was there, their greatness knows."

The Malaspinas built the village of Speloncato. Subsequently to the year 1019, five counts of this house had come to Corsica—Guglielmo, Ugo,

Rinaldo, Isuardo, and Alberto Rufo. The family is spread in numerous branches over the Italian countries.

In later times the democratic constitution of the Terra del Commune deprived the barons of their power in Balagna. The Corsican popular assemblies (*veduta*) were frequently held here, in the Field of Campiolo. At one of these vedutas, the brave Renuccio della Rocca displayed a degree of heroic fortitude which deserves our admiration. Filippini narrates the incident. Renuccio was in the act of addressing the assembly, when his son, a youth of fourteen, who chanced to be riding over the field, was hurled by his startled horse upon the point of the lance carried by a squire who rode behind him. The dying youth was brought to his father. But Renuccio, with unaltered mien, continued in his speech to rouse his countrymen to insurrection against Genoa. This Spartan self-command, the heroism of Gaffori, the heroism of Leoni of Balagna before the tower of Nonza, always remind me of the manly firmness of Xenophon. The news that his son Gryllus had fallen in battle, came to Xenophon when he was engaged in offering sacrifice. The father, overcome at first by the sudden intelligence, took the sacrificial wreath from his head; but when he was told that his son had fallen bravely fighting, he immediately replaced it, and calmly continued his act of worship. Indeed, these stout-hearted Corsicans seem more Spartan than the Spartans themselves.

I found in Balagna a great many fields of grain already cut—a beautiful sight in Corsican regions. Everywhere, especially in the vicinity of the villages, are the most luxuriant and magnificent groves of chestnut, walnut, and almond trees, gardens of oranges and citrons, and wood on wood of olives. The excellent road keeps close by the foot of the mountains, and from all points the traveller enjoys the finest views towards the sea or into the hills. The largest villages of Balagna are Muro and Belgodere; the latter of which owes its name to its beautiful situation. Belgodere might be a sanctuary of Pallas, it lies embosomed in such luxuriant groves of her favourite tree.

It is said that there is no district throughout the whole of Italy where the olive attains such a size as it does in the Balagna. The thickness of its stem, its abundance of branches, and the quantity of fruit it produces, are equally astonishing. It is mighty as a beech, and in the heat of noon you rest cool under its shelter. The olive is a tree that one cannot but love. It has not the imposing magnificence of the oak or the plane; its bole, its grayish green, long, narrow leaves, remind us of our own homely willow; but it is laden with riches—with the very fat of the earth, and it is associated with all the poetry of human culture. Sitting under a gray olive by the sea-strand, we are transported to the sacred, sunny East, where our fancy has been at home ever since we turned over the leaves of the picture-Bible, and heard a mother's stories of the Mount of Olives at Jerusalem. How often have we imagined to ourselves those olive-groves! Then, again, in the whispering of its branches, we hear the wisdom of Minerva, and the poetry of the Hellenes, and are borne away to the land of Homer, of Pindar, of Æschylus, to the Muses and gods of Olympus. The olive is thus doubly dear to us as at once a Christian and a Hellenic tree; its branch is more precious than that of the laurel, it is the beautiful symbol of prosperity and peace, and a man's first prayer to the immortal gods should be: Send into my life the green olive-branch. They send us all kinds of them, the laurel-branch, the myrtle-branch; and they send also the cypress-bough; with humility be the award received.

There are various species of olives in the Balagna—the Sabine (*Sabinacci*), the Saracen (*Saraceni*), and the Genoese (*Genovesi*);—named according to their descent, like noble families of Signori. The third family is the most common. It is ascribed to the Genoese, who, during the government of Agostino Doria, compelled the Corsicans to plant olives in great numbers. This is therefore at least one beautiful and peaceful memorial of Genoese rule in Corsica. When the olive was first introduced into Corsica, I am unable to say. One of the complaints in the epigram of Seneca is, that the gift of Pallas does not exist on the island. Yet it appears to me hardly credible that the olive was not cultivated on the island before Seneca's time. The Corsican olives have at present the reputation of resisting better than all others the changes of the weather; the great Humboldt awards them this praise. They require little attention. The oldest branches are cut off to strengthen the tree, the soil about its roots is loosened, and manure is laid round the trunk. The olives are collected when they fall off. Twenty pounds of olives produce five pounds of clear oil. This is put into large jars, in which it stands till the month of May. The olive-tree yields abundantly every three years.

The birds come and carry away the olive kernels to the four winds of heaven, scattering them over the face of the country. The island thus becomes covered with wild olive-bushes, which flourish lustily on mountain and in valley, waiting to be improved. In the year 1820, an attempt was made to count them, and their number was said to be twelve millions. The richest olive-districts at the present time in Corsica are Balagna, Nebbio, and the country round Bonifazio.

We left the province of Balagna at the village of Novella. At this point the road bends into the mountainous interior, and for hours the Diligenza rolls on through narrow valleys, and between barren rocky hills, not a hamlet in sight, till we reach Ponte alla Leccia in the valley of the Golo, where the principal highways of Corsica, from Calvi, from Ajaccio, and from Bastia, meet. You now drive along the Golo, through a pleasant valley. To the right lies the pastoral district of Niolo, the present canton of Calacuccia—a remarkable region, encircled by lofty mountains, in which lie the two lakes of Neno and Ereno. The district forms a natural stronghold, for it opens only at four points, towards Vico, Venaco, Calvi, and Corte. A steep road, called the *Scala di Santa Regina*, leads to Corte. In Niolo live the strongest men in Corsica, patriarchal shepherds, who have faithfully preserved the customs of their forefathers.

There are many remarkable places on the road to Corte, as for example, Soveria, the home of the brave family of the Cervoni. It was Thomas Cervoni who rescued Pasquale Paoli at the cloister of Alando, when he was besieged there by the furious Matra. The reader will remember that Cervoni, who was at feud with Paoli, had his weapons put into his hands by his own mother, who, threatening to curse him if he refused to obey her, drove him from the house to rescue his foe. Cervoni hastened to the besieged convent, and Matra was slain. It is no ordinary pleasure to wander through a country like this island of Corsica, where there is not a city or village, a mountain or valley, which is not associated with some deed of heroism.

Cervoni's son was the talented general, who, as officer at Toulon, won his first laurels along with Napoleon. He distinguished himself at Lodi; in the year 1799, he was commandant of Rome. It was he who announced to Pope Pius VI. that his power was at an end, and that he must leave Rome. Cervoni made his name terrible in that city, as is evinced by an incident related by Valery. He once in the Tuileries stepped up to Pope Pius VII. at the head of the Generals, and complimented him. His fine voice and beautiful Italian pronunciation astonished the Pope, and he said a great many flattering things to Cervoni. The latter hereupon remarked: "*Santo padre, sono quasi Italiano.*" "Oh!" "*Sono Corso.*" "Oh! oh!" "*Sono Cervoni!*" "Oh! oh! oh!" and at the mention of the dreadful name the Pope receded horror-stricken to the fireplace. In the year 1809, a cannon-ball carried away the head of Marshal Cervoni at Regensburg.

Near Soveria stands Alando, famous as connected with the name of Sambucuccio, the ancient legislator and Lycurgus of the Corsicans, and founder of their democratic constitution. The scarcely distinguishable ruins of his castle are shown upon a rock. In 1466, four hundred years later than

Sambucuccio, one of his descendants was vicegerent of the Corsican nation. Some of the Caporali resided in this quarter, in the neighbouring Omessa. Originating as tribunes of the people, and intended in the democratic system of Sambucuccio to defend the rights of the communes, they succumbed in the course of time to a malady that never fails to undermine and destroy the wisest human arrangements—ambition and the love of self-aggrandizement, and became like the seigniors, the most oppressive petty tyrants. In Filippini's time, we find that historian still complaining that the Caporali were the most dreadful scourges of Corsica.

Chestnuts thrive around Alando, but the region is poor. Black sheep and goats find their nourishment on the mountain heaths. Their wool is here made into the Corsican pelone.

After crossing the Alluraja, a lofty range of hills between the rivers Golo and Tavignano, we descend, on an admirable road, towards Corte.

CHAPTER II
THE CITY OF CORTE

The arrondissement of Corte, the central district of the island, embraces fifteen cantons and 113 communes, and contains a population of 55,000. The town itself has about 5000 inhabitants.

Corte is an inland city with a situation not less imposing than those of the Corsican seaports. The panorama of brown hills in the midst of which it lies, the citadel on an inaccessible and rugged crag, give the town an air of iron defiance. Mountains rise on every side in the most varied forms. To the north the heights are low, and mostly dome-shaped, covered with copsewood, or fields of grain. The summer has clad these hills in a dark brown, and the region thus wears an aspect of the utmost sternness. They are the last spurs of the ranges that form the watershed between the Golo and Tavignano, and separate two valleys, the pastoral dale of Niolo, and the valley of the Tavignano. At the opening of the latter, where the Tavignano is joined by the Restonica, lies Corte. Three high and craggy hills command the entrance to this valley. Both rivers have forced a channel for themselves through deep ravines, and rush into one another over fragments of shattered cliffs. There is a stone bridge over each.

The little city has only one main street, which is newly built, and is called the Corso; an alley of elms gives it a singularly rural appearance. And here too I was astonished at the lonely seclusion, the idyllic stillness, that so peculiarly characterize the Corsican towns. You really believe yourself in the farthest nook of the world, and cut off from all connection with its ongoings.

The city is venerable from its associations with events in Corsican history. In the time of Paoli it was the centre of his democratic government, and in ancient times the residence of Moorish kings; it was important in every period as the central point of the island, and as possessing a fortress which frequently decided the course and issue of a campaign.

The citadel has a singular appearance. It is the Acropolis of Corsica. It stands on a black, steep, and rugged crag, which rises over the river Tavignano. Walls, towers, the old town—which the citadel encloses—all look black, ruinous, and desolate. They have been battered in a thousand sieges. This castle of Corte has been assaulted and defended oftener than Belgrade. The brave Vincentello d'Istria laid the foundations of the present structure, in the beginning of the fifteenth century. The loop-hole is still shown from which the Genoese suspended Gaffori's son, to deter his father from continuing his cannonade of the fortress. Enacting itself on and around this grim, giddy height, how wild must have been that heroic scene! The action of Gaffori is one of the noblest traits to be found in the range of Corsican history, which, as I have already said, for every instance of magnanimity in Greeks and Romans, can produce another no way inferior. The spirit that has animated this Corsican people, has proved itself no less heroic than that which we admire in Brutus and Timoleon; but the acts of national and individual heroism which this spirit produced, have lain buried in the obscurity of the period and the locality.

The name of Gaffori is Corte's fairest ornament, and his little house, still standing pierced with balls, the most splendid monument the city can show. This house preserves another heroic association, connected with Gaffori's brave and high-souled wife. The Genoese, whose constant policy it was to use the families of dreaded Corsicans as hostages, and to oppose natural affection to love of country, on one occasion took advantage of Gaffori's absence from home to attack his house, in order to secure the person of his wife. But she instantly barricaded the door and window, and, with a few friends who had hurried to her assistance, defended herself, musket in hand, for days against the Genoese, who showered a storm of bullets upon the house. The little garrison was reduced to the utmost extremity, and her friends counselled her to capitulate; Gaffori's wife, however, conveyed a cask of powder into a cellar, and seizing a match, swore that she would blow up the house the moment they ceased to fire upon the besiegers. Her friends, who knew her desperate courage, continued their resistance, and at length Gaffori himself appeared with a band of Corsicans, and rescued his wife. After the murder of Gaffori, this woman took his son, the boy who had once been bound to the walls of the castle, and made him swear to hate the Genoese and avenge his father. Hamilcar did the same with his son Hannibal in ancient times.

In this house of Gaffori's, Carlo Bonaparte lived with his wife Letitia in 1778; it was a house worthy to give origin to a Napoleon.

Many memories of Paoli are connected with a house which bears the name of the Palazzo de Corte, and was the seat of Paoli's government, and his residence. Here is the room in which he worked, a mean-looking little place enough, as beseemed the legislator of the Corsicans. They tell that the great man, who was not safe from the balls of the assassin, kept the windows of this room always barricaded; and in fact, the window-shutters are still to be seen lined with cork, as they were in his time. The National Assembly had decreed him a guard of twenty-four men, acting in this like the ancient democracies of Greece; he had another body-guard always in the room beside him, consisting of six Corsican dogs. I cannot help being reminded here of his contemporary and admirer Frederick the Great, and how he too, in his cabinet, was always surrounded by dogs; but these were kept for amusement or ornament merely—the pretty Biche, and the graceful Alcmene, and other greyhounds. The scene is characteristically different. If Paoli were painted in the company of his dogs, as Frederick the Great has so often been represented surrounded by his, it would make rather a wild picture: the Corsican hero in his mean-looking cabinet, writing by the fireplace, wrapped in a coarse woollen gown, behind a barricaded window, grim, shaggy wolf-hounds crouched upon the floor—there we have a Corsican historical *genre* painting.

In another room, formerly the hall where the Council of Nine sat, are preserved some very interesting relics; the rods, to wit, which were to have supported the canopy of Paoli's throne. Paoli and a throne? Impossible! Had the great democrat a hankering after kingly emblems? So it is affirmed; the story is as follows:—One day workmen were seen erecting a throne in the National Palace. It was of crimson damask, hung with gold fringes, and supported, above the Corsican arms, a golden crown, so placed that when Paoli seated himself, it stood over his head. To suit the throne, there were nine smaller crimson chairs, for the members of the Council of Nine. When the councillors had assembled in the hall, the door of Paoli's room opened, and Paoli, as it is said, in a magnificent robe of state, his head covered, and his sword by his side, entered, and moved towards the throne. A murmur of astonishment and displeasure instantly arose among the councillors, followed by a deep silence. Paoli stopped, was disconcerted, and he never took his seat upon the throne.

I have found so many confirmations of this story, that it seems to me almost presumption to doubt it. If it is true, it is a remarkable trait in the character of the great man, and at least a proof that human weakness everywhere asserts its sway, and that no mortal is safe from the moment when he may be overcome by vanity and outside show. Paoli and a throne— there can hardly be a greater contradiction. Liberty and the Corsican people were the noble man's loftiest throne, and no potentate ever occupied one more glorious than that plain arm-chair on which Paoli sat, the legislator and deliverer of a people.

His enemies have accused him of aiming at regal authority, but they wrong him in this, and Paoli's history gives the lie to the charge. Did he wish, perhaps, by means of regal emblems, to secure from foreign countries and from his own people a greater degree of respect for the state over which he presided, and which still bore the time-honoured appellation of the Kingdom of Corsica? We have no other instances of his indulging in kingly pomp. He, and all the other members of the government, went about in the common dress of the country; their clothes were of the Corsican wool, they lived like the simplest commoners. The heads of the state were distinguishable from the people only by their superior intelligence, and it was merely to give the French, in matters of exterior as well as in those of more importance, the impression of a regular and formal government, that he ordered the members of the Supreme Council to wear a distinct dress, a green coat, gold-laced — green and gold being the Corsican colours. He and they put on this official dress for the first time, when French officers came first to Corte. The country's rulers were to appear in a manner becoming their dignity. This was, however, a concession to French etiquette which we cannot but lament, because in making it Paoli ceased to maintain himself superior to appearances, and abolished the beautiful democratic equality which had previously expressed itself even in dress, by some pieces of gold lace. The Corsicans were entitled to wear their woollen blouse with greater pride than the French their glittering uniforms. Trifling and subordinate as these matters may in themselves appear, they nevertheless furnish material for thought. For time makes unessential differences essential, and of extrinsic makes intrinsic. There is in time an invisible influence for evil, which gradually stains all that is pure, dwarfs all that is great, debases all that is noble. In this world of ours, it is so and not otherwise; exalted virtue is a phenomenon confined to the period of *struggle* towards a great aim. In Corsica it has often made me sad to think, that all those heroic exertions of its people, all those battles for freedom, have proved fruitless; and that now, in the land of Sampiero, of Gaffori, and of Paoli, "the vain nation" bears rule. Yet it would have been an experience still more sad, had the state of Paoli sickened of itself, and yielded to human selfishness. For my part, I do not believe that it would have escaped this universal fate. For true freedom exists only in Utopia. Mankind appears to be capable of it only in the highest, most sacred moments.

On one occasion Paoli received in this Palazzo Nazionale a very splendid embassy. A ship of Tunis had stranded on the coast of Balagna, and Paoli had not only restored to the shipwrecked strangers all the property of which the peasantry of the region had deprived them, but hospitably entertained them, and sent them home to the Bey of Tunis under the conduct of two officers, and well supplied with every necessary for their journey. The Bey thereupon sent an embassy to Paoli to thank him, and convey to him the assurance that he would remain eternally his and his country's friend, and that no Corsican would ever sustain injury within the bounds of his territories. The ambassador from Tunis kneeled down before Paoli, and, putting his hand to his forehead, said in Italian, *Il Bey ti saluta, e ti vuol bene*— the Bey greets thee, and wishes thee well. He brought him as presents, a beautiful, splendidly caparisoned horse, two ostriches, a tiger, a sabre set with diamonds; and after residing some days in Corte, returned again to Africa.

Close to Corte lies the old convent of the Franciscans—a ruin of considerable size. In Paoli's time, the Corsican parliament assembled in the church of this convent; and from its pulpit not a few noble patriots have lifted their earnest voices. Many and not vain sacrifices were made to liberty in this church, and her name was not heard as an empty phrase. Those who called upon it, also died for it. In the year 1793, a general assembly of the Corsicans had met on the open ground before the convent; the time was stormy, for the grayhaired Paoli stood impeached of high treason by the National Convention of France. Pozzo di Borgo, that unrelenting enemy of Napoleon—like him, a citizen of Ajaccio—climbed upon a tree, and delivered a powerful and fiery speech in defence of Paoli, whose accusers, the furious clubbists, Arena and the Bonapartes, were here declared infamous.

At the present day, wandering about in the streets of the little city, which are silent as the grave, and beneath whose shady elms here and there, poor-looking Corsicans idle in dreamy listlessness, one can hardly believe that scarcely a hundred years ago such an obscure, secluded nook was the seat of the most enlightened political wisdom of the age.

Paoli founded a university in Corte; and he here called the first Corsican printing-press and the first Corsican newspaper into existence. From this university knowledge and enlightenment were to spread like a flood of light over the mountains, and into all the valleys of Corsica, dispelling the mediæval barbarism of her inhabitants. I have already, in the History of the Corsicans, mentioned this university, and spoken of its high merits as a patriotic institution. Many of Corsica's ablest men have been its pupils— talented advocates, who form in this island the majority of the literary class. Carlo Bonaparte, Napoleon's father, studied at this university. The young institution fell, however, when the country lost its freedom. Paoli on his deathbed set apart a legacy for its restoration, and with the help of this capital a sort of college was re-established in the year 1836. There are at present a director and seven professors for the sciences connected with it, but its condition is not very flourishing. An institution of this academic kind is also perhaps less suited to the wants of Corsica than good commercial schools.

I found among the Corsicans many learned and highly cultivated men, and here in Corte I became acquainted with a gentleman, the extent of whose reading in the literature of the Romanic languages astounded me. He is the son of one of the brave captains who, after the battle of Ponte Nuovo, remained in arms till the last moment, and whom I have mentioned by name. His memory is so retentive, that he knows by heart the best passages of all the great Italian, French, and Latin authors, and that it is a slight matter for him to repeat whole pages of Tasso or Ariosto, and long extracts from Voltaire or Macchiavelli, or from Livy, Horace, Boileau, or Rousseau. Talking with him of literature on one occasion, I asked him if he had ever read any works of Goethe. "No," said our well-read friend, "Pope is the only English author with whom I am acquainted."

Some gentlemen, whose agreeable acquaintance I made at the *table d'hôte* of my inn, among them an artist, the only Corsican painter with whom I became acquainted on the island, took me to the marble quarries in the vicinity of Corte. A quarry of this kind was discovered not long ago in the rocks above the Restonica. The stone is of a bluish colour, with reddish-white veins, and is available for architecture and ornaments. We found the workmen occupied in getting a large block, of which a pillar was to be made, down the hill. It was laid on rollers, and shoved by means of the Archimedean screw to the edge of the incline, at the foot of which the blocks are dressed. The large and beautiful stone slid rapidly down, enveloping itself in a cloud of dust, and as it forced its way onwards, rung clear as a bell. At the foot of the hill on which this rich quarry lies, the Restonica turns a mill that cuts the marble into plates. Seven days are required to cut a block into thirty of these. In Corte, therefore, Seneca's assertion is now disproved—*non pretiosus lapis hic cæditur*—here no costly stone is hewn. Speaking generally, however, the philosopher's words are still applicable, for Corsica's treasures of beautiful stone have remained dead capital.

CHAPTER III
AMONG THE GOAT-HERDS
OF MONTE ROTONDO

— — — —"tomo un puño de bellotas en la mano, y mirandolas atentamente sotto la voz a semejantes razones: Dichosa edad y siglos dichosos aquellos a quien los antiguos pusieron nombre de dorados." — Don Quixote.

I had formed the resolution of ascending the highest mountain in Corsica, Monte Rotondo, which lies about half a day's journey to the south-west of Corte, and may almost be considered as the middle point of the island. Although the excursion was described to me as most fatiguing, still I hoped to find a clear day and sufficient remuneration for my trouble. But what I most of all wished was, some insight into the still entirely primitive life of the herdsmen.

I hired a guide and a mule, and, provided with a little bread and some calabashes of wine, early on the morning of the 28th of July I rode into the hills. The road, a shepherd's track, never leaves the valley of the wild Restonica, from its confluence with the Tavignano, close by the town, up to the very summit of Monte Rotondo, where it has its source. The bed of this beautiful mountain-stream, is, during most of its course, a ravine of gloomy and impressive character. In the vicinity of Corte, it expands into a valley of considerable breadth, in which chestnut and walnut trees thrive. As you ascend, it grows narrower and narrower; the walls of rock on each side rise in black, gigantic masses, shadowed with dark-green, natural wood, of old pines and larches.

My sure-footed mule clambered safely up the narrowest paths along the very edge of abysses; and a glance downwards into these, where the Restonica foamed milk-white far below, had something in it both of terror and of beauty. A magnificent forest of pines and larches received me as the sun got higher. Very picturesque are these giant trees—the pine with its broad, green roof, and the larch, like the cedar of Lebanon, gnarled, soaring, and rich in branches. Tall erica, box, and wild myrtles, covered with a snow of blossoms, clustered in profusion round their mighty stems. And the fragrance of all those medicinal herbs, in which the mountains of Corsica are so rich, made the air of the woods balsamic and refreshing.

My guide kept on before me at a rapid pace. I sometimes almost shuddered, when I saw myself alone with him in this wilderness of woods and rocks, and he threw a backward glance on me. He was an ill-favoured fellow, and had a villanous eye. I learned afterwards that there was blood on his hands—that he was a murderer. A year previously he had stabbed a Lucchese dead, with a single thrust, on the market-place of Corte.

Riding for hours through these romantic mountain-solitudes you hear nothing but the rushing of the streams, the screaming of falcons, and now and then the clear whistle of a goat-herd calling to his goats.

The herdsmen live in caverns or in huts, on the declivities of Monte Rotondo, to the topmost ridge of which their flocks clamber. The highest community of shepherds is to be found at an altitude of 5000 feet above the level of the sea.

After three hours' ride I reached the first of these singular stations—the Rota del Dragone. Descending from the edge of the ravine towards the water, I saw a black, sooty cave before me, running, like a vault, into the cliff, below enormous blocks of granite—a few paces from its entrance the furious Restonica, chafing itself to madness among huge fragments of rock; all around, crag above crag, and dense forest. A wall of uncemented stones formed an enclosure round the entrance of the grotto. A fire was burning in the cave, round which cowered the shepherd family. A miserable-looking woman seemed to be engaged in mending some article of dress; beside her a fever-sick boy lay wrapped in a brown blanket of goat's wool, from which his pale face and glittering eyes looked out inquiringly.

The herdsman had come out of his cave, and hospitably invited me to alight, and refresh myself with new milk and cheese. I willingly accepted his invitation, and proceeded to inspect the interior of this singular cavernous abode. The grotto, I found, ran a considerable way into the mountain, affording room for a flock of two hundred goats and sheep, which the herdsman every evening brings in to milk. It was so exactly the cave of Polyphemus, that it almost seemed Homer must have taken his description from it. Every item of the description was here, even the rows of dishes full of milk, and more than a hundred flat round cheeses arranged on fresh leaves. Only Polyphemus himself was wanting; for mine host, however robber-like and wild he might look in his shaggy habiliments, was hospitality itself.

"Do the bandits ever pay you a visit?" I asked the Troglodyte. "Sometimes they do," said the man; "when they're hungry. You see the stone here on which I sit?—two years ago a couple of bandit-hunters concealed themselves in my cave; they were after Serafin. But Serafin stole in upon them through the night, and with two stabs he made them both cold upon this stone; then he went his way again into the hills."

My guide hinted that it was time to go. I thanked the herdsman for his refreshment, and rode off, not without a shudder.

The path, which now took us through the Restonica to the other bank, became constantly steeper and more difficult. At last, after a ride of two hours, I reached, thoroughly damp with mist, and during a magnificent thunderstorm, the last of the pasturing-stations on the lower heights of Rotondo. Its name is Co di Mozzo.

I had heard a great deal about the shielings of Monte Rotondo; and the pictures of them my imagination drew were original enough, slightly idyllic perhaps—little huts in the green pine-forest, or on flowery Alpine slopes, with all proper pastoral adjuncts. But now, as I rode up in the midst of thunder and lightning, and through a drizzling rain, I saw nothing but a wild waste of titanic fragments of stone—a confusion of vast granite blocks clothing the sides of a huge, gray, desolate cone. A light smoke was rising from among the stones. The gray of the watery clouds, the pale lightnings, the roll of the thunder, the rushing of the Restonica, and the deep melancholy of the gray hills, were irresistibly saddening.

Some storm-battered larches stood on the steepest edge of a naked ravine, through which the Restonica foamed and tumbled from block to block. All around, nothing but the dreariest cliffs; and one grand glimpse into the mist-filled valley out of which I had ascended. My eye sought long for the huts towards which the guide was pointing. At length I detected them among the rocks, and advancing, I soon had before me this most singular of pastoral communities. It consisted of four dwellings, erected in the most primitive manner conceivable, probably with less architectural skill than the termites or the beavers expend on their houses.

Each of these huts consists of four stone walls, built without mortar. They are about three feet in height, and support a sloping roof of sooty stems of trees and boards, on which heavy stones are laid to keep them in their places. An aperture in the front wall serves as door and principal chimney; but the smoke issues through the roof and the walls wherever it finds a chink. An enclosure of stones surrounds a narrow space before the hut, and within this space, dishes of various kinds stand; also, in one corner of it rises the *palo*—a rude stake with projecting pegs, on which hang pots and kettles, clothes, and strips of goat's flesh.

Some shaggy dogs sprang out as I rode up, and forthwith the men, women, and children crept from their huts, and curiously eyed the stranger. They looked picturesque enough in the midst of the stony waste; the *pelone*, their shaggy, brown mantle flung about them, the red *baretto* on their heads, and their bronzed features looking out from their dark bushy beards.

I called to them: "Friends, bestow your hospitality on a stranger who has come over the sea to visit the herdsmen of Co di Mozzo!"

In friendly tones they returned: "Evviva!" and "Benvenuto!"

"Come into my hut," said one, "and dry yourself at the fire; it is warm in there." I immediately twisted myself through the door, curious to see the interior of such a habitation. I found myself in a dark chamber, about fourteen feet in length and ten in breadth—wholly without furniture, not a stool, not a table, nothing but the black naked ground, the black, naked stone walls, and such a smoke of pine-wood as, I thought, it must be impossible to live in. Close by the wall a huge log was burning, and a kettle hung above it.

Angelo, my host, spread a blanket which I had brought with me on the floor, and gave me the place of honour, as near the fire as possible. Soon the whole family had cowered about it—Angelo's wife, three little girls, my host, myself, and my guide. The hut was full. Meanwhile, Angelo threw some pieces of goat's flesh into the kettle, and Santa his wife brought cheese and milk. Our table equipage was as original and pastoral as you choose; it consisted simply of a board laid upon the ground, on which Santa placed a wooden bowl of milk, a cheese, and some bread. "Eat," said she, "and think that you are with poor herd-people; you shall have trouts for supper, for my son has gone a-fishing."

"Fetch the broccio," said the shepherd; "it is the best we have, and you will like it." I was curious to see what the broccio was; I had heard it praised in Corte as the greatest dainty of the island, and the flower of all the hill-products. Santa brought a sort of round covered basket, set it before me, and opened it. Within lay the broccio, white as snow. It is a kind of sweet, curdled, goats' milk; and eaten with rum and sugar, it certainly is a dainty. The poor herdsmen sell a broccio-cake in the city for one or two francs.

With our wooden spoons we wrought away valiantly at the broccio—only the wife and children did not share. Crouching thus on the ground at the fire, in the narrow, smoke-filled hut, wild and curious faces all about me, the wooden spoon in my hand, I began humorously to celebrate the life of the shepherds among the hills, who are contented with what their flocks yield them, and know not the wretchedness of *mine* and *thine*, nor the golden cares of palaces.

But the honest *pastore* shook his head, and said: "*Vita povera, vita miserabile!*" —a poor life, a miserable life!

And so it really is: these men lead a wretched life. For four months of the year—May, June, July, and August—they burrow in these cabins, destitute of everything that makes life human. In *their* world occur no changes but those of the elements—the storm, the clouds, the thunder-shower, the hail, the heat; in the evening, a robber-story by the fire, a melancholy song, a *lamento* to the pipe, a hunting-adventure with the muffro or the fox; high above them and around them the giant pyramids of the hoary Rotondo, and the starry magnificence of the sky; in their breast, perhaps, despite the *vita povera*, an uncomplaining, serene, pious, honest human heart.

With the dawn of day these poor people rise from the hard ground—on which they have been sleeping in their clothes, and without other covering— and drive their herds to the pastures; there they consume their scanty meal, of cheese, bread, and milk. The old people, who remain at home, lie in the hut by the fire, occupied with some simple household work. In the evening, the flocks return and are milked; light falls, and it is time to go to sleep again.

The snow and rains of September drive the herdsmen from their mountain cabins. They descend with their flocks to the coast and the paese, where they have usually more habitable dwellings, in which frequently the wives and children stay all summer. My hostess Santa was the only female in the pastoral community of Co di Mozzo, which consists of six families. "Why," I asked her, "did you come up from the paese to this gloomy hut?" "Look you," put in Angelo, "she came up to refresh herself." I was on the point of laughing outright, for the smoke in the hovel was bringing tears to my eyes, and the atmosphere was infernal. So, after all, I was to view the wretched heap of stones as a summer villa, to which the family had retired to refresh itself! "Yes," said Angelo, as he caught my sceptical look; "below, it is warm; and up here, we have the mountain wind, and the clear stream, fresh and cold as ice. We live as the merciful God grants." I began to have respect for Angelo and his philosophy. His speech was serious and laconic; and he was taciturn, as it becomes a philosopher to be.

Angelo was owner of sixty head of goats, and fifty sheep. The quantity of milk drawn from these is inconsiderable. In summer it is barely sufficient to support the family. The broccio and the cheese, sold below, furnish bread, and the coarsest clothing. Winter is a hard time, for the milk goes to feed the kids and lambs. Many a shepherd, however, has a flock of some hundreds. When the sons and daughters have to be portioned, it is a fortunate thing if the luck of the patriarchs can be had, so that the flocks multiply. The dowry of a shepherd's girl consists in twelve goats if she is poor; if she is wealthy it ranges higher, according to her parents' means.

The weather had cleared up. I stepped out of the cabin, and drew long breaths of the fresh air. The shepherds sat here and there on the stones, smoking their little wooden pipes. They are in the habit of choosing the oldest, or the most respected of their number, to preside in the community, and arbitrate in all disputes. This circumstance, which I discovered accidentally, surprised me; for it allowed me, in this little democracy of shepherds, a glance into the primitive condition of human society, and the beginnings of political life. It seems six men cannot live together without regulating their society, and developing laws. I greeted the little stumpy podestà most reverently; and as I contemplated him in silence, I thought him more venerable than Dejoces, the first and wisest of all the kings of the Medes.

Near the cabins I remarked smaller covered huts of stone, of a round or of an oblong form. These were the storehouses. Angelo opened a little door in his, and creeping in, beckoned me to follow; I contented myself with peeping in. I saw the flat cheeses lying on green twigs, and white balls of goats'-milk butter in little baskets.

I sat down on a stone, and commenced sketching the cabins. The whole community came round me, and looked on with expressions of the liveliest delight. Every one now wanted to have his portrait taken, in order that it might afterwards be "printed" in Paris, as they said. They would have it that I was from Paris; and I could not make it intelligible to them, that besides Paris, there was another country called Germania. "Germania, then," said my host, "is your paese; and this paese has kings, and it belongs to Paris." There the matter had to rest.

The afternoon sun shone warmly, and tempted me into the hills. I took the children with me—Antonio, a boy of thirteen, shaggy as a bear; Paola Maria, and Fiordalisa. Fiordalisa means Lily-flower. Let the reader picture to himself this Lily-flower of Monte Rotondo: she has seen twelve summers; her dress is considerably tattered, her dark hair hangs wild about her brown face, her eyes are clear and keen as a falcon's, her teeth are white as ivory, and she climbs the rocks barefoot with the agility of a chamois. We botanized along the Restonica. I espied some beautiful red pinks on a ledge that I could hardly have reached, and I pointed to them. "Aspettate! wait!" cried the Lily-flower; and she was off like lightning up the cliff, and presently she was down again with a handful of the pinks. The children now emulated each other in climbing and dancing on the perilous crags like so many elves; fear seemed a thing quite unknown to these little mountain-sprites. As we were crossing the Restonica on our return home, Lily-flower sprang into the stream, and took the wild fancy of splashing me with water, which she did most unsparingly. I found the red foxglove growing in great abundance in these hills—my little elves brought it me in armfuls; and when we got home, we encircled the smoking hut with a garland of the poisonous beauties—a decoration that it had probably never before met with. This was to be a holiday token on the cabin that a guest was there, since with good men it is always festival when their house shelters a guest.

Lily-flower's delight in the garland was unbounded. "To-morrow," she said, "when you are up on the hill, you will find a blue flower—the most beautiful flower in all Corsica."

"If you say it, Fiordalisa, then it must be true, and to-morrow I shall find the blue wonder-flower."[L]

Evening came on in the great, silent wilderness. Weary with my day's fatigues, I sat down before the cabins, and contemplated the changeful play of the clouds. Mists ascended from the ravines, and, attracted or repelled by the mountains, rolled themselves together in the valleys, or dispersed, and were lost among the clouds trailing slowly from above along the hill-tops. The flocks and herds were coming in. I saw with pleasure the long lines of the graceful black goats, and the black sheep, to which the poor shepherds owe their subsistence. Each herdsman drove, or drew them by a peculiar clear call, into an enclosure beside his cabin, and there milked them. This operation is managed with astonishing rapidity: the herdsman sits in the centre of the herd, and catches one goat after another by the hind legs. He calls every animal by its name; he knows each exactly. The mark of ownership is generally on the ear. Forty head of goats, belonging to my host, yielded only a single moderate pailful of milk.

The herds remain within the enclosure during the night. The shaggy dogs protect them, not from the wolf, which is not found in Corsica, but from the fox, which is remarkably bold and powerful among the hills, and attacks the lambs. My host's Rosso and Mustaccio were two magnificent dogs.

Meantime the eldest son had returned with a number of beautiful trouts, and Angelo busied himself with supper. I noticed that it was always the man who cooked, and not his wife. Was this in honour of his guest? For the position of woman in general in Corsica is low and menial. As I was thinking of this, it occurred to me that in Homer the men perform all similar operations—put the meat on the spit, roast it, and bring it to the table; so that I had living and acting before me, the man of the epic and primitive epoch of culture. In Corsica are to be found the men of Homer and the men of Plutarch.

We had a bread-soup, cheese and milk, and, in honour of the guest, roasted goat's flesh. For this classic goat-herd took the flesh from the *palo*, and, after the fashion of ancient times, stuck it on a spit, and, kneeling, held it over the glowing fire. Carefully, from time to time, a piece of bread was pressed upon the dripping fat, that the precious juice of the sweet loin-pieces might not be lost. He cooked the trouts in a broth of goat's flesh; and when they were ready, he set them before me, and ladled me forth from the mighty ladle as much as heart could desire. I saw it in the children's eyes, that this was no ordinary meal; and it would have refreshed me still more admirably, had they been allowed to share it.

It was night in the cabin. I was puzzled to imagine how our sleeping was to be arranged within the narrow limits. But that was soon managed. My blanket was spread for me on the ground, and I stretched myself on it, beside the innermost wall; I was at a loss, however, for something on which to rest my head. I looked at Angelo. "Divine and wise Angelo," I said, "give ear. I have never, I swear to you, been a Sybarite, yet am I accustomed to pillows. Could not your hospitality provide me with some such convenience?" Angelo pondered; then he handed me his zaïno or shepherd's bag of goatskin, and spoke the winged words—"Now sleep, and *felicissima notte!*"

Gradually the others laid themselves down, wife and children, on the naked earth, leaning their heads on the wall. Angelo lay nearest the threshold; beside him the youngest child Maria; then Santa his wife, Lily-flower, Paola Maria, and myself. So we all lay peaceably together, our feet turned towards the fire. It was not long till they were all asleep, and I lay contemplating with satisfaction this happily slumbering family of Gymnosophists, and mused on the words of the wise Sancho, when he praised the inventor of sleep, "the mantle that covers all human care, the food that appeases hunger, the water that extinguishes thirst, the fire that warms the cold, the cold that alleviates the heat—in short, the universal money for which all things may be bought, the beam and scale that equalizes king and shepherd." The fire shed a red glow over the singular group. I lamented that I was not a painter. But the intolerable heat and smoke of the pitch-pine would not let me sleep. I rose from time to time and stepped over the sleepers into the free air. I may say this was stepping from hell into heaven—for I walked straight into a cloud that had descended on the hill, and enveloped the cabins.

The night was chill and moist; but the clouds passed off, and the infinite sky threw its myriad lights on the mists, on the craggy heights, and the dark larches. I sat long beside the rushing Restonica, whose tumultuous din broke the impressive silence of the still, pure night. The spirit of solitude had never come so near me as it did that night among the black crags, at the brink of a headlong brook, far up among the clouds and mists, face to face with primitive nature, lost in a foreign island girt with many a mile of sea. In such moments, the feeling of loneliness becomes oppressive, and the sudden thought alarms the soul, that the human being is but an insignificant atom; and that perhaps this spiritual atom may in an instant lose and forget its connexion with all related to it, and remain lonely in void space. But the soul is not thus to be overcome; it spreads its wings for the distant home, there regains its serenity, and loneliness has fled. I listen to sounds that seem to be borne to me from the hills; they sound sometimes like wild laughter—it is the mad Restonica that is so unquiet. These stones are the dumb witnesses to ancient, dreadful birth-pangs, offspring of the fieriest embraces of Uranus and Gaea.

The cold air drove me again to the fire. Overcome with fatigue, I at last fell asleep, when I was suddenly awakened by the clear voice of Santa, who cried several times, *Spettacoli divini! spettacoli divini!* She was putting the children to rights; they had flung themselves about into all sorts of comic positions. Divine spectacles they were certainly. Lily-flower lay rolled up like a snake half over her mother; Paola had thrown her arm about my neck. The child had perhaps heard an owl in her sleep, or seen the vampire in a dream, that comes to suck the heart's-blood.

I spent the rest of the night sitting looking into the fire, and amused myself with imaginary representations of the heretics whom the Holy Catholic Church has burned to the honour of God. Now this is quite an endless amusement.

CHAPTER IV
THE MOUNTAIN-TOP

The day was dawning. I went out and refreshed myself in the waves of the sleepless Restonica, which sprang young and fresh from rock to rock, and hastened down into the valley. The young stream has a beautiful life. After a merry career of twelve hours through ever-green woods, it dies in the waters of the Tavignano. The Restonica gained my affections. I know the whole story of its life; for I have accompanied it in a single day, from its first leap to the end of its course; and many a glorious draught did it afford me. Its water is as clear, as fresh, and as light as ether; and is renowned far and wide throughout the land of Corsica. I never drank better water; it was more grateful than the noblest wine. There is such a keen quality in this incomparable stream, that it cleans iron to the purity of a mirror in the shortest time, and preserves it from rust; Boswell mentions that the Corsicans of Paoli's time laid their rusty gun-barrels in the Restonica to clean them. It makes all the stones and gravel that it washes milk-white; and its channel and banks glitter with such stones down to its confluence with the Tavignano.

On asking my guide to ascend with me now to the summit of Rotondo, he confessed that he did not know the road. Angelo, therefore, became my guide. We began the ascent between three and four o'clock in the morning. It was less dangerous but infinitely more fatiguing than I had supposed.

A number of ridges that rise one above the other, have to be surmounted before we reach Trigione, from which the ascent of the highest peak commences. These successive heights form a mighty scala—a stair piled by the hand of Nature—of colossal steps of primeval reddish granite; huge Titans, storming heaven with rocks in their giant hands, might be fit to stride them. Block lies here over block, vast and formless as chaos, and towering upwards and upwards in such endless masses of monotonous gray, that the heart almost quails, and the foot refuses to go farther. The rains of autumn have, in many places, given the granite such a remarkable smoothness, that it presents large surfaces with all the polish of a mirror. The water was running in a thousand little channels, in exhaustless abundance. Tree vegetation, however, here ceases, and only alder-bushes mark where the young Restonica is collecting its waters.

In two hours we had climbed Trigione, and the white snow-covered summit lay before us. Its steep and jagged cliffs form an incomplete circle (hence the name Rotondo—round), partly hollowed out, like a crater; and where this huge wild amphitheatre of rocks opens, lies a little dark lake, the Lago di Monte Rotondo, encircled by gentle green slopes; an ice-cold draught in a giant beaker of granite. Snow-fields rise from the lake to the summit—a strange sight, and producing a peculiar impression, in the hottest dog-days, under a southern sky and the 42d degree of latitude. They were covered with a crust of ice, and perceptibly cooled the air near them. But though I was in the region of eternal snow, I found the temperature pleasantly cool and bracing, and by no means uncomfortably low.

The summit appeared to the eye near enough, yet it took us two full hours' climbing, often on our hands and feet, over the shattered fragments of rock, before we reached it. The most difficult part of it was the ascent over a strip of snow, on which we could not keep our footing. We succeeded, however, by dint of hammering steps in the icy crust with sharp stones, in making cautious progress. At length, much exhausted, we reached the extreme peak, a torn and rugged obelisk of gray rock ending in a slender pinnacle, clinging to which one manages to support himself on the giddy and somewhat perilous height.

From this highest point of Corsica, then, 9000 feet (exactly 2764 metres) above the sea level, I saw the greater part of the island, and the sea far below washing its coast on both sides—a sight of inexpressible grandeur, once to have enjoyed which may justly be to any man a life-long source of pleasant thought. The horizon which the eye can take in from Rotondo is much grander and more beautiful than that afforded by Mont Blanc. The view ranges far over the island itself into the glittering distances of the sea, over the Tuscan islands to the mainland of Italy, which in clear weather shows the white Alps of the northern lakes, and the entire bend of the coast from Nice to Rome. On the other side rise the mountains of Toulon, and the wondrous panorama thus includes within its magic circle, mountains, seas, islands, the Alps, the Apennines, and Sardinia. I was not so fortunate as to have the prospect presented to me in its entire magnificence, for the clouds that rolled themselves unceasingly up from the ravines, and the exhalations, deprived me of part of the distance. To the north I saw the peninsula of Cape Corso stretching itself into the sea like a dagger; to the east the level coast country descending in easy lines, the islands of the Tuscan sea, and Tuscany itself; to the west the Gulfs of Prato, Sagone, Ajaccio, and Valinco. Ajaccio showed itself very distinctly on its tongue of land in the beautiful bay—a row of little white houses, that looked like swans swimming in the sea. The sea itself seemed an ocean of light.

Southwards the broad-breasted Monte d'Oro shuts out the view of the island. A great many peaks, little lower than Rotondo, and, like it, crowned with glittering snow, were visible on every hand, as the finely-formed Cinto, and Cape Bianco towards the north—the highest summits of the district of Niolo.

From such a comprehensive point of view the island itself shows like an enormous skeleton of rocks. Monte Rotondo does not lie within the main mountain-chain which traverses the island from north to south—it belongs to a subsidiary range running towards the east; nevertheless from its summit the spectator commands the entire gigantic net-work of cells that forms the mountain-system of the island. He sees the main chain close before him, and from this backbone the ribs running out on each side in parallel ranges, with valleys between, which are inhabited and cultivated. Each of these valleys is traversed by a stream, while from the principal range run also the three largest rivers of the island—towards the east coast, the Golo and Tavignano; towards the west, the Liamone.

Glancing from the summit of Rotondo on the scene in the immediate vicinity, the eye is startled and affrighted at these vast and desolate wastes of rock, and the giant ruins of shattered crag and cliff lying around. Huge blocks are tumbled about here in a wild chaos, like monuments of the struggle of the spirits of the elements with the light of heaven. Frightfully steep walls of rock form a net-work of dreary valleys. In the centre of most of them lies a little motionless lake, blue, gray, or deep black, according as it receives light from the sky or shadow from the cliffs. I counted several such lakes not far off, Rinoso, Mello, Nielluccio, Pozzolo, from which brooks run to the Restonica, and Oriente, the principal fountain-head of the Restonica itself. Farther to the north-west I had before me the famous pastoral highlands of Niolo, the most elevated basin of the island, with its black lake Nino, from which the Tavignano flows.

These diminutive lakes are all of great depth, and swarming with trout.

As you stand on the summit you hear a continual sound of rushing waters; part of them are forcing their way under ground. This rigid, blasted wilderness, we perceive, overflows with living fountains, which descend to bless the valleys, and there make culture and human society possible; far down on the lower declivities of these mountains the eye catches here and there a paese and green gardens, and patches of yellow field.

Clouds began to gather round the peak; we had to descend. Returning, we took the difficult route by the Lago di Pozzolo. In this direction rises, black and jagged, the colossal Frate, the mightiest granite pyramid of Rotondo. Chaotic debris covers its huge base, which sinks into the dreary glen of the Pozzolo. That blue wonder-flower, which Fiordalisa had said I should find, was growing in the crevices of the rocks. Angelo had plucked one, and cried to me: *Ecco, ecco la fiore?* —see, see the flower! I took it from his hand; it was our Forget-me-not. On the summit of Rotondo itself, I saw camomile, the amaranth, and the ranunculus, growing in abundance, and our own violets graced the very edge of the snow-fields.

It was with great difficulty that we succeeded in scrambling over the stones of Frate, and a strip of snow threatened at last to block up the way altogether. The goat-herd proposed making a *détour* to avoid it, but as a North-Prussian I was not inclined so readily to succumb, and could not resist the temptation of a capital slide. I accordingly placed myself on Angelo's pelone, and made the descent. I had thus the pleasure of a little sledging-trip beneath the summer glow of an Italian sun, and under the 45th degree of latitude.

We breakfasted at the foot of another cone, and, refreshed with some bread, and a draught from a neighbouring brook, pursued our way downwards. I looked round in vain for the wild animals that haunt the rocks of Monte Rotondo—the Muffro namely, or wild sheep—and the bandits. Although Angelo assured me there were plenty of them in the clefts and ravines that we passed, I could discover none. The only wild creature I saw on these heights was the pretty mountain-finch of Monte Rotondo—a bird with gray body, and red, white, and black wings.

The Corsican wild sheep, the Muffro or Mufflone, is one of the most remarkable products of the island. It is a beautiful, strong-limbed animal, with spiral horns, and silky hair of a brownish-black. It inhabits the highest regions of eternal snow, mounting constantly higher as the summer sun melts the snow from the hills. By day it frequents the shores of the lakes, where it finds pasturage; at night it retires again to the snow. The muffro sleeps on the snow, and the female drops its young on the snow. Like the chamois, the muffro posts sentinels while feeding. Sometimes, in severe winters, when deep snow covers their pasture-grounds, these wild sheep appear in herds among the tame goats, and they are frequently to be seen in the valleys of Vivario, Niolo, and Guagno, feeding peaceably among the flocks of the shepherds. The young animal may be tamed, the old not. They are frequently hunted, and when shots are heard echoing from rock to rock up among the hills, people know that men are stalking the muffro or the bandit. Both are lawful game, brothers of the mountain-fastnesses, and both climb to the eternal snow.

After a descent of three hours we reached the cabins, and the foul atmosphere of these wretched hovels contrasted so disagreeably with the pure ether I had been breathing, that I did not rest more than an hour till I had the mule saddled, and put myself on the road for Corte. I bade the good people of Co di Mozzo a hearty farewell, and wished that their flocks might increase and multiply like the flocks of Jacob. They accompanied me to the gate of the enclosure; and as I rode away, men and children saluted me with an honest burst of *evvivas*.

A ride of some hours brought me once more to the region of chestnuts and citrons, and I had thus, in one day, from the heights of perpetual snow to the gardens of Corte, travelled through three distinct zones of climate, which was like journeying from the arctic winter of Norway to the countries of southern Europe.

CHAPTER V
VENDETTA OR NOT?

I was not destined to leave the quiet Corte without some slightly unpleasant recollections, and that owing to my guide of Monte Rotondo. It was not till after I had returned to the town that I learned to what a furious and passionate individual I had trusted myself. Although he had told me a falsehood, and, proving to be unacquainted with the road to the summit, had compelled me to take the goat-herd Angelo as guide, I gave him the full hire we had agreed on. But the fellow, in the most impudent way, demanded half as much again. The vehement language on both sides drew the notice of some Corsican gentlemen, who took my part. "This is a stranger," said one of them to the guide, "and with us the stranger is always in the right." I replied to the polite speaker, "that I claimed my rights not as a stranger, but as a man, and that I should instantly have recourse to the authorities of the town, if the rascal continued to molest me." The latter threw his wages on the table, and stormed out of the room, exclaiming that he should know how to have his revenge on the German. On this the landlady of the locanda came to me and bade me be on my guard, as the fellow was passionate beyond all bounds, and last year had stabbed a man in the market-place.

Somewhat anxious, I asked the reason. "Because," said the landlady, "the Lucchese had struck his little brother for hanging on to his cart, as children do. The boy ran with his complaint to his brother, who instantly rushed out with his dagger, and murdered the other with one blow."

"How was he punished?" "With five months' imprisonment; for somehow or other the murder could not be properly proved." "Now, I confess—*la giustizia Corsa è un poco corta*—your Corsican justice is a little short; but, my good woman, you knew the ungovernable temper of this man—you knew he had already shed blood, and yet you yourself engaged me this devil for a guide, and allowed an unarmed stranger to enter the hills with him!"

"I thought, sir, you would see it in his eyes, and I gave you a wink once or twice, too. The fellow had offered himself, and if I had been the reason of your sending him away, then *I* should have got myself into trouble."

I now remembered that the good woman had asked me as I was going off with the guide: "When do you expect to return?" and that when I said, "In two days," she shrugged her shoulders, and seemed to intimate something with her eyes.

"Very well," I said to the woman, "I shall not give the man a single quattrino more than was agreed on. On that my mind is made up."

He came in the evening and took away quietly enough the money I had thrown down. But although this looked like an admission of his misconduct, I thought it best to maintain a sharp look-out, and did not go beyond the gates after night-fall.

The following evening I took a walk in the company of a Corsican officer whose acquaintance I had made. Outside the gate I witnessed a slight specimen of Corsican temperament. A youth of about fifteen had tied a horse to a fence, and was throwing stones at it, quite beside himself with rage, and howling out his fury like some maddened beast. The poor animal had probably offended him by a fit of obstinacy. I stood looking at him, and provoked at such malignant brutality, at last called to him to cease. Instantly my companion said to me: "For Heaven's sake come away, and be quiet." I obeyed, not a little struck with the scene, and the suppressed tones in which my companion had addressed me. This, too, was a glimpse of the state of Corsican society.

Shortly after, the youth flew past on the horse like a demon, his hair streaming, his face on flame, his eyes still sparkling with fury.

I felt deeply at that moment that I was among barbarians, and a sudden longing for Florence and its mild Italians filled me.

But there was still another disagreeable little incident in store for me. We had not gone a mile further into the hills, when I saw my guide walking along a height a little distance from the road, his gun upon his shoulder. He sat down on a rock, resting his piece across his knee. I did not know whether he still bore me a grudge, and meant mischief, but it was possible. I pointed him out to my companion, and continued my walk past him, not choosing to show any signs of fear; but I felt uncomfortable. "He will not shoot at you," said the officer, "unless you have offended him by some injurious word. But if you have done that, no saying what may happen; these men will stand no insult." He did not shoot, for which I was obliged to the bloodthirsty vampire, or the poor devil, let me rather call him—for nature sins here more than man. The blood that is shed among the Corsican hills is seldom shed from such a despicable motive as lust of gold—almost always from false notions of honour. The Corsican Vendetta is a chivalrous duel for life and death.

CHAPTER VI
FROM CORTE TO AJACCIO

Travelling from Corte to Ajaccio, you keep ascending for several leagues till you reach Monte d'Oro; the road leads southwards through a beautiful and well-cultivated undulating region, full of magnificent chestnut-groves. Nothing can be more cheerful than the landscapes of the canton of Serraggio, formerly the pieve of Venaco. Brooks which descend from Monte Rotondo water here a lovely green country, on whose eminences little hamlets stand, as Pietro, Casa Nova, Riventosa, and Poggio.

Poggio di Venaco preserves the memory of the handsome Arrigo Colonna, who was Count of Corsica in the tenth century. As the traveller wanders onwards, he lights every now and then on romantic old traditions, which keep his imagination busy, and form great part of his pleasure. Arrigo was so beautiful in person, and courteous and graceful in manner, that he was called the Bel-Messere; and by this name he still lives in the mouths of the people. His wife, too, was a beautiful and noble woman, and his seven children were all fair and young. But his foes were resolved to rob him of his authority, and a fierce Sardinian conspired with them against his life. One day, the assassins fell upon him and stabbed him, and they took his seven children and threw them all into the lake "of the seven bowls." When this wicked deed had been done, a voice was heard in the air, which wailed and cried, "Bel-Messere is dead! Luckless Corsica, hope for no happiness more!" All the people raised a lament for Bel-Messere; but his wife took shield and spear, and hastened at the head of her vassals to the castle of Tralavedo, to which the murderers had retired, and she burned down the castle, and put all the murderers to the sword. Still many a night on the green hills of Venaco nine ghosts may be seen wandering about; these are the ghosts of Bel-Messere, his wife, and the seven poor children.

It was Sunday. The people were walking about in the villages, or, oftener, they were to be seen, like their fathers in times long gone by, sitting round the church;—a beautiful picture in the Sabbath stillness, men peacefully keeping the holiday of God's rest. But even on Sunday, and before the church-door, there comes a sudden musket-shot sometimes, and then the scene changes.

In the neighbourhood of Vivario the country becomes wilder, and the eminences more considerable. Many a passer-by stops a while at the threshold of the little church of Vivario, and looks at a gravestone there. A verse of the Bible in Latin is engraved on it—*Maledictus qui percusserit clam proximum suum, et dicet omnis populus amen*—Cursed be he that smiteth his neighbour secretly, and all the people shall say, Amen. The stone tells a Vendetta story of the seventeenth century; under it the avenger of blood lies buried. Blessed be the memory of the priest of Vivario, who took this curse from the Bible and engraved it upon the stone. They say it is the talisman of Vivario, for the last Vendetta of the village is thereon inscribed. Would that the hand that wrote it had been the hand of a giant, and had written in giant letters over all Corsica—*Maledictus qui percusserit clam proximum suum, et dicet omnis populus amen!*

In a lonely and desolate part of the mountains of Vivario stands a little blockhouse, with a garrison of ten men. The large valley of the Tavignano ends here, and a range of heights forms the water-shed between it and the Gravone, which flows in the opposite direction, towards Ajaccio. On the boundary line between the two valleys stand the two snow-capped mountains, Monte Renoso and Monte d'Oro, which latter attains an elevation only a few metres less than that of Rotondo, and surpasses it in grandeur of form. For many hours the traveller has this mountain constantly before his eye.

The road passes between the two mountains, through the glorious forest of Vizzavona. It consists mainly of larches, which are frequently 120 feet in height, and twenty-one in thickness. Of all the fir species this mighty, broad-branched, fragrant larch is probably the finest, next to the cedar; and as I have no acquaintance with the cedars of Asia I may say that the Corsican larch is the most imposing tree I ever beheld. To see it in its silent, gloomy majesty on the mighty granite rocks of these hills was always a high enjoyment for me. It well befits this imperial tree to stand on granite. It towers high above the cliffs, which its roots victoriously pierce; and on many spots, known only to the eagle and the wild sheep, it rises in solitary majesty. There are magnificent specimens of various other kinds of firs in the forest, red beeches, and evergreen oaks (*ilex*). It shelters abundance of game, particularly deer, which are in Corsica of no great size; the wild swine frequent the regions nearer the coast, where they are eagerly hunted.

The forest of Vizzavona is, next to that of Aitone in the canton of Evisa, the largest in Corsica. All these forests are in the mountainous districts. Some belong to the state, most of them to the communes. Nothing, comparatively speaking, has yet been made of them. I observed a snake sunning itself by the wayside. Corsica has only two species of snakes, and no poisonous animals except a spider called Malmignatto—the bite of which produces a sudden chill all over the body, and sometimes death—and the venomous ant Innafantato.

It was about noon when I passed through the forest. There was a suffocating heat in the atmosphere, but the wood offered its cool springs. Everywhere they trickle down the rocks to swell the waters of the Gravone; their water is cold and pleasant. Seneca can never have tasted the Corsican mountain streams, else he would not have said in his epigram that Corsica could not afford a draught of water.

At length I reached the ridge of the hills, at the highest point on the road to Ajaccio, 3500 feet above the level of the sea. This is the Foce, or Pass of Vizzavona, frequently mentioned in the Corsican popular songs.

The road now descends into the valley of Gravone. Two chains of mountains confine this fruitful valley. The northern, running out from Monte d'Oro, ends above Ajaccio in the Punta della Parata. It separates the basin of the Gravone from that of the Liamone. The southern runs out in a parallel direction from Monte Renoso, and separates the valleys of the Gravone and the Prunelli. On both sides of the Gravone stand villages on the hills. They have a more cheerful appearance than any I have ever seen in Corsica.

The first village we enter in this canton is Bocognano, which lies near the mouth of the wild gorge of Vizzavona. On every side rise dark, wooded hills with snowy summits; the whole region is of a stern, impressive character. They are herdsmen that dwell here—poor men, but stout in heart and strong in arm. They live on milk, or on chestnuts. Many manufacture the pelone. Every one goes armed in this district. The sight of these powerful men, with their double-barrels and carchera, and in the brown woollen blouse, accords well with the gloomy Alpine heights and the pine-forests all around. These Corsican highlanders look as if they were made of iron, like the fusils which they carry. The people here seemed to be still sticking fast in all the rust and rudeness of the Middle Ages.

The road continues to descend towards Ajaccio. At length we descried the magnificent gulf. It was about five o'clock in the afternoon when we gained the neighbourhood of the city. The richer cultivation of the heights, vineyards, and olive-orchards, and the fertile plain of Campoloro, announced the vicinity of the capital of Corsica. It showed itself as a row of white houses stretching into the gulf, at the foot of a range of hills, and surrounded by villas. Through the avenue of elms, which leads along the gulf into the town, I now, with joyous emotion, entered the little native city of the man who convulsed the world.

BOOK VIII
WANDERINGS IN CORSICA

CHAPTER I
AJACCIO

Ajaccio lies at the northern end of one of the most magnificent gulfs in the world. The lines of its two opposite coasts are of unequal length. The northern is the shorter; it runs out in a westerly direction to the Punta della Parata, off which lie the Isole Sanguinarie, or Bloody Islands. The southern side of the gulf stretches from north to south in a long and very irregular line to Cape Muro, on rounding which you enter the Bay of Valinco.

No villages are seen on the northern shore; on the southern but few, with here and there a solitary tower or a lighthouse. Lofty hills rise over the northern end of the beautiful gulf; at their base lies the valley of the Gravone, ending towards the sea in the fertile plain of Campo di Loro. The situation of Ajaccio has an astonishing resemblance to that of Naples.

It is said that Ajaccio is one of the oldest cities in Corsica. According to the fable of some chroniclers, it derives its name from the Telamonian Ajax; according to others, it was founded by Agazzo, the son of the Trojan prince Corso, who wandered with Æneas into the western Mediterranean, carried off Sica, the niece of Dido, and thus gave the island the name of Corsica. Ptolemy places the ancient city of Urcinium on the Gulf of Ajaccio, supposed to be the Adjacium of the earliest period of the Middle Ages, a town which is always mentioned along with the oldest in the island — with Aleria, Mariana, Nebium, and Sagona, cities which now no longer exist.

The ancient Ajaccio, however, did not occupy the site of the present town; it lay on an eminence farther to the north. The hill is called San Giovanni; on its summit lie the ruins of an old castle, named *Castello Vecchio*, and there formerly lay near them the remains of an ancient cathedral, in which it was customary for the bishops of Ajaccio to be consecrated, long after it had fallen into decay. These ruins have vanished; nothing now betrays the former existence of a city on this spot. But many ancient Roman coins have been found in the vineyards; also oval-shaped sarcophagi of terracotta, always containing a skeleton and a key. It is said that the vaulted tombs of the Moorish kings were also formerly shown here; but they have disappeared.

The new town and the citadel were founded by the Bank of St. George of Genoa in the year 1492. It was the residence of a lieutenant of the Governor of Bastia, and did not become the capital of the island till the year 1811, when it was elevated to its new dignity at the instance of Madame Letitia and Cardinal Fesch, who wished in this way to give distinction to their own and the Emperor's birthplace.

The best view of the town and its environs is from the hill of San Giovanni. It presents one of the prettiest pictures that can be imagined, and is equalled by no other city in Corsica. The distance is incomparable. Cloud-topped hills stretching far into the interior, the majestic gulf in azure splendour, an Italian vegetation and a southern sky—no finer combination could be thought of; and here in the midst of it lies a quite idyllic, silent, innocent little town of 11,500 inhabitants, concealed among the verdure of its elms, the mistress of a region which seems intended to be the environment of one of the capitals of the world.

Ajaccio lies on a tongue of land, the extremity of which is occupied by the castle. Portions of the town stretch on each side of this tongue along the gulf. The avenue of elms and planes which leads into the city is continued along its main street—the Cours Napoleon, which is properly the prolongation of the road from Corte. Part of it has had to be blasted through the rocks, two of which still stand at the entrance of the town, close to the houses. In the Corso itself the elms give place to orange-trees of considerable size, which give the street a rich and festive look. The houses are high, but destitute of architectural merit. The gray jalousies are characteristic; this is the colour preferred in Corsica, while in Italy they are usually of a lively green. The gray gives to the buildings a dead, monotonous air. All the more considerable edifices of the Corso stand on the right side; the little Theatre, the Prefecture—a handsome building—and the military barracks.

The rural quiet pervading these streets of Ajaccio surprised me; but their names speak loudly to the traveller, and relate the history of Napoleon. You read Cours Napoleon, Rue Napoleon, Rue Fesch, Rue Cardinal, Place Letitia, and Rue du Roi de Rome, which last awakens mournful recollections. The memory of Napoleon is the proper soul of the town, and you saunter onwards, out of one little street into another, musing on the wonderful man and his childhood, and soon you have wandered through them all. The Rue Fesch runs parallel with the Cours Napoleon; the former leads to the spacious Place du Diamant, which lies on the shore, and has beautiful view of the gulf and its southern coast; the latter ends in the market-place (*du marché*), and leads to the harbour. These are the two principal streets and squares of Ajaccio. Narrow lanes connect them, and intersect the whole of the tongue of land. The silence invites memory and thought, and silently the mirror of the blue gulf stretches away before the view. You see it from almost every street. The eye is nowhere imprisoned by walls, for the main streets are wide, the squares spacious, planted with green trees; and the sea, and green olive-clad hills, which rise close upon the city, look in upon you wherever you go or stand. Ajaccio is at once an inland and a coast town— you live there in the heart of Nature.

In the cool of the evening, the Corso and Diamond Place grew livelier. The military band began to play in the Place; the people gathered here and there in groups, or moved about. Most of the women wore black veils, those of the middle classes were enveloped in the black faldetta. It was easy to imagine you were in some city of Spain.

The Ajaccians have the finest promenades in the world, whether they choose the beautiful esplanade which has so romantic a name, or the walks along the gulf among alleys of elms, and through vineyards and olive-gardens. I know few promenades from which so fine a view is to be had as that from the quiet Place du Diamant in Ajaccio. Immediately in front of it the murmuring sea; towards the land cheerful rows of houses; among them, a stately military hospital and a handsome Catholic College; close over these houses a green hill. A stone breastwork runs along the side next the gulf; a few steps bring you to the strand, which is fringed by an alley of trees.

I found nothing in Ajaccio more pleasant than to wander about on the Place du Diamant in the evening, when the west wind blew fresh over the gulf, or to sit on the breastwork, and feast my eyes on the magic panorama of sea and hills. The sky of Italy is then lit up with a brilliance as of fairy-land; the air is so clear that the Milky Way and the planet Venus throw long lines of radiance across the gulf, and the waves reflect a mild splendour. Where they are in motion, or are furrowed by a passing skiff, they tremble with phosphorescent sparks. Above, the shore wraps itself in night; the beacons gleam from the headlands, and on the hills you see in many places great fires blazing. They are burning copsewood there—a practice common in the month of August, in order to gain land for tillage, which is at the same time manured by the ashes. These fires continue to burn for days. During the day they roll white clouds of smoke over the hills, at night they glare over the gulf like volcanoes, and then the resemblance to the Gulf of Naples becomes striking. A magnificent illumination may thus be enjoyed every evening on the Diamond Place of Ajaccio.

The market-place is no less beautiful, though it affords a less comprehensive view. You see from it the safe and beautiful harbour, confined by a granite mole erected by Napoleon. On the side of the harbour, a beautiful quay of granite bounds the market-place, which, planted with trees, has a look of rural peace. At its entrance stands the principal fountain in Ajaccio, a large cube of marble, from the sides of which the water gushes into semi-circular basins. It is thronged from morning till night with women and children drawing water; and I could never look on these groups without being reminded of Old Testament scenes of the same character. In warm countries, the wells are the very fountains of poetry and sociable intercourse; well and hearth are the time-honoured centres round which human society has always gathered.—The women here do not draw their water in the antique vessels of metal used in Bastia, but in cask-shaped pitchers of terracotta, the handles of which lie across the mouths. These pitchers are also ancient; and another kind of earthenware pitcher, common in Ajaccio, with a long slender neck, has a thoroughly Etruscan look. The poor inhabitants of the barren island of Capraja support themselves partly by making these vessels, which are sent to great distances.

On the same market-place, behind the fountain, close upon the harbour and before the handsome town-house, stands a marble statue of Napoleon, on an excessively high and disagreeably tapering pedestal of granite. The inscription is as follows: "His native city to the Emperor Napoleon, on the 5th May 1850, the second year of the presidency of Louis Napoleon." Ajaccio had long been endeavouring to raise a monument to Napoleon, and always in vain. The arrival of a statue in Corsica was therefore an event of no small importance for the island. It chanced that the Bonaparte family on one occasion sent Signor Ramolino the statue of a Ganymede. The people seeing it as it was taken out of the vessel, took the eagle of Ganymede for the imperial eagle, and Ganymede himself for Napoleon; they assembled in the market-place, and demanded that the statue should forthwith be placed on the above-mentioned fountain, that they might at last have the great Napoleon in marble in the market-place. The worthy Corsicans, in thus turning the Trojan youth Ganymede into their countryman Napoleon, certainly seem to give some colour to the old fable of the chroniclers, that the Ajaccians are descended from a Trojan prince.

The beautiful statue of Napoleon, by the Florentine Bartolini, was originally intended for Ajaccio; but a disagreement arose about the price (60,000 francs), and Bartolini's work never became one of the ornaments of Ajaccio. The statue of Napoleon in the market-place is by Laboureur, and is only of mediocre merit; but its position, in full view of the gulf, gives it an admirable local effect. It is a consular statue. The consul looks from the pedestal upon the sea, turning from his little native town to the world-embracing element. He wears the Roman toga, and on his head a wreath of bays; his right hand grasps a rudder, which rests upon a ball representing the globe. The idea is happy; for in sight of the gulf the rudder appears a quite natural symbol, and is doubly significant in the hand of an islander. The mind of the beholder dwells here not on the history of the complete, but of the incipient ruler; for he sees around him the little world of Ajaccio, in which the mightiest European man went about as child and youth, unconscious who he was, and for what fate had destined him. Then the memory wanders from the market-place to the gulf, and sees the ship anchor there, which bore the General Napoleon Bonaparte from Egypt to France. During the night he sat on board that vessel, eagerly reading such newspapers as could be procured for him in Ajaccio; and it was here that he formed the resolution to seize that rudder with which he was to rule not France alone, but an empire and a hemisphere, till it broke in his hand, and the man of Corsica went to wreck on the island of St. Helena.

Very few vessels, some luggers, and one or two schooners, lie in the harbour. Not, like the Bay of San Fiorenzo, exposed to the maestrale, or north-west wind, but protected by its shores from every storm, this magnificent gulf is capable of sheltering in its roads the largest fleets. But the port is completely dull, and destitute of trade. Once a week, on Saturday, comes a steamer from Marseilles, and brings news of the world, and supplies of necessary articles. I have often heard Corsicans complain that the native city of Napoleon, though possessing the advantages of an incomparable situation, and an excellent climate, was nothing more than an ordinary little provincial town of France. You only need to walk round the market-place, where most of the shops are, on the ground-floors of the houses, to see how slow the sale of goods is, and how limited the native industry. You do not see a single shop where articles of luxury are sold—nothing but the most indispensable handicrafts, such as shoemaking and tailoring; and the wares that look most like to articles of luxury, seem old-fashioned and spoiled.

I found only one book-shop in Ajaccio: it was kept by a dealer in small wares, who sold soap, cordage, knives, and baskets as well as books. The town-house, however, contains, for Ajaccio, a highly considerable library, of 27,000 volumes. It was founded by Lucian Bonaparte, and the opinion is, that he has done greater service to his country in connexion with this library, than by his epic in twelve cantos: *La Cyrneïde*. The prefecture also possesses a valuable library, which is particularly rich in archives and important documents of Corsican history.

In the town-house is also preserved the collection of pictures which Cardinal Fesch bequeathed to his native city. It consists of 1000 paintings. The poor citizens of Ajaccio have no proper museum in which to hang these; they have consequently lain for years in a lumber-room. Fesch also proposed to make his house an institution for the Jesuits; latterly he made it a college, which now bears his name. It has a principal, and twelve teachers for various branches of science and literature.

Ajaccio is very poor in public institutions and public buildings. Its most important edifice is the house of the Bonapartes.

CHAPTER II
THE CASA BONAPARTE

The narrow street of St. Charles issues upon a little square. An elm stands there before an oldish three-storied house, the plaster of which has been coloured a yellowish-gray; it has a flat roof, and a balustrade above it, a front of six windows in breadth, and doors that look greatly decayed. On the corner of this house you read the words: "*Place Letitia.*"

No marble tablet tells the stranger who has come from Italy, where the houses of great men always bear inscriptions, that he stands before the house of the Bonapartes. He knocks in vain at the door; no voice answers, and all the windows are closely veiled with gray jalousies, as if the house were in a state of siege from the Vendetta. Not a human being is stirring upon the square; a deathlike stillness rests upon the neighbourhood, as if the name of Napoleon had frightened it into silence, or scared all else away.

At length an old man appeared at the window of a house close by, and requested me to return in two hours, when he should be able to give me the key.

Bonaparte's house, which has, I am assured, sustained but slight alteration, though no palace, has plainly been the dwelling of a patrician family. Its appearance shows this, and it is without doubt a palace compared with the village-cabin in which Pasquale Paoli was born. It is roomy, handsome, and convenient. But the rooms are destitute of furniture; the tapestries alone have been left on the walls, and they are decayed. The floor, which, as is usual in Corsica, is laid out in small hexagonal red flags, is here and there ruinous. The darkness produced in the rooms by the closed jalousies, and their emptiness, made them quite dismal.

Once, in the time of the beautiful Letitia, this house was alive with the busy stir of a numerous family, and brilliant with joyous hospitality. Now, it is like a tomb, and in vain you look around you for a single object on which fancy may hang associations with the history of its enigmatic inhabitants. The naked walls can tell no tale.

I do not know when the Casa Bonaparte was erected, but it can hardly be very old. It was built, no doubt, when the Genoese were supreme in the island, perhaps when Louis Quatorze was filling the world with his own fame, and with the fame of France. I thought of the time when the master of the craftsmen who erected it pronounced over the house, on its completion, the customary blessing, and when, according to ancient usage, the family for whom it had been built was solemnly conducted into it by an assemblage of kinsfolk—all alike unconscious that the whim of fortune would one day shower upon its roof the crowns of kingdoms and of empires, and that it was yet to cradle the race of princes who were to share among them the thrones of a continent.

The excited fancy seeks them in these rooms, and sees them assembled round their mother, children in no respect differing from ordinary children— boys who toil over their Plutarch and their Cæsar, schoolmastered by their grave father, or their granduncle Lucian, and three young sisters who grow up thoughtlessly, and rather wild, like their playmates, in the half-barbarous island-town. There is Joseph, the eldest, and there Napoleon, the second son, with Lucian, Louis, and Jerome; there Caroline, Eliza, and Paulina, the children of a notary of moderate income, who is constantly and to no purpose carrying on lawsuits with the Jesuits of Ajaccio about a contested property, of which, with his large family, he stands in great need. For it is a matter of much anxiety to him, how his children are to be provided for. How will they prosper in the world? and in what way secure for themselves a respectable livelihood?

And lo! these same children one day put forth their hands, one after another, and grasp the mightiest crowns of the earth, tear them from the heads of the most unapproachable majesties of Europe, wear them before all the world, are embraced as brothers and brothers-in-law by emperors and kings, while great nations fall submissive at their feet, and abandon to the sons of the notary of Ajaccio their country, their wealth, and their blood. Napoleon is European Emperor, Joseph king of Spain, Louis king of Holland, Jerome king of Westphalia, Paulina a princess of Italy, Eliza a princess of Italy, Caroline queen of Naples. In this little house were so many crowned potentates born and brought up; their mother a woman whose name the world had never heard, daughter of a citizen of a small, obscure, provincial town, Letitia Ramolino, who married at the age of fourteen a man as little known to fame as herself. It may be said with truth, that in her labours this mother travailed with the world's history.

There is no fable in all the Arabian Nights apparently more fabulous than the story of the Bonaparte family. That this romance has, however, realized itself in the quiet, sober days of our modern era, must be regarded as a great fact in history, and as a piece of great good fortune. The history of humanity, clogged with political precedent, and paralysed by bureaus and red tape, has thereby been shaken with earthquake force into fresh activity, and flushed with a new life, and man has been shown to be stronger than a supposed political necessity. Human power and human passion have been freed from the spell under which the traditional limitations of rank had bound them, and it has been proved that the individual, though born among the dust, may become anything and everything, because men are equal. That the history of the Bonapartes should appear fabulous is the fault of the mediæval tinge that still attaches to our ideas of life, and of the received notions as to the impassable barriers interposed by social difference. Napoleon is the political Faust. His historical greatness does not lie in his battles, but in his revolutionary nature. He overthrew the political gods of tradition. The history of this predestined man is therefore very simple, human, and natural, but it cannot yet be written.

History, too, is Nature. There is a chain of causes and effects, and what we call genius, or a great man, is always the necessary result of definite conditions.

More than a thousand years of almost uninterrupted conflict between Corsica and her oppressors preceded the birth of the great conqueror Napoleon, in whose nature this rock-bound island, and this insular people, steeled in conflict, and forcibly thrown back upon itself by the narrow space to which it was confined, created for themselves an organ whose law was—illimitedness. The ascending series was this: the Corsican bandit, the Corsican soldier, Renuccio della Rocca, Sampiero, Gaffori, Pasquale Paoli, Napoleon.

I entered a little room with blue tapestry, and two windows, one of which, with a balcony before it, looked into a court, the other into the street. You see here a wall-press, behind a tapestried door, and a fireplace with a mantelpiece of yellow marble ornamented with some mythological reliefs. In this room, on the 15th of August 1769, Napoleon was born. It is a strange feeling, hard to put in language, which takes possession of the soul on the spot hallowed as the birthplace of a great man. Something sacred, mystic, a consecrated atmosphere, pervades it. It is as if you were casting a glance behind the curtain of Nature, where she creates in silence the incomprehensible organs of her action. But man discerns only the phenomenal, he attempts in vain to ascertain the *how*. To stand in silence before the unsearchable mysteries of Nature, and see with wonder the radiant forms that ascend from the darkness—that is human religion. For the thoughtful man nothing is more deeply impressive than the starry sky of night, or the starry sky of history. I saw other rooms, the ballroom of the family, Madame Letitia's room, Napoleon's little room where he slept, and that in which he studied. The two little wall-presses are still to be seen there in which his school-books stood. Books stand in them at present. With eager curiosity I took out some of them, as if they were Napoleon's; they were yellow with age—law-books, theological treatises, a Livy, a Guicciardini, and others, probably the property of the Pietra Santa family, who are related to the Bonapartes, and to whom their house in Ajaccio now belongs.

It is well to review in connexion with this house the early history of Napoleon, about which our information is still insufficient. I shall relate what I know of it by hearsay or reading. I am largely indebted to the lately published work of the Corsican Nasica—*Mémoires sur l'Enfance et la Jeunesse de Napoléon jusqu'à l'age de vingt-trois ans*. It is dedicated to the uncle's nephew, and is written without talent or insight, but contains facts which are undoubtedly correct, and some valuable documents.

CHAPTER III
THE BONAPARTE FAMILY

The origin of the Bonaparte family can no longer be precisely ascertained. Low flattery has availed itself of the most ridiculous means to procure Napoleon ancient and dignified ancestors. A pedigree has even been constructed beginning with Emanuel II., the eighth Greek emperor of the house of the Comneni, whose two sons are said to have emigrated under the name of Bonaparte after the fall of Constantinople, first to Corfu, then to Naples, Rome, and Florence. From them, as this ridiculous fiction will have it, the Corsican Bonapartes are descended.

It has been historically proved that the Bonapartes figured among the seigniors of the Italian cities during the Middle Ages. The Bonapartes were inscribed in the Golden Book of Bologna, among the Patricians of Florence, and in the book of the nobility of Treviso. When Napoleon became son-in-law of Austria, the Emperor Francis ordered active researches to be made as to the position occupied by the Bonaparte family in Italy during the Middle Ages; and sent his son-in-law some documents purporting to prove that the Bonapartes had been for a long period the lords of Treviso. Napoleon expressed himself as obliged, but replied that he found himself sufficiently honoured in being the Rudolph of Hapsburg of his race. On another occasion he declined the ancient patents of nobility which were being palmed on him, with the words: "I date my nobility from Millesimo and Montenotte."

It is quite uncertain when the Bonapartes came to Corsica. Muratori quotes a document of the year 947, in which three Corsican seigniors—Otho, Domenico, and Guido—gift their estate of Venaco in Corsica to Silverio, Abbot of the cloister of Monte Cristo; a Messer Bonaparte signing the instrument in Mariana, along with other witnesses. The family, or rather a branch of it, would therefore seem to have come to Corsica at an early period. Others, perhaps, followed in later centuries, for the Tuscan Bonapartes were partly Guelphs and partly Ghibellines, and were alternately expatriated with the one or the other faction. It is known that some of them removed to Sarzana, in the district of Lunigiana, where they entered into the service of the powerful Malaspinas, with whom, as I am disposed to believe, they came over to Corsica. Another branch remained in Tuscany, establishing itself there permanently—first in Florence, and afterwards in the little town of San Miniato al Tedesco, which lies upon the road to Pisa. The family had its tomb in the Church of San Spirito at Florence; and I saw there, in the piazza of the convent, a stone with the inscription, in antique lettering—

> S. di Benedeto
>
> Di Piero di Giovanni
>
> Buonaparte. E di sua Descendenti.

The coat of arms above the inscription bears two stars, one in its upper and one in its lower division, significantly enough—for the star has twice ascended over the house of Bonaparte.

Members of his family were still living in San Miniato in the time of Napoleon. After his expedition from Leghorn, he found in the little town the last of that branch of the Bonapartes, in the person of an old canon, Filippo Bonaparte, who made the young hero his heir, and died in the year 1799.

As regards the Bonapartes of Ajaccio, they can be traced with certainty as far back as Messire Francesco Bonaparte, who died in the year 1567. Without doubt, the Corsican branch of the family came over from Sarzana.

The following little table gives Napoleon's ancestry so far as it is known with certainty:—

Francesco Bonaparte. 1567.

|

Gabriele Bonaparte Messire.
Built towers in Ajaccio against the Saracens.

|

Geronimo Bonaparte Egregius, *procurator nobilis*.
Head of the Senators of Ajaccio.

|

Francesco Bonaparte.
Capitano of the Town.

Sebastiano Bonaparte.   Fulvio Bonaparte.

Carlo Bonaparte, *nobilis.*

Ludovico Bonaparte, 1632,
Married Maria of Gondi.

Giuseppe Bonaparte.
Senator of the Town.

Sebastian Bonaparte, *magnificus.*
Senator of the Town, 1760.

Luciano Bonaparte,
Archidiaconus.

Carlo Maria Bonaparte,
Born 29th March 1746, Father of Napoleon,
married Letitia Ramolino.

The Bonapartes played no part in Corsican history. Influential in their own city, and honoured with titles of nobility by the Genoese, to whom Ajaccio was subject, they confined themselves to a share in the civic administration of the town. It is not till Carlo Bonaparte that the name acquires consideration throughout the whole of Corsica, and becomes to a certain extent historic.

Napoleon's father was born, as we have seen, on the 29th of March 1746, at Ajaccio, in a stormy time, when the Corsicans were mustering all their force to shake off the detested yoke of Genoa. Gaffori was then the leader of the Corsicans, and Pasquale still in banishment at Naples. It had become customary with the Bonapartes of Ajaccio, to send their children to complete their education in Tuscany, and particularly to let them study in Pisa. For the Bonapartes remembered their Florentine nobility, and never ceased to assert it. Carlo Bonaparte himself, called himself Nobile and Patrician of Florence. The young Carlo studied first at Paoli's newly founded University in Corte; and then went to Pisa, where many of his countrymen were his fellow-students. He studied jurisprudence; and it is said of him, that his talents and learning procured him respect, and his generosity attachment. Returning to his native country after graduating as Doctor of Laws, he soon became the most popular advocate in Ajaccio.

Carlo Bonaparte, with his prepossessing exterior, powerful intellect, and fervid eloquence, was not long in attracting the attention of Paoli, whose perception of character was acute. He began to employ him in business of state. In the year 1764, the young advocate became acquainted with the most beautiful girl in Ajaccio, Letitia Ramolino, at that time fourteen years of age. Both were warmly attached to each other; but the Ramolinos belonged to the Genoese party, and would not consent to their daughter's marriage with a Paolist. Paoli himself, however, interfered, gained the good-will of the parents, and obtained their permission. Letitia's mother had, as widow, married a Signor Fesch, captain of a Swiss regiment in the service of Genoa; Cardinal Fesch was their son.

Paoli, meanwhile, made the young Carlo Bonaparte his secretary, and took him with him to Corte, the seat of government. Letitia followed unwillingly. Corsican liberty was on the eve of its extinction; the French had already entered the island, after the treaty of Fontainebleau; and in the critical position of affairs, a parliament had assembled to decide upon the course to be followed. Carlo Bonaparte, in a fiery, patriotic speech, demanded war against France.

After the defeat at Ponte Nuovo, when the flight had become universal, and the French were already in the vicinity of Corte, some hundreds of families of the higher classes sought refuge on Monte Rotondo, and among them Carlo Bonaparte and his wife, who was then pregnant with Napoleon. The mountain presented a mournful spectacle of despairing, defenceless fugitives, of terrified women and children, who believed that their last hour was come. Several days of anguish and uncertainty passed in these rocky wilds among the goat-herds. At length French officers appeared on the mountain with a flag of truce, sent by Count Devaux, who had occupied Corte. They announced to the fugitives that the island had been conquered, that Paoli was about to leave it, and that they had nothing to fear, but might descend from the mountain to their homes. The fugitives immediately sent a deputation to Corte, at the head of which were Carlo Bonaparte and Lorenzo Giubega of Calvi, to obtain passes providing for the safety of all their families, furnished with which the deputation returned to Monte Rotondo, and brought their friends away.

Bonaparte descended with his wife into the little pastoral district of Niolo, taking this difficult route for Ajaccio. They had to pass the river Liamone, which was swollen, and Letitia was in danger of being drowned. Only her own courage and the activity of her attendants rescued her from the stream. Carlo Bonaparte now purposed to accompany Paoli, his patron and friend, into exile, holding it dishonourable to remain in Corsica now that the common fatherland had fallen under the yoke of the French. But the entreaties of his uncle, the Archdeacon Lucian, and the tears of his wife, induced him to relinquish this despairing thought. He remained on the island, returned to Ajaccio, and there, under the French government, became assessor in the Supreme Court. Marbœuf showed him many marks of distinction; and it was through his influence that Carlo procured for his eldest son Joseph a place in the seminary of Autun; and for his second son Napoleon, a cadetship in the military school of Brienne. It was Marbœuf, therefore, the conqueror of Corsica, who made the career of the young Corsican, Napoleon Bonaparte, possible. He was a frequent visitor at the house of the Bonapartes, and spent many agreeable hours in the society of the beautiful Madame Letitia; this, and the patronage which the French Count bestowed on Napoleon, gave occasion to the scandalous reports circulated by the enemies of the latter, that the gallant Frenchman had enjoyed the favours of Napoleon's handsome mother.

Marbœuf was himself, however, under obligation to Carlo Bonaparte. For when General Narbonne-Fritzlar was intriguing in Corsica against his countryman, in order to obtain the command of the island, Bonaparte had by his courage and energy prevailed with the French ministry to retain Marbœuf as governor. The count repaid this service with his friendship, his good offices, and the recommendation of the young military scholar Napoleon, to the influential family of Brienne. Carlo Bonaparte showed his attachment to Marbœuf in every possible way; I have read a sonnet of his addressed to the count, which I shall not communicate, as it contains nothing characteristic;—any cultivated Italian can write a tolerable sonnet in his native language.

In the year 1777, Napoleon's father was made deputy of the nobility for Corsica, and travelled to Paris by way of Florence. He visited the French capital a second time, in order to bring to a conclusion his process with the Jesuits of Ajaccio in regard to certain properties. While prosecuting this business he died, in February 1785, in his thirty-ninth year, of the same malady in the stomach, which was to prove fatal to his son Napoleon. The incoherent dreams of his deathbed ran always upon Napoleon—a proof that he centred his hopes upon this son; he cried, dying: "Where is Napoleon; why does he not come with his great sword to help his father?" He died in the arms of his son Joseph. They buried him in Montpellier. When Napoleon had become Emperor, the citizens of this town offered to erect a monument to his father. But Napoleon replied to their proposal, that they should allow the dead to rest; for if a statue were raised to his father, now so long dead, his grandfather, and his great-grandfather, might with equal justice demand a similar honour. Louis Bonaparte, King of Holland, afterwards had his father's body disinterred and deposited in St. Leu.

Napoleon was at school in Paris, when Carlo Bonaparte died. The following is the letter which the youth of sixteen wrote to his mother on the occasion:—

"Paris, *March 29, 1785.*

"My dear Mother,—Time has to-day somewhat calmed the first outbreak of my sorrow; and I hasten to convince you of the gratitude with which your constant kindness to us has inspired me. Console yourself, my dear mother. Circumstances demand it. We shall redouble our care and our grateful attention, and shall be happy if we can in any degree compensate to you by our obedience, for the incalculable loss of a beloved husband. I conclude, my dear mother—my grief compels me; while, at the same time, I beg you to moderate your own. My health is excellent, and I pray Heaven every day that yours may be equally good. Give my respects to aunt Gertrude, Minana Saveria, Minana Fesch, &c.

"P.S.—The queen of France was confined of a prince, named the Duke of Normandy, on the 27th of March, at seven o'clock in the evening.—Your very devoted and affectionate son,

"Napoleon de Bonaparte."

If this laconic epistle of the young Napoleon is genuine, it is of some value.

Carlo Bonaparte was a man of brilliant talent and clear intellect, an impassioned orator, a patriot, and yet, as we have seen, capable of adapting himself to circumstances, and not wanting in political prudence. He was fond of splendid living, and his expenditure was lavish. Madame Letitia was only thirty-five years old at his death, and had already borne him thirteen children, five of whom were dead. Jerome was an infant in the cradle.

The Archdeacon Lucian now became the head of the house and proved himself a careful and frugal steward of the family property. The Bonapartes owned some lands, some vineyards, and herds.

CHAPTER IV
THE BOY NAPOLEON

"I too am a mortal man
Like others, born
Of the race of him who was first made."

Wisdom of Solomon.

We dwell with singular interest on the childhood of extraordinary men; the imagination pleases itself with the picture of the boy still lost among his play-fellows, and unconscious of his destiny. We are tempted to guess, in the physiognomy of the child, the traits that mark his future greatness as a man; but childhood is a deep mystery; who shall distinguish in the soul of a child the form of the genius or the demon that sleeps therein?—who prophesy of the mysterious power that is suddenly to determine the vast and slumbering forces, and send them forth commissioned into space and time?

I once saw in Florence the marble bust of a boy. The innocent smile on the childish face attracted me, and I contemplated it with pleasure. On the pedestal was inscribed: Nero.

Little is known of Napoleon's infancy. His mother Letitia was in church at the festival of the Assunta of the Virgin when she felt the first pangs of approaching labour. She immediately hastened home; but had not time to gain her own room, and gave birth to her child in a small cabinet, on a temporary couch of tapestry representing scenes from the Iliad. Gertrude, her sister-in-law, attended her. It was eleven o'clock in the forenoon when Napoleon came to the world.

He was not baptized till the 21st of July 1771, nearly two years after his birth, along with his sister Maria Anna, who died soon after. It is said that he resisted vehemently when the priest was about to sprinkle the consecrated water on him; perhaps he wanted to baptize himself, as at a later period he crowned himself, taking the crown from the hands of the Pope when he was about to set it on his head.

His boyhood showed symptoms of a vehement and passionate temperament, and he was at perpetual variance with his eldest brother Joseph. In these childish quarrels Joseph had always the worst of it, and was rudely handled; and when he ran to complain, Napoleon was declared to be in the right. Joseph became at last quite submissive to his younger brother, and the family began very early to look upon Napoleon as taking the lead among his brothers and sisters. The Archdeacon Lucian said to Joseph on his deathbed, "You are the oldest of the family, but there stands its head— you must not forget that."

We are willing enough to believe that the boy Napoleon showed a quite indomitable passion for everything military, and that this born soldier liked nothing so well as to run by the side of the soldiery of Ajaccio. The soldiers had a pleasure in seeing the boy go through the exercise beside them, and many a grayhaired veteran lifted him in his arms and caressed him for imitating the drill so valiantly. He teased his father till he purchased him a cannon, and the toy was long shown in the house of the Bonapartes with which he used to make his mimic battle-thunder, and play the cloud-compelling Jove. He soon began to exercise empire over the youth of Ajaccio, and, like Cyrus with the shepherd-boys of the Medes, and Peter the Great with his play-fellows, he formed the children of Ajaccio into a regiment of soldiers, who bravely took the field against the youngsters of the Borgo of Ajaccio, and fought sanguinary engagements with stones and wooden sabres.

In the year 1778, his father took him to the military school of Brienne, where the afterwards celebrated Pichegru was his master. It is known that Napoleon here at first showed himself quiet, gentle, and diligent. His impassioned temperament broke out only occasionally when his delicate sense of honour was touched. His quartermaster one day condemned him for some fault to eat his dinner on his knees in the woollen dress of disgrace, at the door of the refectory. Such a dinner was more than the pride of the young Corsican could stomach; he had an attack of vomiting and a fit. The Père Petrault immediately freed him from the punishment, and made it matter of complaint that his best mathematician was treated so shamefully.

In 1783, Napoleon went to the military school of Paris to complete his studies, already a completely-formed character, highly cultivated, glowing with the fires of genius and of youth, his head full of the heroes of his favourite Plutarch, and his heart penetrated with the deeds of his great Corsican forefathers. Society had already begun to ferment, and coming great events threw their shadow forward on the time. It was a period worth living in, heaving with mighty energies, big with change, and full of creative, Titanic impetuosity; it had given Nature the command to prepare great men.

The young officer, Napoleon Bonaparte, joined his regiment in Valence in the year 1785. His soul, profoundly though uncertainly stirred, needed expression. He wrote on the theme proposed for a prize essay by the Academy of Lyons: "What are the Principles and the Institutions which we must give to mankind to make them happy?"—a favourite subject in that humanistic period. Napoleon wrote anonymously. When he had become Emperor, and Talleyrand had extracted the paper from among the archives of Lyons to flatter the potentate, he threw it into the fire. Sentimentality was one of the features of the age, and we see that the young philanthropist did not escape without paying tribute to his time. What if Napoleon should have become the popular author of a sentimental romance in the vein of Richardson and Sterne? He had undertaken a journey to Mount Cenis with his friend Demarris, and on his return, agreeably excited by his little love-affair with Mademoiselle Colombier of Valence, who gave him secret rendezvous and very innocent banquets of cherries, he sat down to write a Sentimental Journey on Mount Cenis. He did not get far with it; but this fit of tender susceptibility in Napoleon is remarkable—and had he not "The Sorrows of Werther" with him in Egypt?

Still body and soul a Corsican, he also wrote in Valence a History of the Corsicans—a theme that suited the young Napoleon well. The manuscript exists in an incomplete state in the Library at Paris, and is now about to be published. Napoleon sent his manuscript to Paoli, whom he admired, and who was at that time living in exile in London. The following is part of the letter to his great countryman, which accompanied it:—

"I was born when our country died. Three thousand Frenchmen infesting our island, the throne of freedom sinking in waves of blood— such was the detested spectacle that first shocked my gaze. The groans of the dying, the sighs of the oppressed, the tears of despair, surrounded my cradle from the moment I was born.

"You left Corsica, and with you vanished the hopes of better fortune; slavery was the tribute we had to pay to conquest. Under an accumulation of burdens—under the threefold chain of the soldier, the legislator, and the tax-gatherer—our countrymen lived on in contempt,... despised by those who had the reins of government in their hands. Is not this the most cruel torture that any one possessed of feeling can have to suffer?

"The traitors to their country—the venal souls whom the love of base hire corrupts—have disseminated calumnies against the national Government, and against you personally. Authors adopt them, and transmit them as truths to posterity.

"Reading them, I was fired with indignation, and I have resolved to dissipate these mischievous falsehoods—the children of ignorance. An early-commenced study of the French language, attentive observation, and *memorabilia* extracted from the papers of the patriots, put me in a position even to hope for some success.... I shall compare your Government with the present.... I shall paint the betrayers of the common cause, with the pencil of shame, in black.... I shall summon those in power before the bar of public opinion, give the minutest details of their vexatious system of oppression, disclose their secret intrigues, and, if possible, interest the virtuous minister who at present governs the State, for the lamentable fate which keeps us so cruelly prostrate."

Such are the sentiments and language of the young Corsican, Napoleon—the revolutionary democrat and scholar of Plutarch. In his History of the Corsicans, he says in one place: "When his country is no more, a high-spirited citizen should die." These were, in those days, no mere phrases from Tacitus; they were the glowing language of a young soul capable of all that was great and noble. There is hardly another character whose development—rapid as the flush of youth and genius can make it—we follow with the same passionate delight as we do that of the young hero, Napoleon, till about the peace of Campio Formio. We see a more than ordinary man—a demigod passing before us, still uncontaminated by the foul touch of selfishness—till the fair picture gradually becomes blurred, and we class it with those of ordinary despots. For no greatness endures, and Macchiavelli is right: "There are none but ordinary men." Other youthful literary attempts of Napoleon are mentioned by his biographers, and they are now to be printed; among them two novels, *Le Comte d'Essex*, and *Le Masque Prophête*, and a dialogue on Love, entitled *Giulio*.

Napoleon visited Ajaccio every year, and made his influence be felt on the education of his brothers and sisters. They were brought up simply, after the fashion of their country, and with a primitive strictness. "It was almost," says Nasica, "as if you were living in a convent. Prayers, sleep, study, refreshment, pleasure, promenade—everything went by rule and measure. The greatest harmony, a tender and sincere affection, prevailed among all the members of the family. It was in those days a pattern to the town, as it afterwards became its ornament and boast."

The Archdeacon Lucian managed the family affairs economically; and it cost the young Napoleon great exertion to obtain a little additional money to meet his expenses. But he obtained it. The whole family felt the influence of the young man, and was subject to the sway of this born ruler. It is characteristic—since empire was his destiny—that he, the second-born, has not only the mastery of his younger brothers and sisters, but even of his elder brother, and that his interference has a decisive effect on their upbringing. It was soon quite well understood that the young Napoleon was to be obeyed.

I find an authentic letter of Napoleon to his uncle Fesch, afterwards the Cardinal, dated from Brienne, the 15th July 1784. The boy of fifteen, in writing here as to the career on which his eldest brother Joseph ought to enter, speaks in the clearest and most sensible way of the circumstances necessary to be taken into account. The letter is sufficiently well worth reading—especially if we consider that the Joseph of whom so many doubts are therein expressed, afterwards became King of Spain.

NAPOLEON TO HIS UNCLE FESCH

"My dear Uncle,—I write to inform you of the journey of my dear father over Brienne to Paris, where he has gone in order to take Marianne (afterwards Eliza of Tuscany) to St. Cyr, and to re-establish his health. He arrived here on the 21st with Lucian, and the two demoiselles whom you saw: he has left Lucian here. He is nine years old, and three feet, eleven inches, ten lines high: he is in the sixth in Latin, and will learn the various branches taught in this school; he shows much talent and willingness, and we may hope that something will come of him (*que ce sera un bon sujet*). [Lucian was the only one of the family who scorned a crown.] He is healthy, he is strong, lively, and thoughtless, and, in the meantime, his masters are content with him. He knows French very well, and has completely forgotten his Italian; but he will write to you along with this, and I shall say nothing to him, that you may see how matters stand with him.

"I hope he will write to you oftener now, than he did when he was in Autun.... I am confident my brother Joseph has not written to you yet. How could you expect it? He sends my dear father, when he does write to him, at most two lines. He is, in truth, quite changed. He writes to me, however, frequently. He is in the rhetoric class; and he would do better if he were diligent, for the master told my dear father that there was no one in the college (at Autun) who showed more talent than he in physics, rhetoric, or philosophy, or who could make so good a translation. In regard to the profession he is to follow, you know he at first chose the clerical. He kept by this resolution up till the present hour, but he now wishes to serve the king. In this he is wrong, on several grounds.

"1. As my father remarks, he has not courage to face the dangers of a battle; his weak health does not allow of his enduring the fatigues of a campaign; and my brother looks at the life of a soldier only from the garrison side. Yes, my dear brother will make an excellent officer in garrison. Well, as he is light-minded, and therefore clever at making frivolous compliments, he will always, with his talents, make a good figure in society—but in a battle? It is about this my dear father is dubious.

> Qu'importe à des guerriers ces frivoles avantages?
>
> Que sont tous ces trésors sans celui du courage?
>
> A ce prix fussiez vous aussi beau qu'Adonis,
>
> Du Dieu même du Pinde eussiez-vous l'éloquence,
>
> Que sont tous ces dons sans celui de la vaillance?

"2. He has received an education for the clerical profession; it is too late to forget it. The Bishop of Autun would have given him a large benefice, and he was certain to have become a bishop. What an advantage for the family! The Bishop of Autun has done all he could to prevail on him to stay, and has promised him that he never would have cause to repent it. In vain!—he persists. I commend his resolution, if he has a decided taste for this profession—the finest of all professions—and if the Great Mover of human things (*le Grand Moteur des choses humaines*) had, in forming him, given him, as He has given me, a decided inclination for a military life.

"3. He wishes to obtain a commission; that is very well, but in what corps? In the marine, perhaps. 4. He knows nothing of mathematics. It would take him two years to learn them. 5. The sea does not agree with his health. Perhaps among the engineers? Then he would require four or five years to master what is necessary. Moreover, I think that to work and be occupied the whole day does not suit the levity of his disposition. The same reason exists for his not joining the artillery as for the engineers, with the exception that he would only have to work eighteen months to become *élève*, and as many to be made officer. Oh! but that is still not his taste. Let us see, then—doubtless he wishes to join the infantry. Good! I understand; he wants to have nothing to do the whole day but wear the pavement; but what is an insignificant infantry officer?—a *mauvais sujet* for three-fourths of his time. And neither my father, nor you, nor my mother will hear of this, nor my uncle the archdeacon, for he has already given some little specimens of lightheadedness and extravagance. It follows that a last attempt must be made to gain him for the clerical profession; if this cannot be done, my dear father will take him with him to Corsica, where he will be under his own eye. They will try to make a law-clerk of him. I conclude by begging that you will continue your good-will towards me; to make myself worthy of it will be my chief and my most agreeable duty. I am, with the most profound respect, my dear uncle, your very devoted and very obedient servant and nephew,

"Napoleon de Bonaparte.

"*P.S.*—Tear this letter.

"We may hope, nevertheless, that Joseph, with the talents he possesses, and the sentiments with which his education must have inspired him, will think better of it, and become the stay of our family. Represent to him a little these advantages."

Have we not almost a right to doubt that a boy of fifteen can have written so self-conscious, so clear and decisive a letter? It has never hitherto been published anywhere but in the work of Tommaseo—*Letters of Pasquale Paoli*—where I found it; the author says he owes it to Signor Lucgi Biadelli, councillor at the Supreme Court of Bastia. The letter appears to me to be an invaluable document; we seem to be present at the family council of the Bonapartes, and have all its members vividly before our eyes. Monsieur Fesch in Ajaccio, when he received the letter with the news about the giddy Joseph, wore his woollen blouse, and had his little wooden pipe in his mouth, precisely as many eye-witnesses remember to have seen him. Later, he wore the cardinal's hat; and the light-headed young Joseph became king of Spain.

We can recognise, in the Napoleon of this letter, the future tyrant of his family. We here find him caring for his brothers—pondering over their prospects; afterwards, he gave them kingly crowns, and demanded unconditional obedience. The plain citizen Lucian, and Louis King of Holland, alone withstood his tyranny.

CHAPTER V
NAPOLEON AS ZEALOUS DEMOCRAT

When Napoleon came on a visit to Ajaccio, he liked to live and work in Milelli—a little country-house in the neighbourhood of Ajaccio belonging to the family—where the old oak-tree may still be seen under which the stripling Bonaparte used to sit and dream, and anxiously revolve his plans of life.

The French Revolution came, the storming of the Bastille, the overthrow of the existing state of things.

The young Napoleon threw himself, with all the force of his impassioned nature, into the excitement of the time. Destiny, however, did not mean him to exhaust his energies in the struggle of the revolutionary parties; it had reserved him for something else. At a distance from Paris, and on his own little island, he was to play a merely preparatory part in the first stormy agitations of the new period. Corsica became his school.

We find him in Ajaccio as a young, enthusiastic revolutionist, declaiming in the clubs, writing addresses, helping to organize the national guard—in short, playing the great politician precisely in the way we are acquainted with from our own experience.

Ajaccio was at that time the centre of the Corsican revolutionists; the house of the Bonapartes their place of meeting; the two brothers, Joseph and Napoleon, undisputed leaders of the democracy. The little town was in a state of wild uproar. The commotion appeared to General Barrin, at that time in command of the island, of a threatening character; and he sent Gaffori's son, Marshal Francesco Gaffori, to check it. Gaffori was by no means successful in this; on the contrary, he was glad to find hospitality and protection in the house of Bacciocchi, afterwards Prince of Lucca and Piombino.

Napoleon and Joseph, meanwhile, assembled the democratic party in the Church of San Francesco, and prepared a congratulatory address to the Constituent Assembly, which contained at the same time the bitterest complaints of the oppressive character of the existing administration in Corsica, and expressed an urgent wish that the island should be declared an integral part of France.

Napoleon understood his time: renouncing his Corsican patriotism, he became decidedly French, and threw himself into the arms of the Revolution.

He returned to Valence in 1789; and soon after he is again in Ajaccio, where the active Joseph, while the national guard was in the process of formation, was zealously exerting himself to obtain an officer's commission. Marius Peraldi, the richest man in Ajaccio, and an enemy of the Bonaparte family, was made colonel of the national guard, and Joseph an officer.

It had in the meantime been proposed in Corsica to recall the exiles; and by the exertions of the two brothers Bonaparte and the Abbot Coti, the Corsican General Assembly was induced to name four deputies, who were to meet Paoli in France, and conduct him to the island. Among these was Marius Peraldi, and both Napoleon and Joseph accompanied the deputation.

When Paoli arrived in Paris, the Constituent Assembly had already (1st December 1789) incorporated Corsica with France, by a decree which for ever put an end to the political independence of the island. Mirabeau and Saliceti—Corsican deputy for the Third Estate, afterwards the celebrated statesman, and minister of Murat in Naples—proposed the resolution.

Napoleon himself hastened to Marseilles to welcome Paoli, and was witness to the tears of joy which the noble patriot shed when he again set foot on his native soil in Cape Corso. An assembly met in Orezza to deliberate on and regulate the affairs of the island. Napoleon and his foe, the young Carlo Andrea Pozzo di Borgo, earned here, at the elections, the first honours as public speakers. Carlo Bonaparte's son could not but attract the attention of Paoli, who, astonished at the exuberance of intellectual resource and unerring judgment of the young man, is said to have expressed himself with regard to him in these terms: "This young man has a career before him; he needs nothing but the opportunity, to be one of Plutarch's men." It is related that Paoli on one occasion entered a locanda, and finding the rooms in disorder, was told in explanation by the landlord that a young man, by name Bonaparte, had been lodging there; had written day and night, and constantly torn what he wrote to pieces; had run restlessly up and down, and at last started off for the battle-field of Ponte Nuovo.

The young Napoleon had left no stone unturned to procure his brother Joseph the presidency of the district of Ajaccio, travelling as an adroit partisan through the villages of the region, soliciting votes, and spending money.

In Ajaccio he was indefatigably occupied in keeping the republican club at the due heat, and thwarting the priests and the aristocrats. A sanguinary struggle took place between the two parties in the little town; Napoleon's life was endangered, and an officer of the national guard was killed by his side. He narrates the details in a manifesto of his own composition. Blood continued to be shed for several days and several times the lives of Joseph and Napoleon were a stake.

Napoleon was considered the soul of the club of Ajaccio. Reminding us of the young politicians of our late popular commotions, we see him fulminate a stinging address against an aristocrat—Count Matteo Buttafuoco, the same who had invited Rousseau to Vescovato, and who, during the Corsican war of independence, had served in the French army, and lent the enemies of his country his arm against his country's cause. He was deputy of the nobility for Corsica, had voted in Versailles against the union of the Estates, and made himself odious by other votes of aristocratic and unpopular tendency. Against this man the young Napoleon wrote a manifesto in his country house at Milelli, which he printed in Dôle, and then sent to the club of Ajaccio. The pamphlet, rhetorical and impassioned, but substantially based on fact, is a notable contribution to our acquaintance with Napoleon. It has all the bold, poetic exuberance of diction characteristic of young revolutionists; and as I read it in this solitude of Ajaccio, it awakened in me amusing recollections of the years 1848 and 1849. But it is more than the mere pamphlet of a young demagogue—it is a preparatory exercise for the imperial edicts; it is the Emperor himself trying his wings. This manifesto is indispensable if we are desirous of insight into the nature and growth of Napoleon in the earlier periods of his development.

LETTER OF MONSIEUR BONAPARTE TO M. MATTEO BUTTAFUO-CO, CORSICAN DEPUTY TO THE NATIONAL ASSEMBLY

"Monsieur,—From Bonifazio to Cape Corso, from Ajaccio to Bastia, is but one chorus of curses upon you. Your friends hide themselves, your relatives disown you; and even the prudent man, who never allows himself to be mastered by popular opinion, is this time carried away by the general indignation.

"What is it you have done, then? What are the crimes that can legitimate an animosity so universal, and a desertion so complete? This, Monsieur, is precisely what I am about to investigate, by the aid of light which you yourself shall supply.

"The history of your life, at least since you were thrown upon the stage of public affairs, is known. Its main features are drawn here in characters of blood. There are details, however, not so generally known; I may therefore make mistakes, but I count upon your indulgence, and on your correcting them.

"After entering the service of France, you returned to see your relations; you found the tyrants beaten, the national government established, and the Corsicans, animated by the most generous sentiments, emulating each other in making daily sacrifices for the public weal. You, Monsieur, did not allow yourself to be led astray by the general ferment; far from it; you listened only with compassion to the babble of fatherland, freedom, independence, and constitution, with which the demagogues had been puffing up our meanest peasants. Profound reflection had taught you to estimate at its proper value this artificial excitement, which can only be maintained at the expense of the community. Of course the peasant must labour, and not act the hero, if he is not to die of hunger, but to bring up his family, and respect the authorities. As regards the persons who by their rank or good fortune are called to rule, it is impossible that they can for any length of time be so stupid as to sacrifice their ease and their influence to a chimera, and that they should stoop to pay court to a cobbler, for the sake of playing the Brutus. However, when you fell upon the project of gaining the friendship of Monsieur Paoli, it was necessary you should dissemble. Monsieur Paoli was the centre of all national movement. We will not deny him talent, nor even genius, of a certain kind; he had for a while made the affairs of the island flourish; he had founded a university, in which, for the first time since the creation, perhaps, those sciences which further the development of the mind were taught among our mountains; he had increased our means of defence by establishing an iron-foundry and powder-mills, and by erecting fortifications; he had opened ports which by encouraging commerce enlivened agriculture; he had created a marine which favoured our communications, while it was destructive to our enemies—and all that he had thus begun, was but the indication of what he would one day have accomplished. Harmony, peace, and freedom were the forerunners of national prosperity—had it not been, that, as *you* had discovered, an ill-organized government, constructed on a false basis, was the still surer omen of the misfortunes into which the nation was to be plunged.

"Paoli's dream was to play the Solon, but he copied his model badly. He had put everything into the hands of the people, or its representatives, so that one could not exist except at its pleasure. Strange mistake, to subordinate to a day-labourer, a man who by education, birth, and fortune, is destined to rule! Such a palpable perversion of reason cannot fail, in the long-run, to produce the ruin and dissolution of the body politic, after it has brought it into uproar by every species of abuse.

"You succeeded according to your wish. Monsieur Paoli, continually surrounded by hot-headed enthusiasts, did not conceive it possible that a man could have any other passion than the fanaticism of freedom and independence. Through certain French introductions, you procured his intimacy, and he did not take time to test your moral principle by anything deeper than your words. By his influence you were chosen to conduct the negotiations in Versailles, in regard to the settlement of affairs which was effected through the mediation of the French cabinet. Monsieur de Choiseul saw you and understood you. Men know in an instant how to estimate souls of a certain stamp. Very soon you transformed yourself from the representative of a free people into the agent of a satrap. You communicated to him the instructions, the projects, the secrets, of the cabinet of Corte.

"This conduct, which people here find base and shameless, I, for my part, find quite simple; after all, in every sort of affair, the important point is to have a clear eye and a cool judgment.

"The prude judges the coquette, and thereby makes herself ridiculous; that is her history in a few words.

"A man of principle would judge you very severely; but you do not believe in men of principle. The common man, who is constantly misled by virtuous demagogues, can have no consideration from you, who do not believe in virtue. Your own principles alone must pronounce sentence upon you, like the laws upon a criminal; but those who know what supple policy means, find nothing but the greatest simplicity in your mode of acting; we come to the same result as before, therefore—in every sort of affair we must first see clearly, and then judge calmly. As to other matters, you can defend yourself no less victoriously, for you have not coveted the reputation of a Cato or Catinat; it is sufficient for you to resemble a certain class; and, with this class, it is a received dogma, that he who can have money and does not use it, is a simpleton, since money procures all the pleasures of the senses, and nothing is of any value but these pleasures. The liberal Monsieur de Choiseul accordingly was sufficiently pressing in his offers, whereas your own ridiculous country, according to its pleasant custom, repaid your services with the honour of serving it.

"When the treaty of Compiègne had been concluded, Monsieur de Chauvelin landed with twenty-four battalions on our coasts. Monsieur de Choiseul, who attached the utmost importance to the speedy accomplishment of the objects of the expedition, became so uneasy that he could not conceal his anxiety from you—you advised him to send you here with a few millions. As Philip took cities with his sumpter-mule, you promised to overcome every obstacle, and produce complete subjection.... No sooner said than done; you hastened over the sea, threw off the mask, and, with money and promotion in your hand, you opened communications with those whom you considered most accessible.

"The Corsican cabinet had no idea that a Corsican could love himself more than his country—it had intrusted you with its interests. As you, on the other hand, had no idea that a man could *not* love money and himself more than his country, you sold yourself and hoped to buy every one else. Profound moralist! you knew the price of each man's fanaticism. A few pounds of gold more or less, were for you the shades of difference in character!

"You deceived yourself, however; the weak were perhaps shaken, but they were shocked at the frightful thought of lacerating the bosom of their country; they imagined they saw their fathers, their brothers, or their friends, who had perished in its defence, rising from their graves to overwhelm them with curses. These ridiculous prejudices were powerful enough to check you in your career. You sighed that you had to deal with a childish people; but, Monsieur, such refined sentiments as yours are not given to the multitude, and they live on in poverty and wretchedness, while the prudent man, as soon as circumstances become in any degree favourable to him, knows how to rise. And that is pretty nearly the moral of your history.

"In giving account of the obstacles which interfered with the fulfilment of your promises, you proposed that the Royal-Corse regiment should be sent here. You hoped that its example would convert our too good and too simple peasantry; that it would accustom them to a thing in which they found so much that was repulsive—but you were deceived in this hope too. Did not Rossi, Marengo, and some other fools, excite such an enthusiasm in this regiment, that the collective officers declared, in an authentic document, that they would rather send back their commissions than break their oath, or be unfaithful to still more sacred duties?

"You found yourself compelled to set the example yourself. Not at all disconcerted, you threw yourself into Vescovato, at the head of some friends and a detachment of French soldiers; but the terrible Clemens hunted you from the nest. You retired to Bastia with the companions of your adventure, and with your family. This little affair did not bring you much honour; your house, and the houses of your associates, were burnt down. In your place of security, you mocked at these impotent exertions of a dying cause.

"It is boldly affirmed here, that you wished to arm the Royal-Corse against its own brothers. And, in the same spirit, people are inclined to call your courage in question, on account of your slight defence of Vescovato. These are useless imputations. For the first is an immediate consequence, is a means for the execution, of your projects; and as we have affirmed that your mode of acting has been very simple, it follows that this incidental accusation is done away with. As regards your want of courage, I do not see that this is proved by the action of Vescovato; you did not go there to make war in earnest, but to encourage, by your example, those of the opposite party who already wavered. And then, what right had people to demand that you should have risked the fruit of two years' good behaviour, in order to let yourself be killed like a common soldier? But you must have been moved when you saw your house, and the houses of your friends, become the prey of the flames. Good God! when will silly mortals cease to take everything so seriously? When you allowed your house to be burnt, you compelled Monsieur de Choiseul to compensate you. The issue has confirmed the correctness of your calculations; you have been paid far beyond the value of what you lost. It is true, complaints have been made that you kept everything for yourself, and gave only a trifle to the wretched men you had corrupted. In order to know to what length you were capable of going, we only require to see how far you could go with safety; now, poor people, who were so much in need of your protection, were neither in a position to assert their claims, nor even to see clearly the wrong that was done them; they dared not exhibit their discontent, and rebel against your authority; detested by their countrymen, their return would not have been so much as safe. It is, therefore, natural that when you found a few thousands of dollars among your fingers, you did not allow them to slip through; that would have been stupid.

"The French, defeated notwithstanding their gold, their commissions, the discipline of their numerous battalions, the lightness of their squadrons, and the skill of their artillery, routed at Penta, at Vescovato, at Oreto, at San Nicolao, at Borgo, Borbaggio, and Oletta, retired behind their entrenchments completely discouraged. The winter, the time of their repose, was for you, Monsieur, a period of the greatest diligence; and though you could not triumph over the obstinacy of prejudices deeply-rooted in the minds of the people, you succeeded in corrupting some of their leaders, whom you robbed of their nobler sentiments, though with difficulty; and this, and the thirty battalions that Monsieur de Vaux brought with him in spring, made Corsica bow her neck to the yoke, and forced Paoli and the most enthusiastic to retire.

"A number of the patriots had fallen in the defence of their independence, others had fled a proscribed country—now the loathsome nest of tyranny; but many had neither died nor been able to flee, they became the objects of persecution. Souls that had proved themselves superior to corruption were of another stamp. The French supremacy could only be secured by their complete extinction. Ah! this plan was but too punctually executed. Some died the victims of supposititious crimes; others, betrayed by those to whom they had extended their hospitality and their confidence, expired upon the scaffold, repressing their tears. Great numbers, immured by Narbonne-Fritzlar in the jail of Toulon, poisoned by bad food, tortured by their chains, loaded with every species of misusage, lived for some time in the spasms of the death-struggle, only to see death slowly approaching.... O God, witness of their innocence, why hast Thou not made Thyself their avenger?

"In this general misery, in the midst of the cries and groans of this unhappy people, you began meanwhile to enjoy the fruits of your labour. Honours, titles, pensions rained upon you; your possessions would have increased still more rapidly if Madame Dubarry, occasioning the fall of Monsieur de Choiseul, had not deprived you of a protector who knew how to estimate your services. The blow did not discourage you; you re-established yourself by your activity in the subordinate bureaus; you saw nothing in it but the necessity of increasing your diligence. People in higher quarters found themselves flattered, your services were so notorious!... Nothing was withheld from you. Not content with the lake of Biguglia, you requested portions of the lands of several communes. How could you rob them of these? people ask. I, for my part, ask: What consideration could you be expected to have for a nation which you knew detested you?

"Your favourite project was the division of the island among ten barons. What! not content with helping to forge the chains of your country, you proposed also to subject it to an absurd feudalism! But I commend you for doing the Corsicans all the harm that was in your power; you were at war with them, and in war it is an axiom to do hurt for your own advantage.

"But passing all this wretched business, let us come to the present, and conclude a letter, the shocking length of which cannot but have tired you.

"The posture of affairs in France was ominous of extraordinary events; you dreaded their effect in Corsica. The same madness with which we were possessed before the war, began again, to your great annoyance, to deprive this amiable people of its senses. You saw what would be the consequence; for, if generous sentiments were to sway public opinion, from an honest man you became a mere traitor; if these generous sentiments stirred the blood of our fiery fellow-citizens, something more wretched still; if a national government followed, what was to become of you? Your conscience accordingly began to make you uneasy. Frightened, cast down, you still did not despair; you resolved to stake your all, but you did it like a man of sense; you took a wife to strengthen your connexions. A worthy man, who, trusting to your honour, had given his sister to your nephew, saw himself deceived. Your nephew, whose paternal inheritance you had devoured to increase a property that should have been his, found himself with a numerous family plunged into misery.

"When you had arranged your private affairs, you threw a glance upon the country. You saw it reeking with the blood of its martyrs, covered with victims, and everywhere breathing nothing but thoughts of vengeance. You saw the reckless soldier, the impudent official, the greedy tax-gatherer, lording it with none to gainsay, while the Corsican, loaded with the triple chain, did not dare to think either on what he was, or on what he might yet be. In the joy of your heart you said to yourself: 'Matters are going on well, the only point is now to preserve them as they are, and forthwith you banded yourself with the soldier, the official, and the farmer of the revenue. All your aims were now centred on obtaining deputies inspired with similar sentiments; for, as concerned yourself, you could not imagine that a nation hostile to you would elect you as its representative. But you were destined to alter this opinion when the writs, with a perhaps intentional absurdity, ordered that the deputy of the nobility should be elected in an assembly composed of only twenty-two persons—all that was necessary was to gain twelve votes. Your associates of the Supreme Council were exceedingly active; threats, promises, caresses, everything was tried: you were successful. Your candidates in the communes were not: your First President was rejected, and two men—in your opinion, of extreme ideas—the one was son, brother, nephew of the most zealous defenders of the people's cause; the other had seen Sionville and Narbonne, and, sighing over his impotence, well remembered the atrocities which he had witnessed—these two men were proclaimed, and met the wishes of the nation, whose hope they became. The secret indignation, the rage, which seized on every one, when you were elected, does honour to your intrigues, and the influence of your associates.

"On arriving in Versailles, you became a zealous royalist; in Paris you saw, to your great affliction, that the government which was being erected on the ruins of the fallen system, was the same which among us had been drowned in so much blood.

"All the exertions of the despotic party were powerless; the new constitution, the admiration of Europe, has become an object of solicitude to every thinking being. There remained for you but one means of rescue, and that was, to make it be believed that this constitution was not fitted for our island, although it was precisely the same as that which had worked so prosperously, and to deprive us of which had cost so much blood.

"All the deputies of the old administration, entering as a matter of course into your cabals, served you with the warmth of men seeking their own interest. You drew up memorials in which you affirmed that the advantages of the existing government among us were matter of experience, and in which it was represented that any alteration was contrary to the wishes of the nation. At this time the town of Ajaccio got wind of your machinations; she raised her head, formed her National Guard, organized her committee. This, intervening so unexpectedly, alarmed you. The excitement spread. You persuaded the minister, of whom you had the advantage in knowledge of Corsican affairs, that it was necessary to send your father-in-law, Monsieur Gaffori, to the island, the worthy forerunner of Monsieur Narbonne; and Monsieur Gaffori, at the head of his troops, had the impudence to attempt to maintain by violence the tyranny which his father, of glorious memory, had by his genius beaten and suppressed. Innumerable blunders disclosed the mediocre talent of your father-in-law: the only art he possessed was that of making himself enemies. On every side people were uniting against him. In this imminent danger you lifted up your eyes and saw Narbonne. Narbonne, seizing a favourable moment, had formed the plan of establishing in an island which he had desolated by unheard-of cruelties, the despotism which tormented his own conscience. You assent: the plan is adopted, five thousand men receive orders; the decree directing the provincial regiment to be increased by a battalion, is despatched; Narbonne himself sets off. This poor nation without arms, without spirit to resist, is delivered, hopeless and helpless, into the hands of its executioner.

"O unhappy fellow-citizens, what detestable intrigues were you to be the victims of! You would not have understood them till it was too late. Where were your means of withstanding, without arms, ten thousand men? You yourselves would have signed the act of your degradation, hope would have fled, hope would have been extinguished, and days of misery would have succeeded each other without intermission. Liberated France would have looked on you with contempt, afflicted Italy with indignation, and Europe, astonished at a humiliation so profound, would have torn from her annals the pages that do your virtues honour. But the deputies of your communes penetrated the design, and put you on your guard in time. A king, who has constantly desired only the happiness of his people, informed by Monsieur Lafayette, that steadfast friend of liberty, of the true state of the case, was able to crush the perfidious machinations of a minister whom revenge ceaselessly spurred on to injure you. Ajaccio showed itself resolute in its address; the lamentable condition into which the most despotic of all governments had brought you had there been so powerfully impressed on people's minds. The hitherto slumbering Bastia awoke at the sound of danger, and seized its weapons with that resolution which has ever characterized it. Arena came from Paris to Balagna full of those sentiments which make a man capable of undertaking everything, and of fearing no danger. His weapons in the one hand, the decrees of the National Assembly in the other, he made the people's enemies turn pale. Achille Murati, the conqueror of Capraja, who carried despair into Genoa itself, and who wanted but opportunity and a wider field to be a Turenne, reminded the sharers of his fame that it was time to win it over again, and that their country needed—not intrigue, which it never understood—but steel and fire. Before the rising din of a resistance so universal, Gaffori withdrew into the nothingness from which intrigue had made him emerge against his will. He remained trembling in the fortress of Corte. Narbonne hastened away from Lyons to bury his shame and his hellish plans in Rome. A few days later, and Corsica is linked to France, Paoli is recalled, and in a single instant your prospects are changed, and a new career offered you for which you would never have ventured to hope.

"Excuse me, Monsieur, excuse me; I took my pen to defend you, but my heart utterly revolted against a system which brought treachery and perfidy in its train. What! son of this same fatherland, have you never had a filial feeling towards it? What! was there no emotion in your heart at the sight of the rocks, the trees, the houses, the neighbourhoods, which were the scene of your sports in childhood? When you came to the world, it carried you on its bosom, it nourished you with its fruits. When you came to years of discretion, it set its hopes upon you, it honoured you with its confidence, it said to you: 'My son, you see the wretched state to which the injustice of men has brought me; collecting my energies in my passionate grief, I once more attain a vigour which promises me sure and infallible restoration; but I am threatened anew; hasten, my son, to Versailles; inform the great king better, dissipate his suspicions, implore his friendship.'

"Well, and what then? A little gold made you a betrayer of the trust your country had reposed in you; for the sake of a little gold you were soon seen with the parricidal sword in your hand lacerating its bosom. Ah! Monsieur, I am far from wishing you any harm; but tremble ... there are pangs of conscience that avenge. Your fellow-citizens, who abhor you, will enlighten France as to your true character. The estates and the pensions, the fruit of your treasons, will be taken from you. Bowed down by age and misery, in the horrible solitude of crime, you will live long enough to be tormented by your conscience. The father will point you out to his son, the teacher to his scholar, and say: "Children, learn to honour your country, virtue, fidelity, and humanity.'

"And she, whose youth, beauty, and innocence they prostitute—her pure and chaste heart trembles under the touch of a polluted hand? Estimable and unhappy woman!...

"Soon the cordons of honour and the pomp of wealth will vanish, and the contempt of mankind will be heaped on you. Will you seek, on the breast of him who is the author of that report, a consolation with which your gentle and loving soul cannot dispense? Will you seek in his eyes tears to mingle with your own? Will your trembling hand, laid upon his heart, try to tell him the emotion of yours? Ah! if you find tears with *him*, they will be tears of remorse. If his heart beats, it will be in the convulsions of the wretch who dies cursing nature, himself, and the hand that leads him.

"O Lameth! O Robespierre! O Petion! O Volney! O Mirabeau! O Barnave! O Bailley! O Lafayette! see, this is the man that dares to sit by your side! Quite drenched in the blood of his brothers, polluted with crimes of every kind, he presents himself shamelessly in his General's uniform, the unrighteous hire of his villanies! He dares to call himself a representative of the nation, he—who has sold it, and you suffer it! He dares to raise his eyes to listen to your discourses, and you suffer it! This the voice of the people!—he had but the votes of twelve aristocrats! This the voice of the people!—and Ajaccio, Bastia, and most of the cantons wreaked that upon his effigy which they would willingly have done upon his person.

"But you, whom the mistake of the moment misleads, whose belief is for the present abused to make you oppose the projected alterations, will you endure the traitor? him who, under the cold exterior of a sensible man, conceals the greed of a lackey? I cannot believe it. You will be the first to drive him forth in shame and disgrace, as soon as you have been made to comprehend that web of knaveries of which he has been the artist.

"I have the honour, Monsieur, to be your very humble, and very obedient servant,

Bonaparte."

"From my Cabinet of Milelli,
"Jan. 23, in the second year."

"From my Cabinet of Milelli"—it sounds quite imperially. The reader will probably find that this bold, unsparing, powerful letter of the youth of twenty-one, half-Robespierre, half-Murat, is in no respect inferior to the best specimens of revolutionary eloquence furnished by the pamphlets of the period.

I may observe here, that of the six Corsican deputies to the Convention, three voted for the perpetual confinement of Louis Capet, two for his confinement till peace was established and his banishment thereafter, Cristoforo Saliceti alone for his death.

CHAPTER VI
NAPOLEON'S LATEST ACTIVITY IN CORSICA

In the year 1790, two battalions were to be formed in Corsica, the soldiers being allowed to name their *chefs* themselves. It is worth noticing on this occasion, how the subsequent Cæsar, Napoleon, holds it for the highest honour, and an almost unattainable piece of good fortune, to become *chef* of a battalion. The difficulties were as great as the energy of the young candidate. The most influential men of Ajaccio were opposed to him, Cuneo, Ludovico Ornano, Ugo Peretti, Matias Pozzo di Borgo, and the rich Marius Peraldi. Peraldi laughed at Napoleon, ridiculed his personal appearance, his diminutive stature, his limited prospects. This made Napoleon furious, and he challenged him. Peraldi agreed to a duel. His rival waited for him till nightfall at the little Chapel of the Greeks, walking restlessly up and down; but Peraldi did not make his appearance; his family had found means to prevent the duel.

The wanderer who now takes his way to the Chapel of the Greeks, to enjoy from it the beautiful view of the city and gulf, sees above him, on the rocks of the shore, a little Ionic temple. I asked what it meant, and was told it was the tomb of the Peraldi. Marius, the rival of Napoleon for a Major's commission, lies buried there. His family has left behind it no other reputation than that of having been one of the wealthiest in Corsica.

Madame Letitia sacrificed half her fortune to procure her favourite son the command of the battalion. Her house was constantly open to Napoleon's numerous party, her table always covered. Mattresses lay constantly ready in the rooms and in the passages, to receive his armed adherents during the night. It was as if the house were in a state of defence from the Vendetta. Matters looked threatening. Napoleon was never so excited as at this period; he could not sleep at night, during the day he wandered restlessly through the rooms, or deliberated with the Abbé Fesch and his partisans. He was pale and abstracted; his eyes full of fire, his soul full of passion. Perhaps he approached the consulship and the empire more calmly than the rank of major in the National Guard of Ajaccio.

The commissary, who was to conduct the election, had arrived, and was lodging in the house of the Peraldi. This was alarming. It was resolved, therefore, on the 18th Brumaire, to have recourse to stratagem. The partisans of Napoleon arm themselves; one of these—the fierce and reckless Bagaglino, armed to the teeth—forces his way at night into the house of the Peraldi, where the family are sitting at supper with the commissary. "Madame Letitia wishes to speak with you," cries Bagaglino threateningly; "and immediately!" The commissary follows him, the Peraldi not venturing to detain their guest; who, carried off by the Napoleonists, is compelled to quarter himself in the Casa Bonaparte, under the pretext that with the Peraldi he was not free. This little *coup d'état* shows us Napoleon complete.

The Casa Bonaparte now held itself ready for an assault; but Peraldi made no attempt. The day of the election came, and the people assembled in the Church of San Francesco. A disturbance arose, Geronimo Pozzo di Borgo was torn from the pulpit, and with difficulty rescued. The result of the election was this: Quenza, a Bonapartist, was made first *chef*—Napoleon, the second. The victory was almost complete, and the unattainable all but attained; Napoleon was second in command of a battalion.

Napoleon lived henceforth only among his soldiers, and he was the soul of his battalion. He now made his practical military studies before engaging in actual warfare, as he had received his political schooling in the clubs. Meanwhile, the irritation between the national battalion and the aristocrats and citizens—the latter worked upon by the priests—grew stronger every day. After seeing the highland Corsicans of the present time, one can form some idea of the nature and appearance of that Quenza-Napoleon battalion. The citizens of Ajaccio may not have dreaded this troop of Montagnards in the process of training altogether groundlessly. On Easter-day, of the year 1792, open hostilities commenced between the battalion and the inhabitants of Ajaccio. The struggle began on the Place du Diamant; the fighting lasted several days, and a great deal of blood was shed, neither the civil authorities nor the military commandant, Maillard, interfering. Napoleon escaped without injury. When quiet was re-established, he drew up a justification, in the name of the battalion, and addressed it to the Department, to the Minister of War, and the Legislative. Three commissaries hereupon appeared in Ajaccio; they returned a favourable report as to the conduct of the battalion, but it was removed from the town. Napoleon went to Corte, where Paoli received him coldly.

In May of the same year, he made a journey to Paris to bring his sister Eliza from St. Cyr. The changes in the political world took him here by surprise, and shattered all the hopes of military promotion which he had thought to realize in Paris. This is said to have produced so powerful an effect on the passionate nature of the young Corsican, as to make him entertain thoughts of suicide. He freed himself from them in a dialogue on self-murder. Napoleon left Paris soon after the frightful 2d of September, and returned to Corsica.

While Dumouriez, therefore, was astonishing the world with the first military achievements of the young Republic, the man who was destined to give new shape to Europe, was exerting himself in the wild Corsica, to make head against the cabals of his opponents—himself forming counter-cabals, and daily exposing his life to the dagger-thrust and the musket-ball. Arrived again in Corte, Paoli received him austerely. The paths of the two had completely separated; for another ambition was now stirring in the soul of the young Napoleon than to tread in the footsteps of the noble patriot. Had he done so—had his heart remained warm for the freedom of Corsica, then perhaps a wild goat-herd, as he pointed out to me some spot among the hills associated with a tale of blood, would have said: "See, it was here the Corsican patriot-leader, Napoleon Bonaparte, fell; he was almost as great as Sampiero."

Paoli gave Napoleon orders to proceed to Bonifazio, and join the expedition against Sardinia. Napoleon obeyed murmuringly. He remained eight months in Bonifazio, to make the necessary preparations, as far as they had been committed to him. On the 22d of January, the day after the execution of Louis Capet, Napoleon almost lost his life in Bonifazio. Some marines—a furious rabble from Marseilles—had landed, and commenced a quarrel with the Corsican battalion; and when Napoleon hastened up to prevent bloodshed, they received him with shouts of *ça ira!* cried out that he was an aristocrat, and, rushing in upon him, would have hung him on the lamp-post, had not the Maire, the people, and the soldiers succeeded in putting them to flight.

The enterprise upon Sardinia, of which Truguet was commander-in-chief, undertaken with a view to frighten the court of Turin, proved utterly futile. It is affirmed that Paoli had a share in its ill success. It is true that he had sent a thousand of his National Guards, under the command of his most trusted friend, Colonna Cesari; but, as the latter himself afterwards admitted, he had said to him: "Remember, O Cesari! that Sardinia is the natural ally of our island; that it has, under all circumstances, supplied us with victuals and ammunition, and that the King of Piedmont has ever been the friend of the Corsicans and their cause." The squadron, under the command of Colonna, at length left the harbour of Bonifazio, and made sail for the island of Santa Maddalena. Napoleon was next in command under Colonna, and was intrusted with the artillery. The young officer burned with impatience; it was his first deed of arms. He was one of the foremost to jump ashore, and he threw, with his own hand, a fireball into the little town of Maddalena. But the admirable measures he had taken proved completely fruitless; the Sardinians made a sortie; Colonna immediately ordered the retreat to be sounded.

The young Napoleon wept for rage; he made the most vehement representations to Colonna, and when the latter listened to him with cool indifference, Napoleon turned to some officers, and said, "He does not understand me." "You are an impudent fellow!" thundered Colonna to him. The born soldier knew his duty, was silent, and placed himself at his post. "He is a parade-horse, and nothing more," said he afterwards. Napoleon's first expedition was thus unfortunate, discreditable—a retreat.

On his return to Bonifazio, he learned that Paoli, who now saw himself compelled to throw off the mask, had dissolved the Quenza battalion. This occurred in the spring of 1793, about the time that the Convention sent Saliceti, Delcher, and Lacombe, to the island as commissaries. Lucian Bonaparte and Bartolommeo Arena had denounced Paoli. But Napoleon had no part in this denunciation; the memory of his father, and his own generous spirit, led him, on the contrary, to defend his great countryman. He himself wrote an apology for Paoli, and sent it to the Convention—an action that does him honour. This remarkable document has been preserved, though in a somewhat defective state. We have the defence, it appears to me, as Napoleon first threw it off, previously to giving it a complete form.

NAPOLEON'S LETTER TO THE CONVENTION

"Representatives!—You are the true organs of the people's sovereignty. All your decrees are dictated by the nation, or receive their effect immediately from the nation. Every one of your laws is a benefit, and earns for you a new claim on the gratitude of posterity, which owes to you the Republic, and on that of the world, which will date from you its freedom.

"A single decree that you have passed has greatly disheartened the city of Ajaccio; that which commands a feeble gray-haired man of seventy to drag himself to your bar, and place himself for a moment beside the impious mover of sedition or the venal self-seeker.

"Paoli a mover of sedition, or an ambitious man?

"Seditious! and with what object? To revenge himself on the family of the Bourbons, whose *perfidious policy* overwhelmed his country with calamity, and *forced himself into banishment*. But was not the end of their tyranny also the end of his exile; and have you not already appeased his wrath—if he still cherished it—by the blood of Louis?

"Seditious! and with what object? To restore the aristocracy of the nobles and the priests? He who, since his thirteenth year ... he who was no sooner at the head of affairs than he destroyed *feudalism*, and knew no other distinction than that of the citizen; he who, thirty years ago, fought against Rome, and was *excommunicated*,[M] who made himself master of the estates of the bishops to give them away, to Venice ... in Italy....

"Seditious! and with what object? To deliver Corsica into the hands of England? he who would not deliver it to France, despite the efforts of Chauvelin, who did not spare titles nor marks of favour!

"Give Corsica to England! What would he gain by living in the mire of London? Why did he not remain there when he was banished?

"Paoli a self-seeker! If Paoli is a self-seeker, *what more can he desire*? He is the object of his people's affection, and they refuse him nothing; *he is at the head of the army*; he is on the eve of the day when he must defend the island against a foreign attack.

"If Paoli was ambitious, then he has gained everything by the Republic; and if he has showed himself an adherent of ... since the Constituent Assembly, what should he do now, *when the people is everything*?

"Paoli ambitious! Representatives! when the French were governed by a corrupt court, when men believed neither in virtue nor in love of country, then certainly it might have been said that Paoli was ambitious. *We made war against the tyrants; it is to be supposed that that was not from love of country and of liberty, but from the ambition of our leaders!* In Coblenz, Paoli must be considered as ambitious; but in Paris—*the centre of French freedom*—Paoli, if people know him well, must be accounted the patriarch of the French Republic; *posterity will think thus*—the people think thus. Follow my advice, silence calumny, and the utterly corrupt men who use it as their instrument. Representatives! Paoli is more than a grayhaired man of threescore and ten—he is infirm. Otherwise he would have gone to your bar to crush his enemies. *We owe him everything*—even the happiness of being a French Republic. He enjoys our constant trust. Revoke, as concerns him, your decree of the 2d of April, and restore joy to this whole people."...

Soon after this, however, the young revolutionist completely quarrelled with Paoli; they became deadly enemies. The aged patriot found in the young man the most violent adversary, not of his person, but of his ideas. It is said that Paoli did not quite know him at that time, and had hinted to him that it was his intention to separate Corsica from France, and effect a connexion with England, that the indignant Napoleon did not conceal his anger, and that Paoli hereupon flew into a furious passion, and conceived the most violent hatred for his opponent. Pasquale's adherents were numerous, and the fortress of Ajaccio was in the hands of his friend Colonna. Paoli and Pozzo di Borgo, then procurator-general, cited before the Convention, defied the summons, and lived now under the ban of the Convention, and at open war with France.

The three representatives now made Napoleon Inspector-general of Corsican Artillery, and instructed him to reduce the citadel of Ajaccio. He attempted it, but all his exertions to conquer the fortress of his native town were in vain. Destiny had planted no laurels for Napoleon in Corsica. During the siege, his life was on one occasion in extreme danger. He had occupied the Tower of Capitello with about fifty men, in order to operate from that point by land, while the vessels of war carried on the bombardment from the sea. A storm blew the fleet out of the gulf, and Napoleon remained cut off from it in the tower, where he had to defend himself for three days, living on horse-flesh, till some herdsmen from the mountains freed him from his perilous situation, and he succeeded in reaching the fleet.

Much disconcerted, he was proceeding to Bastia by land. On the way, however, he learned that his life was threatened, that Marius Peraldi had instigated the people to seize him, and put him into the hands of Paoli, who meant to shoot him as soon as he had him in his power. In Vivario he was concealed by the parish priest; in Bocognano his friends rescued him with the greatest difficulty from the fury of the people; during the night, he escaped through the window from the chamber in which he had hid himself, and at length reached Ajaccio in safety. Here again, however, menaced still more seriously, he fled from his house to a grotto near the Chapel of the Greeks, where he remained concealed for a night. His friends now conveyed him safely on board a vessel, and he reached Bastia by sea. The fury of the Paolists was meanwhile directed upon Napoleon's family. Madame Letitia, terrified at the symptoms of approaching danger, fled with her children to Milelli, accompanied by some trusty peasants of Bastelica and Bocognano. Louis, Eliza, Paulina, and the Abbé Fesch were with her; Jerome and Caroline remained in concealment with the Ramolinos. Still insecure in Milelli, the persecuted family fled during the night to the shore in the vicinity of the Tower of Capitello, to await there the arrival of the French fleet, which had been announced as on its way to reduce the citadel of Ajaccio. The flight through the rugged hill-country was difficult and fatiguing; for there are no paths in that region but over the rocks, through the macchia, and over the mountain-torrents. Madame Letitia held little Paulina by the hand, Fesch preceded with Eliza and Louis; a troop of adherents from Bastelica, the birthplace of Sampiero, marched in advance, and behind them the men of Bocognano, armed with daggers, muskets, and pistols. The family of Napoleon wandering thus through the mountains, reached at length, after great exertions—clambering over rocks, and wading through streams—the shore at Capitello, where they all concealed themselves in the woods.

About this time Napoleon had thrown himself on board a small vessel in Bastia, had out-sailed the French fleet, and landed at Isola Rossa, where many of the herdsmen of his family have their pasturing-grounds. Here learning that his relatives were in flight, he sent shepherds out in all directions to seek for them, and passed the night waiting in the most painful suspense for news. Morning dawned; he was sitting under a rock, anxiously pondering the fate of his friends. Suddenly a herdsman rushed up to him, crying, "Save yourself!" A band of men from Ajaccio, in quest of Bonaparte and his family, was hastening towards him. Napoleon sprang into the sea. His little vessel, a *chebeque*, kept his pursuers off by its fire, and the boat it had immediately lowered took him safely on board.

On the same day Bonaparte sailed into the gulf, and keeping close in shore, he saw people making signals to be taken off. These were his mother Letitia and her children.

The suffering family was conveyed with all speed to Calvi, where hospitable entertainers were found. But the house of the Bonapartes, in Ajaccio, had been entered and plundered by the furious mob. The family owed its rescue entirely to the prudence and foresight of the Corsican Costa, to whom Napoleon in his will bequeathed the sum of 100,000 francs in acknowledgment of the service.

The young Bonaparte himself, called away from a fruitless attempt upon Ajaccio, in which he was not supported by the fleet, also sailed to Calvi; and leaving Corsica from this point, he appears again at Toulon.

Pasquale Paoli himself had thus driven him out into European history. Two men, bitter enemies of each other—Marbœuf and Paoli—that is, despotism and democracy, had guided Napoleon to his special career. When Napoleon became consul, and his star shone the Cynosure of the world, the star of Paoli had long since set. Deeply does it move me when I think of the noble old Pasquale living in forgotten and solitary exile in London, and illuminating his house in unselfish joy, when he hears of the dignity to which his countryman has attained, forgetting his grudge, and hoping that the great Corsican may become a blessing to humanity. In one of his letters, he says: "Napoleon has consummated our Vendetta on all those that were the authors of our fall. I only wish he may remember his country." He remained in banishment; Napoleon did not recall him, perhaps because he feared to excite the jealousy of the French.

In the days of his prosperity, Bonaparte forgot his little fatherland; thankless and weak, like all *parvenus,* who are unwilling to be reminded of the obscure spot that gave them birth. He did nothing for the poor island, and the Corsicans have not been able to forget this. They still remember that the Emperor, when a Corsican once presented himself to him, drily asked him: "Well, how is it in Corsica; are the Corsicans always murdering each other yet?"

He visited his native island only once after that flight from Calvi—on his return from Egypt. On the 29th of September 1799, his ship ran into the harbour of Ajaccio; with him were Murat, who was yet to leave this same harbour under very changed circumstances—Eugene, Berthier, Lannes, Andreosi, Louis Bonaparte, Morge, and Berthollet. He sat there on board, and read the journals during the night and great part of the next day. He was unwilling to land; but his officers were curious to become acquainted with his birthplace, and he at length yielded to their solicitations, and those of the citizens of Ajaccio. A man, who had in his boyhood been one of the spectators of this landing, gave me an account of it. "Look you," said he, "this Place du Diamant was covered with a huzzaing crowd, and the people filled the roofs; they wanted to see the wonderful man, who, a few years before, had walked about these streets a simple officer, and one of the leading democrats of Ajaccio. He alighted at the Casa Bonaparte, and came out afterwards and walked in the Place du Diamant. But I must tell you of a circumstance that does him honour. When Napoleon lived in Ajaccio, the priests and aristocrats were his bitter enemies. He was one day returning to his house, and had arrived just at the corner of this street, when he saw a priest, a relation of my own, standing at the window of yonder house, and levelling a musket at him. Napoleon bent himself that moment, and the ball whizzed over his head into the wall behind;—a moment sooner, and the world would never have seen an Emperor Napoleon. Well, General Bonaparte met that priest on the Place du Diamant. The man, well remembering that he had once shot at him, turned off to one side. But Napoleon saw him, stepped up to him, gave him his hand, and reminded him good-humouredly of old times. Look you, he was no Corsican in that; great men readily forget injuries." Napoleon, however, was a thorough Corsican when he had the Duke of Enghien shot. This deed was the deed of a Corsican bandit, and can only be rightly understood when we know what the custom of the Vendetta in Corsica allows—the murder even of innocent members of an enemy's family. Napoleon could not quite disown his Corsican temperament; and thus we find him romantic, theatrical, adventurous, as the Corsicans in a certain degree are. Egypt, Russia, Elba, are passages in his history in which he was nothing but a great and genial adventurer.

He went out shooting on occasion of that visit to Ajaccio, and spent a day in Milelli, where he wrote the pamphlet against Buttafucco. How many wonderful deeds lay already behind him! how many princes and peoples had the might of his sword and the thunder of his phrases already overthrown! He called his herdsmen about him, and richly rewarded that Bagaglino who had aided him in carrying out his first *coup d'état*. He distributed his herds and his lands. His nurse, too, Camilla Ilari, came to see him: she embraced him weeping; and as she presented him with a flask of milk she had brought, said in her *naïve* and simple way: "My son, I gave you the milk of my heart—take now the milk of my goat." Napoleon gave her a comfortable house in Ajaccio, and a large extent of arable land; and when he became Emperor, he added a pension of 3600 francs. After remaining six days in Corsica, he again sailed from Ajaccio for France.

He never afterwards visited his native island; but fate one day gave him a sight of it, when, a defeated man, whom history had laid aside as no longer available for its aims, he stood upon the narrow cliff of Elba. Then ironic destiny showed him the obscure corner from which, as a child of fortune, he had issued into the world to seek a career.

Later, on St. Helena, his thoughts constantly recurred to Corsica. People on their deathbeds usually wander back in imagination through the course of their lives, and dwell with greatest pleasure on their childhood. He spoke a great deal of his native island. In the Commentaries, he says on one occasion: "My good Corsicans were not contented with me in the time of the Consulate and the Empire. They affirmed I had done little for my country.... Those who hated me, and still more those who envied me, were continually on the watch; all that I did for my Corsicans was cried down as a theft and an injustice to the French. This necessary policy had turned away the hearts of my countrymen from me, and made them cold towards me. I pity them, but I could not act otherwise. When the Corsicans saw me unfortunate, abused by many an ungrateful Frenchman—when they saw all Europe in conspiracy against me, they forgot all, like men of steadfast and incorruptible virtue, and were ready to sacrifice themselves for me if I had wished.... What memories Corsica has left me! I think with joy still on its fair regions, on its mountains; I remember still the fragrance that it exhales. I should have bettered the lot of my beautiful Corsica, I should have made my fellow-countrymen happy; but days of misfortune came, and I have not been able to carry out my plans."

The first question that Napoleon put to the Corsican Antommarchi, his physician, when he entered his room in St. Helena, was: "Have you a Filippini?" Many of his countrymen had been his companions throughout his career; he had raised many to elevated stations—Bacciocchi, Arena,

Cervioni, Arrighi, Saliceti, Casabianca, Abbatucci, Sebastiani. His relation to that Colonna who had been the friend of Paoli, and who had once been hostile to him, was to the last one of intimate friendship. It is said that Paoli had commissioned Colonna to lay an ambuscade for Napoleon near Ajaccio, and take him alive or dead; such, at least, is the report. Colonna refused. He remained the friend of both, of Napoleon as well as Paoli—and that without playing the hypocrite, for he was a high-spirited man. He was the first who knew of Napoleon's flight from Elba; and in the will which he made in St. Helena, the Emperor intrusted to him the charge of his mother. Colonna discharged this trust conscientiously, and till Letitia's death remained with her as her friend and manager of her affairs. He then retired to Vico, near Ajaccio.

The dying Napoleon received extreme unction from the hands of a Corsican, the priest Vignale, who was afterwards murdered in his native island. He died thus among brother Corsicans, who had not forsaken him.

CHAPTER VII
TWO COFFINS

"Where are the princes who held mightiest sway?
Where are the heroes all, the wise and bold?
The world endures when thou hast pass'd away,
And none has read its riddle deep and old.
The course of things is full of teachings wise,
But, reckless still, we close unheeding eyes." — Firdusi.

As I called up before my mind the history of Napoleon, his splendid empire, the peoples and princes that this headlong comet had drawn onward in his train, the flood of events he had thrown upon the world, the influence he had exercised over unnumbered human destinies — there came over me, in his now desolate and silent house, at once a sadness and its consolation.

All those boundless passions that devoured half the world and were not satisfied, where are they, and what power have they now? They are as a dream, as a great fable that Father Time tells his children. Our thanks are due to Time — the silent and mysterious power that again levels all, humbles heaven-aspiring potentates, checks unscrupulous self-aggrandizement, and effectually ostracizes over-grown ambition.

Where is Napoleon? What is left of him?

A name and a relic, which an easily blinded nation now publicly worships. What lately happened beyond the Rhine, appears to me like the celebration of Napoleon's suppressed funeral of 1821.[N] But the dead do not rise again. After the gods have come their ghosts; and after the hero-tragedy, the satyr-farce. The breath of a charnel-house has spread through the world from beyond the Rhine, since they wakened a dead man there.

I went from the house of Letitia to the church where her coffin stands.

The street of the King of Rome leads to the Cathedral of Ajaccio. This church is a heavy building, with a plain facade; above its portal are some defaced armorial bearings. They are, doubtless, those of the extinct Republic of Genoa. The interior of the cathedral has a motley and rustic appearance. Heavy pillars divide it into three naves (*drei Schiffe*); the dome is small, like the gallery.

Near the choir, to the right, a little chapel, hung with black, has been put up. Two coffins, covered with black velvet, stand therein, before an altar, coarsely decorated in the style we find in village churches. Clumsy wooden candlesticks have been placed at the head and foot of each coffin; and above each hangs a perpetual, but extinguished lamp. On the coffin to the left lies a cardinal's hat and an amaranth-wreath; on the coffin to the right an imperial crown and an amaranth-wreath.

They are the coffins of Cardinal Fesch and Madame Letitia. They were brought hither from their Italian tombs in the year 1851. Letitia died in her Roman palace, in the Place di Venezia, on the 2d of February 1836, and her coffin had since stood in a church of the little town of Corneto, near Rome.

No marble, no sculpture, nothing of the pomp of death, adorns the spot where a woman lies who gave birth to an emperor, three kings, and three princesses.

I was astonished at the unconscious irony, the deep tragic meaning that lay, as it seemed to me, in the almost rustic simplicity of Letitia's tomb. It was like a princely tomb in the scenes of a theatre. Her coffin rests on a high wooden platform; the clumsy candlesticks are of wood, the gold is tinsel. The canopy of the chapel would fain look like velvet, but it is of common taffeta, and the long silver fringes are only silver paper. The golden imperial diadem on the coffin is of gilded wood. The amaranthine wreath of Letitia alone is genuine.

I was told that this chapel was merely temporary, and that a new cathedral was to be built, with a beautiful tomb for Letitia. Improbable enough; the Corsicans are very poor, and for my part, I should be sorry to see it. The worthy citizens of Ajaccio do not know how wise they have been. A profound philosophy speaks from this chapel—what sort of crowns were those that Letitia of Ajaccio and her children wore? For one short evening they were princes, then they hurriedly threw away sceptre and purple, and vanished. History itself, therefore, has laid the tinselled crown on the coffin of the daughter of the citizen Ramolino. Let it lie—it is not the less beautiful that it is counterfeit, like the lofty fortunes of the bastard kings that this woman bore.

Never, so long as the world has stood, has a mother's heart beat higher than the heart of the woman in this coffin. She saw her children, one after another, stand at the loftiest zenith of human glory; and, one after another, saw the same children fall. She has paid Destiny its debt.

Truly, it is hard for him who stands by this coffin to restrain his emotion, so sad, so moving is the great tragedy of a mother's heart that lies therein enclosed. What an undeserved fate!—and how came it that, in the bosom of this gay, young, unpretending woman, those world-convulsing forces and those men and city-devouring passions were to ripen?

CHAPTER VIII
POZZO DI BORGO

The house in the street Napoleon, in which the fugitive Murat lived, has been rebuilt in a style of great magnificence. The arms of the Pozzo di Borgo family, above the door, inform us to whom it belongs. After the Bonapartes, these Pozzi di Borgo are the most famous family in Ajaccio; they are of an old and noble stock, and their name began to be of note long before that of the Bonapartes. In the sixteenth century they distinguished themselves in the service of the Venetians. The Corsican poet, Biagino di Leca, who, in his epic called *Il d'Ornano Marte*, celebrates the achievements of Alfonso Ornano, praises also several of the Pozzi di Borgo, and predicts to their race undying fame.

The family has certainly attained a European importance, in the person of Count Carlo Andrea Pozzo di Borgo, the friend of Paoli, and in his youth the friend of the young Napoleon; but later, the unrelenting, the truly *Corsican* foe of the Emperor. He was born in Alata, a village near Ajaccio, on the 8th of March 1768; he studied law in Pisa together with Carlo Bonaparte, and afterwards made himself conspicuous in Corsica, first as revolutionary democrat, then as Paolist. In the year 1791 he was representative for Ajaccio, then Procurator-general and Paoli's right hand. When Corsica allied herself with England, this clever politician was chosen president of the Council of State, under the viceroyship of Elliot. People say that he brought his patron, Paoli, into bad odour with the English, in order to make his own influence supreme. He afterwards left Corsica, made several journeys to London, travelled to Vienna, to Russia, to Constantinople, to Syria; wandering from country to country and court to court, this unwearied foe kept stirring up with ceaseless activity the hatred of the cabinets against Napoleon. Alexander had made him a member of the Russian Privy Council in 1802. Napoleon, in his turn, pursued him with a hatred equally bitter; he longed to have this man within his power—this artful and dreaded antagonist that crossed him at every turn. At the peace of Presburg he demanded that he should be delivered into his hands. Had he obtained this demand, he would have done with Pozzo di Borgo what Charles XII. did with Patkul. Remarkable is this enmity—it is true Corsican Vendetta—Corsican hatred playing a part in universal history. It was Pozzo di Borgo who induced Bernadotte to become the active opponent of Napoleon; it was he who impelled the allies to a speedy march on Paris; it was he who set the King of Rome aside; he who, at the Congress of Vienna, insisted that Napoleon should be banished from the dangerous Elba to a distant island. At Waterloo he fought with armed hand against his great adversary, and received a wound. And when at length his gigantic but now for ever vanquished foe lay dead in St. Helena, he uttered those haughty and terrible words: "I have not killed Napoleon; but I have thrown the last shovelful of earth upon him!"

Pozzo di Borgo earned a Russian coronet, and the honour of remaining the perpetual representative of all Russian states at the court of France. Living in Paris, he became a frank opponent of the reaction, and thereby endangered his relation to the courts. Notwithstanding his career, he was, and remained, a Corsican. I have been told that he never laid aside his Corsican habits of life: he loved his country. It was, one may say, another victory of his over Napoleon, that he took from him the gratitude of his countrymen. Napoleon did nothing for Corsica, Pozzo di Borgo much. He had the works of the two Corsican historians, Filippini and Peter Cyrnæus, published at his own expense, and Gregori dedicated to him a collection of the statutes. Pozzo di Borgo's name is now inseparably connected with the three greatest documents of Corsican history, and is imperishable. He freely spent his large means on charitable foundations, and in general beneficence towards his countrymen. He died a private individual at Paris, on the 15th of January 1842, at the age of seventy-four, at variance with the world about him, sick and sad at heart, and weary of life. He was one of the most skilful diplomatists and clearest heads of the present century.

His immense fortune passed to his nephews, who have bought rich estates in the neighbourhood of Ajaccio. A few years ago, one of them was murdered close to the town. He had the management of the funds devoted by Count Carlo Andrea to benevolent purposes, and had drawn odium upon himself by acts of injustice. I was told, besides, that he had seduced a girl; and that, as he refused to pay a certain large sum demanded in reparation by her kinsfolk, they resolved upon his death. One day when he was driving from his villa to the town, these men stopped and surrounded the carriage, and called to him: "Come out, nephew of Carlo Andrea Pozzo di Borgo!" The unhappy man obeyed instantly. The murderers then coolly completed this summary execution, in broad daylight, and on the open highway, as if it were an act of popular justice against a criminal. Their shots, however, had not quite killed the man. The murderers placed him in his carriage, and bade the coachman drive homewards, that the nephew of Pozzo di Borgo might die in his bed. They then took to the woods, where they met with their death some time after, in a fight with the gendarmes.

Such is one shocking instance of the rude popular justice still so prevalent in Corsica. I shall here relate another. The circumstances excite our astonishment and admiration, but are at the same time exceedingly painful. The scene is Alata, the native village of the Pozzo di Borgo family, a few miles from Ajaccio.

A CORSICAN BRUTUS

Two grenadiers belonging to a French regiment, forming, as Genoese auxiliaries, the garrison of Ajaccio, one day deserted. They fled to the hills of Alata, and kept themselves concealed there in the wild fastnesses, subsisting on the hospitality of the poor but kind-hearted shepherds.

Sacred are the laws of hospitality; he who breaks them is before God and man like Cain.

When the next spring came, it chanced that some officers from the garrison went a-hunting to the hills of Alata. They came near the place where the two fugitives lived in concealment. These latter caught sight of the huntsmen, and cowered behind a rock, lest they should be recognised and perhaps shot down as game. Quite near them a young herdsman was watching his goats. The colonel of the regiment, De Rozières, stepped up to him and inquired if any deserters were concealed in the mountains thereabouts. The herdsman said that he did not know, and was embarrassed. De Rozières began to have suspicions. He threatened the youth with severe punishment—with immediate imprisonment in the Tower of Ajaccio, if he did not tell the truth.

Joseph was frightened; he said nothing, but he pointed to the spot where the poor grenadiers lay hiding. The officer did not understand him. "Speak!" he shouted. Joseph said nothing, but pointed again. The other officers, who had laid hold of the young man, now left him, and hastened in the direction where he had pointed, expecting possibly to find some animal which this stupid mute knew to be lying there.

The two deserters started up and took to flight, but were overtaken and made fast.

Colonel de Rozières gave Joseph four bright louis-d'ors as informer's reward. When the young herdsman saw the gold pieces in his own hand, he forgot, in his childish joy, officers and grenadiers and the whole world; for he had never seen the like before. He ran into his father's hut—called father, mother, and brothers together, and behaved like one out of his wits as he showed them his treasure.

"How didst thou earn this gold, my son Joseph?" asked the old shepherd. The son narrated what had happened. With every word he uttered, his father's countenance grew darker; the brothers seemed horror-struck, and, by the time his story was told, Joseph had grown pale as death.

Sacred are the laws of hospitality; he who breaks them is before God and man like Cain.

The old shepherd threw one terrible glance on his trembling son, and left the hut. He called all his kinsfolk together. When they were assembled, he related to them the circumstances, and requested them to pronounce judgment on his son; for it appeared to him that he was a traitor, and had brought shame on his own house, and all the neighbourhood.

This court of kinsmen pronounced the deed worthy of death, and there was not a dissenting voice. "Wo to me and to my son!" cried the old man in despair. "Wo to my wife that bare me the Judas!"

The kinsmen went to Joseph. They took him and led him to the city-wall of Ajaccio, to a lonely place.

"Wait here," said the old shepherd; "I will go to the commandant, and beg of him the lives of the two grenadiers. Let their lives be my son's life."

The old man went to Colonel de Rozières. On his knees he implored of him the pardon of the two soldiers. The officer gazed on him in astonishment, and could not understand why this compassionate shepherd should weep so bitterly for two foreign soldiers. But he said to him that the punishment of the deserter was death; so the law willed it. The old man rose, and went out groaning.

He returned to the wall, where his friends stood with the unhappy Joseph. "It was in vain," he said, "my son Joseph, thou must die; die like a brave man; and farewell!"

Poor Joseph wept, but he was quiet and composed. A priest had been brought, who confessed him, and endeavoured to comfort the unhappy youth.

It was just the hour when they were scourging the two deserters to death with rods. Joseph placed himself quietly by the wall. The kinsmen took certain aim—and Joseph was dead!

When he had fallen, his old father, bitterly weeping, took the four louis-d'ors, gave them to the priest, and said: "Go to the commandant, and say: "Sir, here you have the Judas-money back. We are poor and honest people, and have executed justice on him who took them from your hand. The laws of hospitality are sacred, and he who breaks them is before God and man as Cain.'"

In Alata and Ajaccio, the noble action of a woman of the Pozzo di Borgo family is still well remembered.

MARIANNA POZZO DI BORGO

In Appietto, near Ajaccio, the people were merrily celebrating the Carnival. According to an ancient custom, still observed in the island, the Carnival-king sat on a throne in the middle of the market-place, a golden crown on his head, and surrounded by his Ministers of State. Tables had been placed there, covered with fruits, wine, and provisions of every sort. For the Carnival-king had vigorously imposed his taxes; it is Corsican Carnival-law that he has the right to tax the families of the village, each according to its means; and this tribute they must pay in wine and viands for the common entertainment.

It was a merry feast, and the wine was not spared. Guitar and violin were not idle, and the young folks were wheeling in the dance.

Suddenly, in the midst of the merriment, was heard a shot and a cry, and the revellers scattered in every direction. A wild tumult arose in the market-place of Appietto. The young Felix Pozzo di Borgo was lying in his blood. Andrea Romanetti had shot him dead—some insulting words had been dropped. Andrea had taken to the macchia.

They bore the dead youth into the house of his mother. The women raised their wail; the guitars were silent.—Felix's mother, Marianna, was a widow; she had seen much trouble. As soon as the youth was buried, she dried her tears, and thought only of avenging him, for she was a woman of a high spirit, and sprung of the ancient house of Colonna d'Istria.

Marianna laid aside her female dress, and put on male attire. She wrapped herself in the pelone, put a Phrygian cap upon her head, girded herself with the carchera, placed dagger and pistols in her belt, and grasped the double-barrel. In all respects she was like a rough Corsican man; but her scarlet girdle, the velvet border of her pelone, and the ornamented hilt of her dagger, which shone with ivory and mother-of-pearl, showed that she belonged to a noble house.

She put herself at the head of her relations, and unrestingly pursued the murderer of her son. Andrea Romanetti flew from bush to bush, from grotto to grotto, and from hill to hill. But Marianna kept close upon his track. In the darkness of night, the fugitive threw himself into his own house in the village of Marchesacchia. Here a girl connected with the family of his enemies detected him, and gave information. Marianna was immediately on the spot. Her relations surrounded the house. Romanetti made a brave defence, but when his powder was exhausted, and his enemies had got upon the roof, and from that side were forcing an entrance, he saw that he was a lost man. He now thought of nothing but the welfare of his soul; for he was pious and God-fearing.

"Stop!" cried Romanetti from the house, "I will surrender; but promise me first, that before I die, I shall have a confessor." Marianna Pozzo di Borgo promised him this.

Romanetti then came out, and gave himself into the hands of his foes. They brought him to the village of Toppa, and there they led him before the house of the parish priest, Saverius Casalonga. Marianna called the priest out, and prayed him to receive the confession of Romanetti, for that after it he must die.

The priest begged the unhappy man's life with tears; but his prayers were fruitless. He then received his confession, and while this proceeded, Marianna lay upon her knees and besought God that He would have mercy on the murderer of her son.

The confession was ended. The Pozzi di Borgo led Romanetti outside the village, and bound him to a tree.

They raised their pieces; suddenly Marianna rushed before them. "Stop!" she cried, "for God's sake, stop!" and she ran to the tree where Romanetti stood bound, and flung her arms round the murderer of her son. "In the name of God," she cried, "I forgive him. Yes, he has made me the most unhappy of mothers, but ye shall do him no further harm, and shoot me rather than him." And she continued to hold her enemy in her embrace, and to protect him with her own body.

The priest came forward; but his words were not needed. The men loosed Romanetti, and from that moment he was free, and his life sacred for the Pozzi di Borgo, so that none ever touched a hair of his head.

CHAPTER IX
ENVIRONS OF AJACCIO

I spent some time in wandering through the country round Ajaccio. The uneven nature of the ground allows you to walk only in three directions— along the shore to the north, inland along the highway to Bastia, and on the other side of the gulf, on the road to Sartene; the mountains close in on the fourth side. Footpaths wind among the vineyards, which adorn in great numbers the country to the north-east of Ajaccio.

In these vineyards are to be seen those curious watch-houses, which are peculiar to Ajaccio, and are called Pergoliti. They are formed of the stems of four young pines, which support a small hut, raised entirely above the ground, and thatched with straw. The watchman bears the dignified name of Baron. He is armed with a double-barrelled gun, and from time to time blows a blast on a conch or a shrill pipe made of clay, for the purpose of notifying his presence, and of terrifying robbers.

One evening, a hospitable old man conducted me into his vineyard on San Giovanni. He loaded me with bunches of beautiful Muscatel grapes, plucked almonds for me, and juicy plums and figs, which grow in luxuriant confusion among the vines. I happened to be passing along the road, when, after the hospitable manner of the country, he invited me to enter his garden. A very benevolent old man he was, and his reverend appearance reminded me strongly of the pictures of old age we find in the poems of Gleim's epoch, the touching simplicity of which often evidences a truer human wisdom than is discoverable in the most popular poems of our own time. Can there be seen a more beautiful picture than that of a cheerful and healthy old man in the garden planted by himself in his youth, the fruits of which he now kindly shares with the weary travellers by the wayside? Yes! thus peaceful and benevolent ought the close of man's life upon this earth to be.

The old man was talkative, praised this and that fruit, and described the processes necessary for raising a juicy growth. The vines are here trained to the height of four or five feet on poles, like beans, and in general four vines are planted with their tops bound together in a square shallow trough.

The grape-harvest was large, but the disease had made its appearance in many places. The wine of Ajaccio is hot, like the Spanish. I found in this vineyard also, for the first time, the ripe fruit of the Indian fig-tree. After these trees have shed their cactus blossoms, the fruit ripens very rapidly. The fig is of a yellowish colour; the rind is peeled off, and only the inside of the fig eaten, which is unpleasantly sweet. Various attempts have been made to extract sugar from them. The power of growth displayed by this species of cactus, which grows in astonishing luxuriance round Ajaccio, is very remarkable. A leaf placed in the ground quickly strikes out roots, and becomes an independent plant. It requires the very least nourishment, and will grow on the thinnest soil.

A beautiful villa, in the castellated style, with Gothic towers, and immense imperial eagles carved in stone, stands near Mount San Giovanni. It belongs to Prince Bacciocchi.

The small fertile plain lying beyond, at the end of the bay, is called Campo Loro. The spirit of a sad event, which occurred in the Genoese war, hovers over this fruitful spot. Twenty-one herdsmen from Bastelica—all powerful men, worthy of Sampiero's canton—had taken up a position here. They made a brave stand against eight hundred Greeks and Genoese, till they were driven to a marsh, where they were surrounded and all killed, except one young man. This youth had thrown himself down among the dead, and, partly covered by the bodies of his companions, escaped slaughter for a time. But the Genoese afterwards came upon the field for the purpose of cutting off the heads of the fallen, and setting them up on the walls of the citadel. They raised the young herdsman, and brought him before their lieutenant. Condemned to death, he, the last of the little band, was led through the streets of Ajaccio with six of his companions' heads hung round him, and was afterwards quartered, and his body exposed upon the wall to the birds of prey.

At one end of this plain lies the Botanical Garden, which Ajaccio owes to Louis XVI., and which was commenced under the superintendence of Carlo Bonaparte. Its original purpose was the acclimatizing of foreign plants, which were intended to be introduced into France. This garden, sheltered by high mountains from the cold winds, and lying exposed to the noonday sun, contains the noblest productions of foreign countries, which, in the warm climate of Ajaccio, thrive in the open air. You can walk here among splendid magnolias, those wonderful plants called poincianas, tulip-trees, gleditschias, bignonias, tamarinds, and cedars of Lebanon. The cochineal insect is found on the mighty Indian fig-tree here, just as in Mexico.

The sight of this beautiful garden transports the mind to tropical regions; and, when standing among these wondrous, foreign trees, with our eyes fixed on the deep blue waters of the gulf, upon which the warm summer air broods, it is difficult not to imagine ourselves on the shores of some Mexican bay. The garden lies near the road to Bastia—the most frequented of all the highroads from Ajaccio. This is especially the case in the evening, when the townspeople return from their occupations in the country.

It was a favourite amusement with me to take a seat on the shore of the gulf, and to observe the passers-by. The women have all good figures, and their features are clear and delicate. I was often struck with the softness of their eyes and the fairness of their complexion. They wear the fazoletto, or mandile as a head-dress; on Sundays it is of white gauze, and contrasts well with the black faldetta. The peasant women generally wear round straw hats with very low crowns. Upon the straw hat they place a little cushion, and in this manner carry easily and conveniently very heavy burdens. The Corsican, like the Italian women, are distinguished by natural grace of deportment. I had frequent occasion to be delighted with the ease and grace of their movements. One day I met a young woman carrying fruit to the town. I requested her to sell me some. The maiden immediately removed her basket from her head, and, with the most perfect grace, requested me to take as much as I wished. With equal delicacy, she declined my offer of money. She was very poorly dressed. Afterwards, every time I met her in Ajaccio she returned my salutation with a grace which would have well become a lady of the noblest birth.

A man gallops past me. His pretty little wife has perhaps just gone before him, laden with a bundle of brushwood or fodder, while her indolent husband has come from the mountains, where he has been doing nothing all day but waiting for an opportunity to shoot some mortal enemy. When I see these half savages alone, or in companies of three or six, on horseback or on foot, all armed with their double-barrelled guns, I can hardly persuade myself that the country is not permanently in a state of war. Even the peasant, who sits on his hay-cart, has his gun slung upon his shoulder. I counted in half an hour twenty-six men armed with double-barrelled guns, who passed me on their way to Ajaccio. The people in the neighbourhood of Ajaccio are known to be the most quarrelsome in the island.

The appearance of these men is often bold and picturesque; often, too, frightfully hideous, and even ridiculous. You see them on their small horses, men of short stature — generally about Napoleon's height — with jet-black hair and beard, deep bronze complexion, in brownish-black jacket of a shaggy material, trowsers of the same sort, their double-barrelled gun on their shoulder, the round yellow zucca — usually filled with water — strapped to their back, the pouch of goat-skin or fox-skin, stuffed with bread, cheese, and other necessaries, the shot-belt buckled round the waist, with the leathern tobacco-pouch attached. Thus is the Corsican horseman equipped; and thus he lies all day in the field, while his wife is hard at work. I could never repress a feeling of annoyance and disgust when I saw these furious fellows — two generally on one horse, spurring him on unmercifully — pass me at a gallop, and turned to look upon the beautiful shores of the gulf, where not a single village is visible. The soil might produce a hundred kinds of fruit, while at present it is overgrown with rosemary, thorns, thistles, and wild olives.

The walk along the shore, on the north side of the bay, is delightful. It is a pleasure, during the prevalence of a light breeze, to watch the waves breaking upon the granite reefs, and covering them with their pure white foam. On the right rise mountains, which, near the town, are covered with olive-trees, but beyond, and as far as Cape Muro, are bleak and desert.

On this part of the coast stands, close to the sea, the small Greek chapel. I have not been able to discover why it bears this name — dedicated as it is to the Madonna del Carmine, and bearing a tablet with the name of the family of Pozzo di Borgo — *Puteo Borgensis* — inscribed upon it. It was probably ceded to the Greeks on their arrival at Ajaccio. The Genoese had settled the colony of Mainotes at Paomia, which lies a considerable distance above Ajaccio. These industrious colonists were continually threatened by the Corsicans. Hating and despising the intruders — whose settlement had flourished in a remarkable degree — they stabbed the husbandman at the plough, shot the vine-dresser in his vineyard, and laid waste the fields and gardens. In the year 1731, the poor Greeks were expelled from their settlement; they fled to Ajaccio, where they were quartered by the Genoese, to whom they had always remained faithful, in three separate divisions of the town. When the island fell into the hands of the French, they were allowed to settle in Cargese. They brought this part of the country into a high state of cultivation, but had hardly time to become properly domesticated before the Corsicans again fell upon them, in the year 1793, set fire to their houses, slaughtered their cattle, destroyed their vineyards, and forced them to flee once more to Ajaccio. In 1797, General Casabianca led the poor wanderers back to Cargese, where they now live in peace and safety. All peculiarities in their manners and customs have disappeared; they speak Corsican, like their troublesome neighbours, and among themselves a corrupt kind of Greek. Cargese lies on the sea, north from Ajaccio, and not far from the baths of Vico and Guagno.

On the same part of the coast are scattered many small chapels, in various forms—round, polygonal, with and without cupolas, and some in the shape of sarcophagi and temples, surrounded by white walls, and overhung with cypresses and weeping willows. These are the country-houses of the dead—family burying-places. Their situation on the sea-shore, in sight of the beautiful gulf, standing, too, among green trees and shrubs, and the elegant Moorish style in which they are built, give a very pleasant and romantic appearance to the country. The Corsican has strong antipathies to being buried in a public churchyard; he follows the ancient custom of the patriarchs, and prefers to rest with his fathers on his own possessions. Thus the whole island is covered with small tombs, often in the most beautiful situations, and heightening greatly the picturesque appearance of the landscape.

Walking further on towards Cape Muro, where the traveller sees, close to the shore, several red granite cliffs—the Bloody Islands, as they are called—on which stand a lighthouse and several Genoese watch-towers, I found some fishermen engaged in drawing a net to land. They stood in rows of from ten to twelve men, each company pulling in a long rope, to which the net was fastened. These ropes are more than a hundred and fifty yards long on each side; the part pulled in is neatly and cleverly arranged in a round coil. In three-quarters of an hour the net was on shore, heavy with fish. When they spread it out on the beach, such a spluttering, and leaping, and bounding, and springing! The fish were mostly anchovies, the largest were ray-fish (*razza*), very similar to our Baltic flinder. They carry a sharp and painful sting at the end of their long tails. The fishermen lay the ray-fish very carefully on the ground, and sever the tail from the body with a knife. They were an industrious and active body of men, of a powerful build; for the Corsicans are as active and useful on sea as among their native mountains. The old granite mountains and the sea develop and determine, on the one side and on the other, the character of the island and its population; and thus the Corsicans are naturally divided into two powerful bodies—herdsmen and fishermen. The fishery in the neighbourhood of Ajaccio is, as in all the bays of the island, of great importance. In April, the tunny coasts along the shores of Spain, France, and Genoa, and makes its appearance in the Corsican channel; the shark is its sworn enemy. It also is often seen in these seas, but it does not come near the shore.

Returning in the twilight from this sea-side walk to Ajaccio, the report of a gun at no great distance among the hills, struck my ear. Presently a man came running up to me and inquired in an excited manner: "You heard the shot?" "Yes." "Did you see any one?" "No." He then left me. Two sbirri passed. "What was it?" I inquired. "Some one has been murdered, we suppose." A walk in the country may be diversified in this island by somewhat dramatic occurrences. Death breathes around one everywhere, and the beauty of Nature herself has here the sad charm of melancholy and gloom.

BOOK IX
WANDERINGS IN CORSICA

CHAPTER I
FROM AJACCIO TO THE VALLEY OF ORNANO

The road from Ajaccio to Sartene is rich in remarkable scenery and peculiar landscape. It runs for a time along the Gulf of Ajaccio, crosses the river Gravone, which falls into the gulf, and winds through the valley of the Prunelli. From all sides the view of the gulf is magnificent, at times unseen, at other times reappearing, as the road pursues its spiral windings among the mountains.

At the mouth of the Prunelli stands the solitary tower of Capitello, with which the history of Napoleon has made us acquainted.

The towns in this part of the country are but few in number: they are called Fontanaccia, Serrola, and Cavro. Cavro is a paese, consisting of several distinct hamlets, in a wild and romantic mountainous country, rich in granite and porphyry, and interspersed with the most luxuriant vineyards. Ten minutes' walk into this mountainous region of Cavro brings us to the scene of the treacherous assassination of Sampiero. The Ornanos chose their place well. There, in a circle, stand high rocks, down the side of which winds a narrow path into the gorge, through which a mountain stream flows, while around grow oaks, olive-trees, and brushwood. On a rock near the place are still visible the ruins of Castle Giglio, where Sampiero spent the night before his death. I looked around in vain for some memorial which might inform the wanderer that in this gloomy spot the most heroic of all Corsicans met his fate. This, too, is a characteristic trait of the Corsican nation; the living memory of the people is the only monument of their wild tragic history. Every rock in the island is a memorial stone; and the Corsicans may well dispense with monumental pillars and tablets, so long as the great events of their history continue to form a living element of their own being. For, when a people begin to decorate their land with statues and with monuments, it is a sure sign that their primeval power is gone. The whole of Italy is at present a mere museum of monuments, statues, and inscriptions; while in Corsica, nature continues to reign, and living tradition has lost none of its power. Indeed, the Corsicans would not even understand the meaning of a statue or a monument; such a thing would appear to them strange and foreign. When a statue—which he declined—was voted to Pasquale Paoli, after his return from England, a Corsican remarked: "As well give an honest man a box on the ear, as offer him a statue."

Near this gloomy spot, however, stood a group of living monuments of the greatness of Sampiero—peasants, with the Phrygian cap of freedom pressed down upon their brows, talking together in the sun. I went up to them, and entered into conversation with them about their old national hero. The people have conferred upon him the most honourable agnomen that could be borne by the son of any nation; for he is never mentioned by any other than Sampiero Corso—Sampiero the Corsican. In a striking manner has the judgment of his countrymen been pronounced in this name—that Sampiero is himself the most complete expression of the character of the Corsican people, and a symbol of the nation's power and greatness. This great man, hewn from the primeval granite of his country, is the perfect representative of the character of the island as of its history—rude valour, unconquerable obstinacy, a glowing love of freedom, patriotism, a penetrating sagacity, poverty without its wants, roughness and violent passion, volcanic emotions, thirst for revenge—leading him even like Othello to murder his wife; and, that no bloody trait (and bloodthirstiness is a remarkable psychological characteristic of the Corsican nationality) in the history of Sampiero Corso may be wanting, we find the completion of the picture in his own violent death. Living several centuries ago, his character could embrace within itself every element of the Corsican nature. The same traits are observable in Pasquale Paoli, but, from the philosophical and humanistic character of the century in which he lived, their manifestations are not so intense nor so peculiarly national.

The eldest of Sampiero's sons continued the war against the Genoese for some time after his father's death, but afterwards emigrated. In the year 1570, Catherine de' Medici appointed him colonel of the Corsican regiment which she had taken into her service. He distinguished himself by his courage in many battles and sieges, under Charles IX. and Henry III. After the murder of Henry, under whom he had been governor of Dauphiné, the League exerted themselves to draw over the influential Corsican to their side; but Alfonso was among the first who acknowledged the claims of Henry IV., and became one of the most powerful supports of his throne. The king created him Marshal of France, and rewarded the fidelity of the hero with his personal friendship. Henry thus writes to Alfonso: "Dear Cousin—Your despatch, delivered to me by M. de Tour, has given me the earliest information with regard to your successful exertions in my town of Romans. By God's grace, few, if any evil consequences have followed from these wicked plots; and, next to him, there is no one who deserves greater praise in this affair than yourself, for you have acted with unparalleled skill and courage. Receive my best thanks. Your present exertions are but the continuation of your usual decided style of action, and they have been attended with the success which always accompanies your endeavours." In the year 1594, Alfonso took Lyons, Vienne, and several towns in Provence and Dauphiné. He was the terror of the anti-royalists; and, honoured and feared for his military genius, he was equally beloved and respected for his uprightness and benevolence. Several French towns, ruined by the plague and the severities of war, were assisted by Alfonso from his own private purse. He died at Paris in 1610, at the age of sixty-two, and was buried in the Church de la Merci at Bordeaux. By his wife, a daughter of Nicolas de Ponteveze, lord of Flassau, he had several children; and one of his sons, Jean Baptiste d'Ornano, likewise rose to the dignity of Marshal of France. His fall, in the period of Richelieu's government, was occasioned by certain court intrigues; the minister threw him into the Bastille, where he died by poison—administered, it is said, by Richelieu's orders—in 1618. In the year 1670, the line of Sampiero's family, which had made its first appearance in France with Alfonso, became extinct.

His second son, Antonio Francesco d'Ornano, met, like his father, a violent end. It was he with whom the unhappy Vannina fled from Marseilles to Genoa, and who was with her when she was murdered by her enraged husband. Antonio Francesco lived, like his brother, at the court of France. Young, of a fiery temperament, and with a strong desire to see the world, he sought and obtained leave to accompany the ambassador of Henry III. to Rome. One day, at cards, a quarrel arose between him and some French gentlemen of the embassy, among whom one M. de la Roggia took the lead. The impetuous Corsican let fall some insulting words; but the Frenchman restrained his anger and concealed his desire for revenge, and the youthful Ornano suspected nothing. A riding-party was soon after formed for a visit to the Colosseum. Here Ornano, after his Italian friends had left him, remained alone with his servant and twelve Frenchmen, half of the number on horseback, and half on foot. M. de la Roggia invited him to dismount and accompany him into the Colosseum. Ornano agreed; but had hardly dismounted from his horse, before the treacherous Frenchmen—those who were mounted as well as those on foot—fell upon him. Though bleeding from several wounds, Ornano defended himself against this unequal force with heroic courage. Setting his back to a pillar of the Colosseum, he made a bold and vigorous stand with his sword, till he was overpowered and fell. The murderers fled, leaving him weltering in his blood. Mortally wounded, he was carried to his own house, where he died on the following day. This event took place in the year 1580. He was never married, and left no descendants.

I visited the tomb of this the youngest son of Sampiero, in the Church of San Chrysogono, in the Trastevere at Rome, where he lies buried, with many other Corsican gentlemen. San Chrysogono is a church belonging to the Corsicans, having been ceded to them several centuries ago, when numerous fugitives from the island settled in Ostia, and upon Tiber-Borgo. Antonio Francesco d'Ornano is said to have been the perfect image of his father; and it is added, that, in addition to his face and form, he possessed also his intrepidity—a virtue for which Sampiero was as celebrated as the Roman Fabricius. History informs us that Pyrrhus plotted to terrify this great general by the sudden appearance of an elephant; and there is a tradition that the Sultan Solyman tried a like experiment with Sampiero. The story goes that one day the Grand Seignior wished to discover for himself whether the accounts he had heard of Sampiero's intrepidity were exaggerated or not. Accordingly, when Sampiero was seated at table with him, one of his attendants, who had received proper instructions, fired off a two-pound cannon under the table, the moment the Corsican hero was about to drink from the goblet of wine he had carried to his lips. All eyes were turned upon him. Not a feature of his countenance altered; and the shot made no greater impression on him than the noise of a cup falling.

Further north from Cavro lies the large canton of Bastelica, separated by a chain of mountains from the canton of Zicavo. This rugged and mountainous country, piled up with immense masses of granite, interspersed with wild valleys shaded by the knotty oak-tree, and hemmed in by the snow-capped peaks of giant mountains, is the fatherland of Sampiero. In Bastelica, or rather in the little village of Dominicaccia, they still show the dark gloomy house in which he was born; his own dwelling was pulled down by the Genoese under Stephen Doria. He is well remembered in this district, and the imagination of the people has consecrated many a natural memorial of his life and deeds. Here it is a foot-mark of the hero in the rock—here the impression of his gun—here a cave, or an oak-tree under which he rested and ate. The inhabitants of this valley are distinguished for their powerful frames and warlike appearance. They are mostly herdsmen—rude natures, with the iron manners of their forefathers, and completely untouched by culture or civilisation. The inhabitants of the cantons of Bastelica and Morosaglia are considered the most powerful men in Corsica—curiously enough, since they are the brothers of Sampiero and Paoli, both of whom were veritable men of the people, without titles and without ancestry.

The mountain-ridge of San Giorgio divides the valley of Prunelli from the broad valley of the Taravo. After passing the crest of the mountain—the Bocca, as it is called—the traveller's eye falls upon two beautiful mountain-valleys thickly studded with hamlets and villages—the valleys of Istria and Ornano. The river Taravo flows through them in a very rocky channel. My memory in vain seeks for some well-known region of Italy, to illustrate to the reader the character of these Corsican valleys. Many parts of the Apennines are somewhat similar. But these Corsican mountains and valleys, with their chestnut-groves, their dark-brown rock-walls, their foaming streams, their black and scattered villages, appeared to me far more sublime, far wilder and more picturesque than any Italian scenery; and, when suddenly the distant shining sea broke upon the view, the scene was not to be compared with the landscape of any other country in the world.

In these mountains dwelt the old noble families of Istria and Ornano, the head of whom local tradition declares to have been Hugo Colonna; the same whom I have mentioned in my history of the island. Many a tower and ruined castle still attest, but in uncertain accents, the glory of their rule. The chief cantons of this district are those of Santa Maria and Petreto.

In Santa Maria d'Ornano was the seat of the Ornanos. Originally the pieve went by the name of Ornano, but it is now called Santa Maria. The country around is beautiful, with green smiling hills, broad rich pastures, and thick olive-groves. This was the native land of the fair Vannina; and here still stands the tall, brown, castellated house where she lived, picturesquely situated on a height commanding the valley. Not far from this house are still to be seen the ruins of a castle, built by Sampiero, with a chapel near it, in which he heard mass. It is said, however, that he never went to the chapel, but contented himself with sitting at a window of the castle when mass was being read. It was built in the year 1554.

CHAPTER II
FROM ORNANO TO SARTENE

The Taravo forms the boundary between the province of Ajaccio and that of Sartene, the most southern of the arrondissements of Corsica. The traveller, on entering it, comes at first to the beautiful canton of Petreto and Bicchisano, which extends along the Taravo to the Gulf of Valinco. The view of this district, and of the bay far below, is regarded by the Corsicans themselves as one of the most magnificent in their romantic island. In general, the country on the other side of these mountains is of a grander and more sublime character, and bears upon it the colossal stamp of primeval nature. In many parts of this canton the traveller meets with ruins of the castles of the lordly house of Istria, but in a sad state of decay, and seldom distinguishable at the first view from the black granite of the surrounding rocks.

On a mountain above Sollacaro stand the ruins of a castle belonging to Vincentello d'Istria—of whom mention is made in the history—deep buried among trees, and thickly shrouded with creeping plants. With this castle is connected one of those wild traditions, which peculiarly distinguish Corsica, as they likewise characterize the terrible times of the Middle Ages. On this spot stood, in earlier times, another castle, in which dwelt a lady, very beautiful, but of a fierce and savage disposition. This lady, Savilia by name, enticed a powerful lord of the family of Istria—Giudice d'Istria—into her castle, after having promised him her hand. Istria entered the castle, and was immediately cast into a dungeon by the lady Savilia. Every morning, she went down to the prison where he was lying, and while she undressed herself before the eyes of Istria, at the grated window of the dungeon, she mocked and scoffed at him with cruel gibes. "Look upon me!" she said; "is this fair body made, thinkest thou, to be enjoyed by a hideous wretch like thee?" And thus she continued, morning after morning, for a long time, till at length Istria succeeded in making his escape. Vowing revenge, he marched with his vassals to Lady Savilia's castle, broke into it, and laid it level with the ground; the fair Savilia he shut up in a hut, which stood at the crossing of several roads, and compelled her to expose herself to every passer-by.

The miserable lady expired on the third day of her captivity. Vincentello d'Istria afterwards built, on the site of the former, the castle whose ruins are at present to be seen there. The family of Colonna still survives in Corsica; in fact, it is perhaps older and more numerous than any other noble family in the world, and its branches have spread over the whole of Europe.

The next pieve—Olmeto—was entirely a fief of the powerful family of the Istrias. The chief town, also called Olmeto, lies at the foot of high mountains, while beyond stretches a magnificent valley, wooded with olive-trees, and washed by the waters of the gulf of Valinco. On Buttareto, one of the most rugged of these mountains, are still shown the ruins of a castle, formerly the residence of Arrigo della Rocca. The view from Olmeto, away over the valley, as far as the gulf, is remarkably fine. There is a peculiar charm in the soft lines of the landscape, and the silence of the dark-brown coast. The view extends to the north as far as Cape Porto Pollo, and on the south to Cape Campo Moro. The name of *Moorish camp*, which is given to the cape and a small piece of land adjoining, on which now stands a watch-tower, carries the mind back to the time of the Saracens, who so often landed here in centuries long gone by. The Corsican arms—a Moor's head, with a band across the brow—dates from the expedition of the Saracen king, Lanza Ancisa, so celebrated in legendary romance. The whole coast is here of a Moorish-brown colour, and over it broods an inconceivable stillness—the deep peace of a summer's day. As I approached the little port of Propriano on the gulf, the spirit of dead times—a spirit so welcome in a desert island-country, again breathed upon me. There stood before me, on the shore, a crowd of Corsicans, all of them strong, healthy, dark-haired fellows; the double-barrelled gun slung upon their shoulders, standing as if in readiness to resist the attack of the Saracen. The sight of these dark and warlike forms, and the melancholy wildness of the shore, transported me completely into the times of the Middle Ages. I could not help remembering a Spanish ballad, which celebrates the prowess of Dragut the Corsair—well known in the history of the Corsican nation. It may well be sung on the shores of this wild gulf, among this stern band of islanders:—

DRAGUT AT TARIFA

In the offing of Tarifa,
Nearly half a league from shore,
Dragut, chief of all corsairs,
Pirate both by sea and land,
Of the Christian dogs descried—

Come from Malta—vessels five.
Cursing all the hated race,
Thus he shouted loud and long—
Al arma! al arma! al arma!
Cierra! cierra! cierra!
Que el enemigo viene a darnos guerra.

Dragut, chief of all corsairs,
Fired with haste a signal-gun—
A signal to the pirate crew,
Who were for wood and water gone.
Then the Christians gave reply
From the galleys and the shore,
And in the haven every bell
Quick took up the 'larum-cry—
Al arma! al arma! al arma!
Cierra! cierra! cierra!
Que el enemigo viene a darnos guerra.

And the Christian captive, who
Despairing wailed his hapless lot,
Felt a gleam of hope light up
The darkness of his prison-gloom.
For a moment Dragut took
Counsel with his captains all:
"Shall we wait, or shall we hoist
Our sails, and put to sea?"
Al arma! al arma! al arma!
Cierra! cierra! cierra!
Que el enemigo viene a darnos guerra.

Then said they all with one accord—
"Wait! wait! let them come on!
What is the ocean but the field
Of pirates' victory?"
Then Dragut shouted loud and long—
"Up, knaves! up to the fight!

Every gunner to his gun!
Load and fire, and load again—hurra!"
Al arma! al arma! al arma!
Cierra! cierra! cierra!

Que el enemigo viene a darnos guerra.

The refrain of this spirited song—"To arms! to arms! to arms! Danger! danger! danger! for the enemy is coming to attack us"—I have preserved in the original Spanish; it would seem somewhat tame in a translated form.

On the 12th of June 1564, Sampiero landed on the shores of this gulf—another note of more peculiar meaning among these warlike echoes of past times.

The country rises gradually from the shore into a rugged mountainous region, covered with huge boulders. Rocks, low brush-wood, the sand upon the shore, and a dead marsh, combine to render this part of the island peculiarly wild and bleak. The evergreen oak, however, and the cork-tree, grow here in great numbers; and the rugged soil brings forth corn and wine. At last Sartene met my view, stretching before me—a wide-extended paese—in melancholy isolation, among melancholy rocks and mountains.

CHAPTER III
THE TOWN OF SARTENE

The town of Sartene contains only 3890 inhabitants. It is the capital of the arrondissement, which is divided into eight pieves or cantons, and has a population amounting to 29,300. Sartene appeared to me a rude country place, with less of the appearance of a town than even Calvi or the little town of Isola Rossa; it does not, indeed, seem to differ in any respect from the other large paeses of the island. The style of building is that in common use in the villages, with the addition of a little ornament. All the houses, and even the tower of the largest church in the town, are built of brown granite, with loam instead of mortar. The church alone has a coating of yellow wash; all the other buildings are of the usual dark-brown hue. Many of the houses are merely wretched huts; and some of the streets, on the slope of the mountain, are so narrow, that two men can with difficulty pass each other. Steep stairs of stone conduct us to the vaulted gate which stands in the middle of the outer wall. I rambled through the streets; they seemed to be inhabited by veritable demons; and I felt as if at some corner I should suddenly come upon old Dis, or were wandering through Dante's city of Hell. In the quarter of Santa Anna, however, there are some elegant houses, belonging to the richer classes; and some have a very pleasant appearance, in spite of the black stone of which they are built. All are quaint, original, and picturesque in the highest degree—effects which they owe to the blunt-cornered, projecting Italian roofs, and the odd Italian chimneys; some in the shape of pillars, with the strangest-looking capitals, others in the form of towers or obelisks. A house with an Italian roof looks remarkably well; and, if its walls are only built of regularly hewn stone, the appearance of it is undoubtedly pleasing. I found my old cabins of Monte Rotondo again in the market-place. They were used for provision-stores. The pompous names of some of the inns—Hôtel de l'Europe, Hôtel de Paris, Hôtel de la France—were ridiculous enough beside these primitive specimens of Corsican architecture.

The name *Sartene* seems to have some connexion with Sardinia or Saracen. No one could give me any information as to the origin of the word. In ancient times, the town was called Sartino; and a local tradition informs us that it was once famous for its mineral springs. At that time strangers flocked to the place for the benefit of these waters. The poor inhabitants of the barren spot died in consequence of hunger—for the strangers seized upon all the produce of the soil. The inhabitants, resolved no longer to endure such a state of things, choked up the springs, abandoned their houses, and built a town higher up among the mountains. If this tradition is a true one, it forms no testimony in favour of anything but Corsican indolence.

Sartene suffered terribly from the Saracens. The Moors, after repeated attacks, surprised the town in the year 1583, and in one day carried off four hundred persons into captivity—the third part of the population at that time. From that date, Sartene has been defended by a strong wall.

To-day, standing in this quiet town, whose inhabitants are talking peacefully together under the large elm-tree, in the quaint, idyllic market-place, one cannot believe that revenge and the fiercer passions could find a lurking-place within its walls. And yet this town, after the Revolution of July, was for many years the scene of a horrible civil war. The citizens have been divided, since the year 1815, into two parties—the adherents of the family of Rocca Serra, and those of the family of Ortoli. The former party is composed of the richer inhabitants, who live in the quarter of Santa Anna; the latter, of the poorer classes occupying the Borgo. Both factions had intrenched themselves, barred their houses, shut their windows, and proceeded to make sorties upon each other, to shoot and to stab one another with the most furious zeal. The Rocca Serrans were the Whites or Bourbonists, the Ortoli the Reds or Liberals; the former had forbidden the opposite party admission into their quarter of the town; and the Ortoli, in contempt of this declaration, had formed a procession, and marched with flags flying into Santa Anna. The Rocca Serrans immediately ran to their arms, and shot at the procession from their windows, killed three men and wounded several others. This was the signal for a bloody combat. The day after, several hundred mountaineers came with their guns to the assistance of the Ortoli, and besieged Santa Anna. The Government despatched a body of soldiers, which had the effect of apparently restoring order. Both parties, however, continued hostilities, and many lives were lost on both sides. The hostile feeling continues to this day, although, after thirty-three years of deadly feud, the Rocca Serrans and the Ortoli, on the occasion of the election of Louis Napoleon as President, held a meeting of reconciliation, where their children were allowed to dance together.

Corsica, with these inextinguishable family feuds, presents the same picture as the Italian cities of Florence, Bologna, Verona, Padua, and Milan, several centuries ago. The Italian Middle Ages still survive in this island; and here still rage the same tumults described so picturesquely by Dino

Compagni in his chronicles of Florence—that war of fellow-citizens, whom, as Dante complains, the same ditch surrounds and the same wall defends. But in Corsica, these feuds are much more remarkable and more terrible; raging, as they do, in districts of so small an extent, in villages with a population of not above one thousand souls, the inhabitants of which are indissolubly connected by the ties of blood and hospitality.

To-day the people of the town are assembled in the marketplace, where an odd sort of scaffolding is being erected, for the exhibition of fireworks, against the 15th of August, the anniversary of Napoleon's christening. It is not improbable that the festival may rekindle the flame, and these black houses may in a few days be transformed into little fortresses, from which shots of death will be scattered around. Here it was political feeling that stirred up the angry passions of the townspeople; in other districts strife has been kindled by a personal offence, or some accidental circumstance of the most trivial nature. The shooting of a goat has occasioned the death of sixteen men, and roused a whole canton to arms. A young man throws a piece of bread to his dog, another man's dog snatches it; and a feud arises between two parishes, with death and murder upon both sides. Causes of quarrel are never wanting at the communal elections, festivals, or dances; these are often extremely ridiculous. At Mariana, in the year 1832, a dead ass became the occasion of a bloody feud between two villages. A procession from one of the villages was proceeding, during Easter-week, to a chapel, on the road to which a dead ass was lying. Upon this, the sacristan began to curse the people who had thrown the ass upon the road, and had thus profaned the holy procession. Immediately there arose a quarrel between the people of Lucciana and those of Borgo—the parish to which the ass belonged; guns were unslung, and shots exchanged; the holy procession was suddenly transformed into a confused mass of combatants. The one parish threw the blame of the dead ass upon the other; the body was dragged from Borgo to Lucciana, and from Lucciana to Borgo; and these pilgrimages were on every occasion accompanied with fighting, shooting, and the furious shouts of battle.

It resembled the combat of the Greeks and Trojans for the dead body of Patroclus. The people of Borgo dragged the dead ass to the chapel of Lucciana, and flung it down at the door of the church; the Luccianese carried it off to Borgo, and after storming the village, fixed it on the church-tower. At last the Podestà seized the *corpus delicti*, already in a state of rapid decomposition, and none the better for its frequent travels, and the dead ass found a quiet resting-place in the grave. The poet Viale has written a comic Epopee on this occurrence, in the style of the Stolen Bucket of Bologna.

A detachment of ten gendarmes is at present stationed in Sartene. The same number is usually posted in the chief town of every canton, and in those villages which are particularly troublesome. The officer of the company was an Alsatian, who had lived twenty-two years in the island, seemingly quite happily, and without any expectation of meeting a countryman in Sartene. Whenever I meet an Alsatian or a Lothringian—the latter always speak very inaccurate German—I feel deep sorrow for these lost German brethren of mine. It always brings a pang to my heart, to think of a branch of the noble old German oak in the hands of the French. This officer had severe complaints to make regarding the dangerous service in which he was employed, and the petty warfare he had to carry on with the banditti. He pointed to a mountain in the distance—the lofty Incudine. "Look," said he, "yonder sits a captain of banditti, whom we have to hunt like a wild sheep. There are fifteen hundred francs on his head, but they are not so easy to win. A few days ago we apprehended twenty-nine men who had been carrying provisions to the fellow. I have them here in the barracks."

"What will be their punishment?"

"A year's imprisonment, if they are convicted. They are herdsmen or mountain-people, friends and relations of the bandit."

Poor Corsica! what, under circumstances like these, is to become of thy industry and thy agriculture!

The view of the dark mountain of Incudine where the poor bandit is sitting, and the recollection of the feuds of Sartene, recall to my mind some stories from the inexhaustible stores of the Corsican romance of revenge. Let us sit down together upon a rock, in sight of these glorious mountains, and the waters of the Gulf of Valinco, and listen to two stories about Corsican guns and their owners.

CHAPTER IV
TWO STORIES OF THE VENDETTA

ORSO PAOLO

The people of the village of Monte d'Olmo were one day celebrating a festival of the Church. The priests had taken their places before the altar, and numbers of devout worshippers had already assembled within the sacred edifice, while not a few still lingered over their gossip outside. Among these latter were the Vincenti and Grimaldi—two families between which a hereditary feud had existed from time immemorial. To-day they ventured to look each other in the face, as the sacred festivity compelled at least a temporary suspension of all animosities.

Somebody started the question, whether or not the priests should be made to wear the capote or cowled cloak of their order during the procession.

"No," said Orso Paolo, of the Vincenti family, "they should be made to do nothing of the kind, for it was never the custom in our forefathers' times."

"Yes," cried Ruggero, of the Grimaldi family, "they ought to wear their capotes, for that is the regulation of our Holy Church."

And the strife for and against capotes waxed hot and noisy, and filled the little square before the church with a din that could not have been exceeded, had a declaration for or against Genoa been the question to be decided. One took the word out of another's mouth; one after another sprang upon the stone bench to defend his opinion in a speech, and the by-standers hissed or applauded, shouted in derision or approbation, according as a Grimaldi or a Vincenti had advocated or denounced the capotes.

Suddenly some one let fall an insulting expression. That moment rose cries of rage and defiance, and every one drew his pistols from his belt. The Grimaldi rushed upon Orso Paolo, who fired among his assailants. Antonio, Ruggero's eldest son, fell mortally wounded.

The music of the holy mass ceased in the church. The people poured out in a body—men, women, and children, the priests in their robes, crucifix in hand.

The entire village of Olmo was one confused scene of flight and pursuit, re-echoing with yells of fury, and the reports of fire-arms. The cries of the Grimaldi were vows of death to Orso Paolo.

Orso had made for the woods with the speed of a hunted deer. But his foes saw his aim; revenge gave them wings, and they succeeded in interposing themselves between him and the hoped-for shelter.

He was surrounded. From every side he saw furious pursuers approaching; already their balls whizzed about his head. It was vain to think of reaching the wood; there was little time to ponder a new plan; he was cut off from the open country; only a house stood near on the mountain-side— the house of his deadly foe Ruggero.

Orso Paolo saw it, and in a moment he had crossed its threshold and secured the door. He had his weapons with him, his carchera was full of cartridges, there was a store of victuals in the house, and he might hold out for days. It was empty too; all its usual inmates had hurried into the village, and Ruggero's wife was occupied with the wounded Antonio. Her second son, still a child, had alone remained in the house, and lay asleep.

Scarce had Orso Paolo intrenched himself here, when Ruggero appeared with all the Grimaldi at his back; but the barrel of Orso's gun appeared at the window, and he was heard to promise its contents to the first that approached the door. No one ran the risk.

In most ungentle mood, they stood before the house uncertain what to do; Ruggero stamped with rage that his deadliest enemy should have found refuge in his own house; the tiger is not more furious when it sees and cannot reach its prey.

The crowd increased every minute, and filled the air with their vociferations; presently the wail of women was heard to mingle with their cries; it was a party carrying the wounded Antonio into the house of a relation. The sight redoubled Ruggero's fury; he rushed into a house, and snatched a firebrand from the hearth, to fling upon his own roof, and consume it and Orso Paolo together. As he swung the brand round his head, and cried to the others to follow his example, his wife threw herself distractedly in his way. "Madman," she cried, "our child is in the house! Would you burn your child? Antonio is at death's door—Francesco lies sleeping within there—will you murder your last child?"

"Let them burn to death together," cried Ruggero; "let the world be burnt to ashes, if only Orso Paolo perish in the flames!"

The shrieking woman threw herself at her husband's feet, clasped her arms round his knees, and refused to let him move from the spot. But Ruggero thrust her from him, and hurled the firebrand into his house.

The fire caught. Soon the flame rose, and the dancing sparks flew about upon the wind. The mother had sunk lifeless to the earth, and they carried her to the house where her son Antonio lay.

But Ruggero stood before his burning house, which was now completely surrounded by the Grimaldi, that Orso Paolo, if he should attempt to escape, might find their bullets in his way; Ruggero stood before his house and gazed into the flames, laughing horribly as they rose and roared, shouting mad shouts of gratified revenge and wild pain, as the beams cracked and fell in—for it seemed to him that every burning beam fell upon his own heart.

Often he thought he descried a form among the flames, but perhaps it was only a wreath of smoke, or a whirling column of fire—then, again, came sounds as of a weeping child. Suddenly the roof fell in with a crash, and smoke and tongues of flame shot up from the horrid ruin towards heaven.

Ruggero, who had been standing dumb and motionless, staring with glassy eye, body bent forward, and arm outstretched toward the house, fell with a groan to the earth. He was borne into the neighbouring house, and laid beside his wounded son. When his consciousness returned, he was unable at first to understand what had happened, but immediately the truth dawned upon him—the glare of his burning home flashed conviction and remorse into his soul, and shuddering, he recognised the dreadful enormity of his deed.

For the space of a minute he stood in deep thought, as if the lightning of heaven had scathed him to the marrow; then with a sudden start, he tore the dagger from his belt, and would have buried it in his breast. But his wife and friends arrested his arm, and deprived him of his weapons.

What had become of Orso Paolo? What of Francesco?

When Orso Paolo found the beams of the roof had taken fire, he began to seek for some place of safety, some hole or vault where he would be protected from the flames. As he wandered from chamber to chamber, he heard the weeping and terrified screaming of a child. He sprang into the room whence it issued. A child sat here upon its bed, and, bitterly weeping, stretched its arms towards him, and called for its mother. It seemed to Orso at that moment, as if the Evil One called to him from out the flames to murder the innocent child, and so punish his foe's vengeful barbarity. "Hast thou not a right of vengeance over the very children of thine enemy? Thy knife, Orso! Extinguish the last hope of the house of Grimaldi!"

A horrid thirst for vengeance glared in Orso's eye as he bent over the child. The glow from the flames bathed himself, the child, the room, in a purple tinge as of blood. He bent over the weeping Francesco, and — suddenly he snatched up the child, clasped it to his breast, and kissed it with a wild fervour. Then, still bearing it in his arms, he rushed out of the chamber, and groped his way through the burning house, seeking some spot of safety.

The house had scarcely fallen in, when the horns of the Vincenti were heard outside the village. The men of Castel d'Acqua, all of them friends or relations of Orso Paolo, had heard of his danger, and were assembled for his rescue. The Grimaldi fled from the scene of the conflagration to the house in which Ruggero, his wife, and Antonio were.

A quarter of an hour of fearful suspense passed away.

Suddenly the market-place of Olmo resounded with a loud and exulting shout, and from a hundred tongues was heard the cry: Evviva, Orso Paolo! Antonio's mother flew to the window; then with a cry of joy she rushed to the door, and after her Ruggero and the women.

Through the midst of the jubilant crowd came Orso Paolo, his face beaming with joy, and the child Franceso clasped tenderly in his arms. His clothes were singed, he was black with smoke, and covered with ashes. He had rescued himself and the child in a vault beneath a flight of stairs.

Ruggero's wife threw herself on Orso Paolo's breast, and flung her arms round him and her little son, with a joy too deep for utterance.

But Ruggero fell upon his knees before his foe, and while he embraced his feet with sobs, begged his forgiveness, and God's.

"Rise, my friend Grimaldi," said Orso Paolo; "may God so to-day forgive us both, as we forgive each other; and here, before the people of Olmo, swear eternal friendship."

The foes sank into each other's arms, and the people shouted exultingly: Evviva, Orso Paolo!

Antonio soon recovered from his wound; and gay were the festivities of that evening in the village of Monte d'Olmo, when the Grimaldi and the Vincenti celebrated their solemn feast of reconciliation. The olive-branch of peace decked the houses, and nothing was to be heard but evvivas and musket-shots, and the music of tinkling wine-glasses, violins, and mandolines.

DEZIO DEZII

When the Genoese were still lords of the island of Corsica, a furious contest arose between the two villages of Serra and Serrale, in the pieve of Moriani. Two houses were at bitter and bloody feud—the Dezii in Serra, and the Venturini in Serrale.

At length they had grown weary of the long war of vengeance, and both families had with solemn oath sworn peace before the Parolanti. Now these Parolanti are worthy men, appointed as arbitrators by the two parties in common; they act as witnesses of the oath of reconciliation; in their hands is lodged the written deed by which amity is ratified, and it is their duty to watch that for the future nothing be done to break the peace. On that godless man who nevertheless does break the peace, falls the scorn and contempt of all the good, and the wrath and vengeance of the Parolanti overtake his house, his field, and his vineyard.

The Dezii and the Venturini, then, had in this manner sworn peace, and a happy tranquillity reigned in the Pieve di Moriani. But as the evil spirit of contention cannot rest, but must ever be blowing upon the ashes, to see if some spark of the old grudge may not yet be awakened, it fell out one day in the market-place of Serrale, that such a spark was kindled in the fierce heart of the old Venturini. Nicolao was a grayhaired man, but in bodily vigour he was young as his sons. He had a dark look, a venomous tongue, and the cramp in his dagger-hand. He met young Dezio Dezii on the market-place—Dezio, the pride and flower of the house of his enemies. He was a comely youth, and of pleasant manners; but his temper was quick and fiery.

This old man with the dark look, addressed sneering and bitter words to Dezio, nor was it known why he should have done so; for the youth had given him no provocation. When the words fell on Dezio's ear, his heart filled with shame and indignation; but he thought on the Parolanti, on his oath of peace, and the gray hairs of Nicolao; and he quieted his swelling heart, and passed silently out of the village of Serrale.

It so happened, however, that on the same evening the old man and the youth met in the open field. When Dezio saw Nicolao approaching, observing that he was unarmed, he left his gun leaning on a tree, that the Evil Spirit might not provoke him to injure a man who carried no weapon; then, going up to old Nicolao, he demanded haughtily the ground of his insult.

The old man replied contemptuously; and after a few fiery words had passed, he seized the youth by the breast, and gave him a blow in the face. Dezio staggered back; the next moment he sprang to his musket, and in another second Nicolao fell, shot to the heart.

The unhappy Dezio fled as if pursued by the avenging angel, and made his way from crag to crag far into the heights of Monte Cinto, where he threw himself, weeping, into a cave.

The Parolanti had hastened to the scene of this deed of blood. They cried, "Wo over Dezio and all his race!" and assembled in a body before his dwelling. His young wife was in the house. They told her that she must leave her home, for it had fallen under the ban of justice; and as soon as the sobbing woman had crossed the threshold, they set the house on fire, and burned it to the ground. They then entered Dezio's chestnut-grove and olive-orchard, and, with the hatchet, barked every tree, in token that the owner had broken his oath and shed blood, and that the curse of angry Heaven had fallen upon him and all that was his. And this they did according to ancient and sacred custom.

The kinsmen of Dezio remained quiet, for they acknowledged that in all this was nought but justice. But Luigione, son of the murdered Nicolao, allowed his beard to grow, signifying thereby that he had resolved to avenge his father's blood. He took his gun, and ranged the hills to find Dezio; and, as he could not come upon his traces, though he lay night and day among the rocks, he took service with the Genoese, who formed the watch in the Tower of Padulella, thinking, that with their help, he might perhaps surprise his foe.

Dezio, meanwhile, lived with the fox, the deer, and the wild sheep, and roamed about in desert fastnesses, every night seeking a new shelter, ever wandering, and ever bearing with him in his heart sadness and alarm. One day he escaped in a ship with sailors, who were his friends, to Genoa. He enlisted in the service of the Genoese, and in this banishment long years went by.

At length there awoke in him a longing to see his native country and his wife. He obtained his discharge, and took with him from Genoa a letter of protection, which ordained that he was to live free and unharmed in Corsica, and outlawed any one that should seek to injure him.

Perhaps, too, Dezio hoped that Luigione's thirst for vengeance had in the course of time gone to sleep. He returned accordingly to his village, found his wife again, and remained quietly within her house. Nobody knew that he had come back; for he never showed himself, going only into the woods, and to lonesome places, where he was certain that no one would meet him. But the shadow of old Nicolao was always by his side.

Weeks and months passed thus, and nobody knew or spoke of Dezio. One day, Luigione, who was famous in these mountains as a hunter, said to his wife, "I dreamt last night that I shot a fox in the hills. I shall go out to-day; perhaps I may have good luck." So he threw his gun upon his shoulder, and went into the hills.

He started a fox. It took cover in a thicket, and Luigione hastened after. The spot was wild and lonely. As soon as he got among the bushes, he found a narrow shepherd's track, which wound about and about, and led him always deeper and deeper into the savage country. Suddenly, Luigione stopped. Below a clump of wild olives, he saw a man lying in deep sleep. Beside him lay his double-barrelled gun and his zucca. A long and bushy beard partly concealed his face. Luigione remained motionless as a statue; but with a feverish eagerness his eyes devoured the sleeping man. The blood shot seething hot to his cheeks, and then again they became deadly pale; his heart was beating so loud that it might almost have given the alarm to the sleeper.

He made a single step forwards—another; he gazed into the stranger's face. Yes; it was Dezio—his father's murderer! A wild smile lit up Luigione's face. He drew the dagger from his belt.

"God has given thee into my hands," he murmured, "that I may kill thee this day. My father's blood be upon thee!" and he raised the two-edged blade. But a swift thought sped like an angel between him and his sleeping foe, and suspended the weapon in the air. The words of the angel were, "Luigione, forbear to murder sleep!"

Luigione sprang suddenly backwards. Then, with a fearful shout, he cried—

"Dezio! Dezio! rise, and stand to thy weapon!"

The sleeper leapt to his feet, and caught up his gun.

"I could have murdered thee sleeping," said Luigione to him; "but it would have been the deed of a villain. Now defend thyself, for my father's blood cries for revenge!"

Dezio, shocked to death, gazed for one moment on the terrible man, then he hurled his gun far into the bushes, tore pistol and dagger from his belt, and flung them both away, and, baring his breast, cried—

"Luigione, shoot, and avenge thy father! Then I shall have rest in my grave! Kill me!"

Luigione looked at his enemy in amazement, and for a while both were silent. Luigione then laid down his gun, went up to Dezio, and offered him his hand. "God," he said, "gave thee into my hand; but I forgive thee. Peace be with the blood of my father! Now, come and be my guest."

The two men went down into the village side by side; and they remained friends. And as Luigione had no children of his own, he stood godfather to the child of Dezio, as a solemn token that they were reconciled before God; and this he did according to ancient custom.

Dezio grew weary of the world, and became a monk. So pure and God-fearing was his walk, that he was beloved by all till the day of his death; and the blessing of his pious and peace-making spirit diffused itself far and wide among the hills.

On his burial-day, the villages of all the region accompanied him to his grave; and still in the pieve of Moriani they speak of Dezio the comely youth, Dezio the murderer, Dezio the bandit, Dezio the monk, Dezio the priest, Dezio the saint.

CHAPTER V
THE ENVIRONS OF SARTENE

Sartene is encircled by a range of bleak mountains, to the north of which stand the Incudine and Coscione. The Coscione is celebrated for its rich pasture-grounds, which are watered by the beautiful streams of the Bianca and the Viola. To these grounds the herdsmen of Quenza bring their flocks in summer, spending the winter on the coast of Porto Vecchio. One of the mountains in the neighbourhood of Sartene is an immense rock of a very remarkable shape; its appearance from a distance is that of a giant lifting his monstrous and misshapen head into the clouds. The mountain goes by the name of the Man of Cogna. In this part of the country are also to be found the remains of Menhirs and Dolmens—those ancient mementos of the Sabian ritual, which are not unfrequently met with in the islands of the Mediterranean, and in countries inhabited by Celtic nations. They consist of stones—not very unlike pillars—placed in a circle, and are here called Stazzone. Corsica has preserved but few remains of these heathen temples; but they are peculiarly abundant in Sardinia. I regretted exceedingly that I had no time, when in Sartene, to pay a visit to these curious remains.

On the surrounding mountains stand ruins of many of the old castles of the brave Renuccio, and the famous Giudice della Rocca. The estates of these old seigniors lay in the neighbourhood of Sartene. The canton of Santa Lucia de Tallano still preserves a memorial of Renuccio in the ruins of the Franciscan convent which was founded by this brave hero, with whom fell the power of the old Corsican barons. In the church is shown the tomb of his daughter Serena, with a marble statue of her in a recumbent posture, a chaplet in her hand, and attached to it a gold purse, as a symbol of her great benevolence.

Among the mountains of Santa Lucia is found that remarkable species of granite—peculiar to Corsica—which goes by the name of Orbicularis. The ground-colour is a grayish blue, but interspersed with black points with a white border, which appear in great numbers on the surface of the stone when broken. I saw some beautiful specimens of this stone. It has, when polished, a remarkably rich appearance, and is of peculiar value in architectural ornamentation. Nature seems to have created this stone in one of her sportive and most genial moods; it is a jewel in the rich mineralogical cabinet of the island. The orbicular granite of Santa Lucia de Tallano has been also deemed worthy of a place in the chapel of the Medicis at Florence, in the decoration of which the rarest and most beautiful stones have been employed.

North-east from Santa Lucia, in the valley of the Fiumiccioli, lies the celebrated canton of Levie, which extends to the small gulf of Ventilegne. The district is mountainous, and tolerably well wooded. It was the abode of several old noble families, particularly that of the Peretti, from whom was descended Napoleon, the friend of Sampiero, and the first of this name mentioned in Corsican history. He was not, however, a relation of Bonaparte. He was killed in a battle with the Genoese.

In Levie stands the town of San Gavino de Corbini, a place well known in Corsican history as the head-quarters of the strange sect of the Giovannalists—those old communists of Corsica, whose theories made such remarkable progress on the island, and who may be considered as the forerunners of Saint-Simonism and Mormonism. Only in a country where the inhabitants still lay in a state of the rudest and most uncultivated nature, and where a belief in the natural equality of man was the dominant trait in the national character—only in a time, moreover, of social disorder, misery, and blood—could the sect of the Giovannalists have found their origin. It is very much to be regretted that the chronicles of the country have not preserved more particular accounts of this remarkable sect. Its appearance seems to be a remarkable trait in the physiognomy of the national history; and transitory as was the phenomenon, I look upon it as forming a strongly-marked line in the portrait of this extraordinary people.

Before taking leave of Sartene, my heartiest eulogies are due to the hospitality of its inhabitants. It was my good fortune to meet with the greatest kindness from these amiable people; their noble and honest confidence cheered my heart, and I spent many a pleasant hour in their society. I could with difficulty tear myself from their hospitality; I accompanied them on their hunting expeditions among the mountains, and, above all, enjoyed myself many a summer day in their beautiful orchards. On leaving Sartene, early in the morning, I was accompanied by all those excellent gentlemen with whose friendship I had been honoured; and when bidding the company adieu, one of them—a cousin of the unfortunate Vittoria Malaspina—placed a note in my hands.

Upon opening it, I found its contents to be as follows:—

"To Signor Ferdinando.

"If you should ever happen to be in danger or in difficulty during your stay in our island, do not forget that you have a friend in Sartene.

Alessandro Casanova."

I preserve this note as a talisman, and at the same time as a testimony to the noble hospitality of Corsica. It was not sufficient for my Sartenese friend to assure me by hand and word that, as his guest, I was under his protection for the rest of my life, but he must needs add to his promise the additional guarantee of a written document.

CHAPTER VI
THE TOWN OF BONIFAZIO

About eight o'clock in the morning I set out from Sartene to Bonifazio, the most southerly town and fortress in Corsica. The road lay along a desolate coast, the hills sloping gradually towards the sea-shore. There is not a village to be seen all the way; and I should have perished from hunger and thirst, had not my travelling companions taken care to furnish themselves with bread and wine before setting out. Who not his bread with joy has eaten, by olive gray or vine-tree seated, He knows you not, ye heavenly powers!

We passed through the vale of Ortoli—everywhere waste hill-country, neither grain nor fruit-tree visible. The olive is no longer met with; cork-tree clumps and arbutus alone occupy the soil. We approached the south coast—still more desolate, if possible, than that which we had left behind us. Not far from the mouth of the Ortoli lies a solitary post-house, and opposite it a ridge of rock, on which stands the Tower of Roccapina. Close beside it, on the sharp edge of the cliff, there is a rugged and irregular rocky mass. It bears a striking resemblance to a colossal crowned lion, and is called among the people, *Il leone coronato*. This singular rock—so conspicuous an object along this line of coast, the first bit of Corsican ground which fell into the hands of Genoa when she wrested the island from the Pisans—stands there as if it were the monument or the arms of the Republic.

From the height here I got my first view of the open sea not far from me, and the coast and hills of Sardinia—a glorious spectacle. The sight of a foreign land suddenly unfolded to the view, here only showing its outline, and there revealing objects with forms characteristic of the country, rouses feelings at once strange and pleasing—anticipation, longing, and doubt. It resembles nothing so much as the fabulous fancy-pictures of childhood. Wholly an island! I stood for long on one of those bare masses of rock, in a violent wind, and in the full glow of the mid-day sun; with a deep feeling of desire, I gazed across the strait on the twin-sister of Corsica. It was entirely wrapt in an ethereal veil of blue; and the sea, stirred by the maestrale, dashed in foaming breakers round its shore.

We rested for a couple of hours, and then resumed our journey farther along the coast. It is much broken up by arms of the sea, and wears a gloomy aspect. Little streams creep sluggishly through morasses into the sea; gray turrets surmount the cliffs which occur at intervals along the coast, and hold solitary watch there. The air is unwholesome. I perceived a couple of little villages on the slope of the hill. I was informed that they were uninhabited; the people, it seems, do not leave the mountains till the first of September.

The sea at this place forms two little gulfs—Figari and Ventilegne. They resemble Fiords, and their coast-lines are often of the most irregular form, rising like rows of ash-gray obelisks.

As we traverse the extreme point of Corsica towards the south-west, the tongue of S. Trinita, terminating in the Capo di Feno, the chalky coast of Bonifazio becomes visible. At the same time, the town itself comes into view, the most southerly and most singular town in the island, snow-white as the coast on which it stands, and perched high upon its rock—an unexpected and surprising spectacle in the midst of the wide and melancholy waste.

The shore all round is stony and shrubby; but for half a league before reaching the town, the traveller passes through olive-groves and orchards, and is astonished to see the blessings which man, when compelled to exert all his industrial power, has been able to win from the limy soil. The little land of Bonifazio gives a full supply of olives which do not yield in quality to those of Balagna. Between chalk-cliffs we drive down to the Marina of Bonifazio, lying on the shore of the gulf. The town itself can now be reached only on foot or on horseback, for we must clamber up the steep rock on a broad path of steps. Cross two drawbridges, and pass through two old gates, and we are in Bonifazio. The fortress and the tower, between which indeed there is no distinction, lie on the flat summit of the rock.

A beautiful greeting does Bonifazio give to the wayfarer who enters through the old gloomy gate; for on the front of one of the towers stands boldly out the grand word *Libertas*. I used to read it often on the towers and houses of Italian towns—a melancholy satire; on many a banner has this word been blazoned. But here it stands proudly and confidently out on those antique turrets, which can tell of so many glorious deeds of arms. I entered the city with the joyful sensation that I was going among valiant and free men. To the present hour the Bonifazians have the character of being the most republican as well as the most industrious and religious of the inhabitants of Corsica.

The site of Bonifazio is quite peculiar. Imagine a colossal white pyramid of rock, formed of horizontal layers planted in the sea, with its base pointing upwards, and supporting high in the air, fortress, towers, and town, and you will have some idea of this Corsican Gibraltar. The façade is deeply excavated; the whole mass seems to cling to the mainland. On two sides the sea foams round it, a narrow inlet shut in by precipitous, inaccessible hills washes it on a third, forming at once, gulf, haven, and fosse. The power of the water has torn up the coast all round, and has washed the rocks into the most grotesque forms. From beneath, viewed from the sea, which in many places has no beach, the coast rising sheer from the water, this gray rock stands out boldly. I descended to look up at it; the waves dashed round its base, the clouds above floated over it; I felt as if the rock were tottering and it was about to fall upon me—an ocular delusion the more natural, as a large mass is washed away from the bottom, and here and there huge layers of chalk blackened by the weather project boldly into the air. As soon as I saw Bonifazio, I at once comprehended how Alfonso of Arragon failed to take it.

It numbers 3380 inhabitants, and, on account of its insular position, contains no communes. Its buildings are of Pisan and Genoese origin. Old, and long inhabited, they resemble ruins more than dwelling-houses. They are built mostly of the material of the rock. They are all white; and as the walls and short towers have the same hue, the spectator has more than enough of the national colour of Corsica. It would be difficult for me to convey a distinct idea of the town itself; for it is impossible to describe this intricate confusion of narrow streets, through which the draught or the sea-breeze is continually whirling the dust, and through which, going down or up hill, one must skilfully steer his course, wandering about in perpetual astonishment at the novelty of the position, especially when the eye, finding an open space, discovers the sea far beneath it as blue as the heavens above. Beams are frequently thrown across from house to house, and dark passages often lead from one narrow street to another.

The wind whistles, and the waves dash their foam round the rock. There is something strangely uncomfortable in the sensation. The consciousness of space—so agreeable to the mind—is here lost. The lonely sentinel yonder paces up and down on the round tower in a whirlwind of lime-dust. I wish to find a piazza—to be among men. But there is no such thing here as a square. The necessary limitation admits of no open spaces; yet, strange to say, the main street is fondly called the Piazza Doria. The Bonifazians no doubt felt the need of a piazza or forum, without which a town is like a house without a family room; they consequently gave that gave that name to the main street. Want of room compelled the Bonifazians to carry their houses to a great height. The stairs are uncommonly steep, on account of the want of depth in the buildings. On many houses I saw the arms of Genoa still carved—a crowned lion-rampant holding a ring in its claw. The old emblem awakes proud memories, like the name of Doria, which still exists in Bonifazio under the form of D'Oria. For this is the proper name of those famous Genoese lords of the great family of Oria. The Corsicans hated Genoa to the death, and, when treating of the old Republic, it will be remembered that we found the same inveterate hate on its part. Every calamity which has befallen Corsica, its moral as well as its physical desolation, they ascribe to Genoa. The Bonifazians, however, are much attached to the memory of the Genoese connexion, and their history makes that quite intelligible.

There is a difference of opinion as to the ancient name of the spot whereon Bonifazio now stands. Some consider it to have been the old *Syracusanus portus*, others the old town of Palæ, the last of the Corsican stations enumerated by Antoninus in the *Itinerary*. The Bonifazio of the present day was founded by the Tuscan margrave whose name it bears. We know that, after a naval victory obtained over the Saracens in 833, he laid the foundations of this town, that it might serve as a barrier against their piratical attacks, for they had been in the habit of effecting descents on this side of the island, from Africa, Spain, and Sardinia. Of the forts erected by that margrave, one still stands—the large old tower, called Torrione; three more tower above the rock. They are all represented on the arms of Bonifazio. At a later period, the town passed into the hands of the Pisans, together with the rest of the island; but the Genoese wrested Bonifazio from them so early as the year 1193. They surprised and took the town during the celebration of a festival. They treated it with great liberality, gave it very free laws, and permitted it to exist as a Republic under their protectorate. In the register of Bonifazio the contract is preserved, which the Genoese procurator in Bonifazio, Brancaleone d'Oria, signed and solemnly swore on the Bible to observe, on the 11th February 1321. According to the terms of this contract, complete freedom of trade and exemption from imposts in Genoese harbours, was granted to the Bonifazians; also, the right of self-government. In their popular assembly they chose a Council composed of the more elderly citizens, hence called *Anziani*; the Genoese podestà, who was annually sent to the town as Syndic or Commissioner, had to conform his decisions to the will of this body. The podestà could neither impose taxes nor introduce any innovation without the consent of the Anziani; nor had he the power of imprisoning any citizen of Bonifazio, whether murderer, thief, or traitor, if he could procure bail. When a new podestà was sent from Genoa, he was never put in possession of the town till he had solemnly sworn an oath on the Sacrament, to preserve inviolable all treaties and statutes of Bonifazio. This deed is signed—*Per Brancaleonem de Oria et per Universitatem Bonifatii in publico Parlamento*—'by Brancaleo d'Oria, and the whole community of Bonifazio, in public Parliament assembled;'—

high-sounding words for a little place, consisting at that time of scarcely a thousand inhabitants.

Thus did this bold little people win for themselves freedom with all its privileges, and were able to preserve it intact on their rock for many centuries.

The Genoese paid every possible respect to the Bonifazians. When one of their vessels entered the port of Genoa, it was customary to ask—"Are you from the district of Bonifazio, or from Bonifazio proper?" Hence the popular saying: "He is a Bonifazian proper." Many Genoese nobles and citizens, induced by these privileges and rights, emigrated to this rock from their lordly Genoa; and, in this way, Bonifazio became in language, manners, and leaning, a Genoese colony. Even now, the Genoese character of the town is visible not only in the armorial ensigns, but in the people themselves.

Calvi too, has, like Bonifazio, remained true to Genoa. Both towns have occupied on this account quite a peculiar historical position, and it is remarkable to find in this fearful sea of Corsican hate, two little islands, as it were, which loved the tyrannical Genoa. Let us not grudge this to the manly Genoese; their old sin-laden but always kingly and great Republic has long since paid its debt to humanity in history, and is no more.

A Bonifazian of the name of Murzolaccio, wrote a characteristic little history of his town in 1625. It may be seen in Bologna, and is an extremely rare book. I have not been able to procure a copy, much to my disappointment, for I have a great affection for Bonifazio. But I will here relate, following the chronicle of Petrus Cyrnæus, the memorable siege of the town by Alfonso of Arragon; for indeed the heroic bravery of the Bonifazians deserves to live in the memory of men together with that of Numantia, Carthage, and, in modern times, Saragossa. I give Peter's description of it, not following him through all his details; I have shortened it also, as it is too long to give entire here.

CHAPTER VII
THE SIEGE OF BONIFAZIO BY ALFONSO OF ARRAGON

Alfonso of Arragon, after he had examined the position of the town, took possession of a high hill lying towards the north; and from it and the sea he kept up a perpetual fire of stones from his bombs. The Spaniards had come with eighty ships, and among them twenty-three triremes; they had forced their way into the harbour after the fall of the two towers which defended it. Now, when a great part of the defences and the walls had been overthrown, and it seemed possible to force a passage into the town, King Alfonso called his captains to a council of war. He was young and fiery, and full of desire to do great deeds. "When Bonifazio has fallen," he said, "all Corsica will be ours, and then we shall sail for Italy." He promised rewards to the first man who should scale the wall and plant his banner on it, and to the second, and the third, and so on to the tenth. The Spaniards heard this with great joy, and prepared themselves for the assault. The Bonifazians suffered much from the missiles and arrows of the assailants; but with stones and long spears they hurled the enemy back into the sea, and held their post bravely. Suddenly the tower Scarincio fell with a fearful crash, and immediately the ships laid themselves close to the breach; the Spaniards sprang upon the wall and planted their standard. In the army of the king, the shout was heard, "The city is stormed." Then the marines might be seen quickly and nimbly clambering up the walls on the masts and yards; and when they came within reach of the houses they cast torches on their roofs. Now, there arose a terrible death-struggle of fugitives, brave citizens who still held their ground, and the assailants all mingled together. But Orlando Guaracchi, the heroic Margareta Bobia, and Chiaro Ghigini rushed to drive back the advancing enemy, and from their posts came Jacopo Cataccioli, Giovanni Cicanesi, and Filippo Campo, and cut down every foe who had pressed into the town, even to the last man. They then threw fire on the ships in the harbour, and the king was repulsed with great loss.

For three days had the struggle lasted, with fire and slaughter without end. Every age and sex laboured to fortify the walls anew, and to fill up the breaches with cross-beams. But alas! the granaries had been consumed. Alfonso, meanwhile, kept throwing arrows into the town with letters attached to them, offering bribes to all who should pass over to him. Two deserted, Galliotto Ristori, a Bonifazian, and Conrado, a Genoese, and they stimulated the courage of the king by telling him that within the town both bread and munitions were failing. Accordingly, the king took possession of another hill near the town; and after drawing a double chain across the mouth of the harbour, to exclude any succours which might come from Genoa, he resolved to reduce the town by blockade. The Doge, Thomas Fregoso, heard that, and equipped a fleet of seven sail; in this way the month of September passed. But the sea was so stormy during the whole of October, November, and December, that the fleet could not leave the harbour of Genoa. The Bonifazians, meanwhile, had been brought to such extremities, by the bombs and catapults, that they were compelled to leave the town, and seek shelter in the grove beside San Antonio, and in the Convent of St. Francis, as the most of their houses were now in ruins; those only remained behind who had to fill the posts of defence.

The king had been strengthened by reinforcements and ships from Spain; but, notwithstanding, he preferred negotiation, and gave a solemn promise to the besieged that, if they would yield to him, they should have permission to live free, and according to their laws. The Bonifazians purposely prolonged negotiations with the ambassadors, and as they looked in wretched plight, pale and exhausted with hunger, and as the Arragonese taunted them with their condition, saying that they would be soon forced to submit, it is said that, in order to give him the lie, they threw bread over the walls down among the enemy's outposts, and sent a cheese made of woman's milk as a present to the king. Alfonso next moved all his engines and ships close to the walls. Two vessels lashed together bore towers. The assault began afresh from the sea and the heights. To oppose the machines on board the ships, the Bonifazians had likewise planted engines on various parts of the ramparts; on the more distant vessels they propelled stones of immense weight; on those more near they threw stones of smaller size and missiles of all kinds, as thick as hail. Although they themselves were almost overwhelmed by the storm of missiles, and many of them lay mangled and dying, they yet persevered with astonishing valour. Those who still retained their strength filled up the places of the fallen—the son that of the wounded father, the brother of the brother; the women brought projectiles, wine, and bread, and carried off the wounded. Arming themselves with shields and lances, too, they took their place upon the ramparts wherever there was a vacant spot. Many of them could not carry off or succour their fallen relations, till they had hurled back the enemy from the walls. The assailants also suffered dreadfully; many were drowned, being dragged into the sea by the swords, hooks, and curved lances, thrown by the besieged upon the floating towers. Very many were dashed to pieces with beams and stones, as they were scaling the walls with ladders. In other places, the besieged threw torches, tow, and pitch upon the enemy, so that often they did not know whither to run, or on what side to defend themselves first.

The Bonifazians were now exhausted by the ceaseless contest, which had already raged without intermission for many days, and the king resolved once more to collect all his strength in order to make a grand assault on the following day. So the fight raged anew, and more terribly than before, for the foe brought every engine, tower, and catapult to bear upon the town, and almost buried it under a shower of stones, arrows, and steel hooks.

Only at the tower of Scarincio the bombarding ceased, for the besiegers feared to overwhelm the Spaniards—who had already at that point forced their way into the town—in the same destruction with the citizens. There, armed women fought untiringly beside the men, and threw harpoons on the assailants. From the ship-towers and the cross-trees, the Spaniards kept up a ceaseless shower of darts, and propelled leaden acorns out of certain cast-metal hand-bombs, which were bored like a reed, and went by the name of Sclopetus. (This is Peter of Corsica's description of a musket, which in those days was a rare, but is now too common a weapon in Corsica.) They threw also showers of sulphur, followed by fire, on the houses and men, so that many were half burnt, and others were precipitated headlong through the breach. In this way the breach, which was near the tower of Preghera, stood open to the foe. As soon as the sulphur-smoke, which had wrapt it in thick darkness, had cleared off, matrons, the unarmed, and crowds of children, could be seen carrying stones and missiles of every kind to the wall, to supply the combatants; when they found the breach deserted, they raised loud cries of lamentation. Then, with wailing and tears, the mother besought her son, the daughter her father, the wife her husband, to return to the breach. The priests and monks also took up arms, and hurled down flaming bundles of tow and slacked lime. This had such great effect that very many, stupified and almost blinded by the dust and the floating vapour, were forced to shoot at random. As the flames subsided a little, the besieged sallied from the gate.

This day had been the most severe which the citizens had yet endured; but it had been a destructive one to the enemy.

As the besieged became from day to day more hardly pressed, the more frequent became the letters despatched to the Doge and Senate of Genoa, begging them to come to the help of Bonifazio. The king, meanwhile, having been again reinforced, gave the signal to his men to renew the assault. By land and sea a fierce onset was then made in seven places at once; but into the city Alfonso could not get. For fresh wall was erected almost as quickly as it was thrown down, and armed men even placed themselves in the breaches, and formed a living rampart. Then the king ordered a mole to be thrown up, eight feet high, running towards the great gate. Thereon was erected a tower of ten stories, so high as to overtop the walls. Under cover of a shower of missiles, the mole and tower were gradually nearing the gate, when one day it was suddenly flung open, and the people sallying out, flung torches and fire on the mound, and fascines into the tower, and in that way destroyed this laborious work, which had already occupied so long a time.

Neither night nor day did the assault slacken; and nothing was for a moment intermitted by the Bonifazians which could retard the progress of the besiegers, whether it was the erection of new walls, or perpetual sallies on the enemy's works. The poor citizens had not a moment's rest; and, quite exhausted by continual exertion, were wasting away with hunger, wounds, and daily and nightly watching. No day passed without burial of the dead; death stood before every eye, and day and night the sound of lamentation was heard. Meanwhile the necessity had become so great, that they were compelled to eat disgusting weeds; and how long were they still to wait for aid from Genoa? The power of endurance which the people of Bonifazio exhibited under hunger and privations the most severe, almost exceeds human conception. Horse and ass-flesh were in those days dainties. Some ate herbs of all kinds—herbs which even the cattle refused to touch—roots and wild fruits, the bark of trees, and animals never before eaten by man. Despairing now of relief, many would have willingly ended their lives, weeping and bewailing, and many of the wounded, too, would have died of starvation on the walls, had it not been for the compassion of the women. For the pious wives of Bonifazio freely gave of their milk to relations, brothers, children, connexions, and godfathers. And there was no one in that beleaguered town who had not sucked a woman's breast.

As up to that moment there had been no signs of any help in their sore extremity, the Bonifazians entered into an agreement that if the Genoese did not come to their relief within forty days, they would deliver themselves up to the Spaniard. They gave two men and thirty children of the noblest citizens as hostages. But it was a matter of great anxiety to the Bonifazians that King Alfonso had not allowed them meantime to send messengers to Genoa. Accordingly, they built a little ship in great haste, and in the darkness of the night they let it down into the sea by ropes, on that side of the rock which fronted Sardinia and was averted from the enemy, and in a similar manner they let down the young men, twenty-four in number, who were to be the messengers and crew. The chief magistrate had given them letters for Genoa, and a great multitude of citizens had accompanied them to the edge of the cliff, wishing them a successful expedition. One after the other, the women gave them their breasts to suck before setting out, for they had no food with them. After many perils by sea, and being long retarded by contrary winds, these bold messengers at last reached Genoa, and informed the Senate that the city of Bonifazio was brought to the last extremity.

Meanwhile, in Bonifazio, they resolved in solemn procession to beseech God for deliverance from the enemy, and for forgiveness of all their sins. The procession walked from the Cathedral of the Holy Mary to St. Jacob's, then to San Domenico, and all the churches in succession; and although the winter cold was very severe, yet all walked barefoot; and as they walked, they sang hymns with great fervour. From an early hour till late at night, prayers were offered up in the churches, and every mind was intently hoping for relief or for some news of the messengers.

At last, on the fifteenth day, the messengers returned to Bonifazio in their little ship, in the darkness of the night, and having given the signal, they were drawn up by ropes. Every one in the city seemed beside himself with joy. As the messengers walked to the Church of the Holy Mary, where the senate sat in council day and night, all the people poured in a living stream after them to hear the news. They delivered the letters of the Doge, which were read by the magistrates, and then taken out to the assembled people. Picino Cataccioli, the chief of the messengers, gave them a detailed account of the expedition, and assured them that the Genoese fleet was all equipped, and only waited for a favourable wind to set sail. The senate of Bonifazio now ordered a public thanksgiving of three days; and the joy in the city was quite uncontrollable when what little grain the messengers had brought back with them was distributed among the people.

Meanwhile, the day of surrender was fast approaching, but the Genoese fleet had not yet made its appearance, and the ambassadors of the king were already pressing the senate to fulfil their agreement. "If, in the following night," declared the Anziani, "the Genoese do not appear, we shall then surrender." Then began a wailing and lamentation of women and children, and great sorrow and dejection filled every mind. But the senate called an assembly that they might learn the sense of the people about the matter. Guglielmo Bobia earnestly maintained that they should hold out, and he conjured the shade of the Count Bonifazio (the founder of the city) to fill the Bonifazians with his spirit, so that none should think of parting with his freedom. Accordingly, they resolved to wait to the last moment. Suddenly a cry arose in the night, that the Genoese were at hand. All the bells began to ring, and fire-signals blazed on every turret; endless shouts of joy rose to heaven. The Spaniards were astonished, and lid not know what to think, as they could see no sign of the Genoese. Their ambassadors lost no time in presenting themselves before the gate at dawn, and demanded the surrender of the city, according to the agreement. The men of Bonifazio, however, replied, that during the night they had received the Genoese auxiliaries; and, behold! armed men displaying the Genoese standard were seen to march thrice along the walls, bristling with lances and sparkling weapons. For all the women had during the past night put on armour, so that the number of the Bonifazians seemed to be trebled. When Alfonso of Arragon saw this, he exclaimed: "Have then the Genoese wings, that they can enter Bonifazio when we occupy every approach?" And again he directed all his engines against the town.

At last, however, on the fourth day after the stipulated period had run out, the Genoese came in reality, and cast anchor in the offing of the strait. Angelo Bobia and a few other brave men swam during the night to their ships, and horrified all with their wasted forms and hunger-pale faces. But the Genoese captains declared that they dared not venture to attack the Spaniards. Bobia laid his fore-finger on his mouth, as if thunderstruck, and then said, "We have trusted in God alone, and in you—you shall attempt it, and we will help you!" The Genoese were afraid.

Alfonso immediately turned a part of his ships towards the Genoese, and directed his missiles upon the harbour, to cut off their entrance. The Genoese ships, however, would not venture to attack the Spanish till the young Giovanni Fregoso, Rafael Negro, and other leading men insisted on their risking an engagement. But especially Jacopo Benesia, the most valorous and daring of them all, decided for the battle. For seven hours the struggle lasted at the entrance of the harbour and before the rock—a fearful struggle—ship lying close to ship, as the confined space rendered it quite impossible to move about; the Bonifazians, meanwhile, hurled down missiles and torches on the Spaniards. At last the Genoese burst through the chain, and forced a passage into the harbour; and indescribable was the joy of the starving people, when seven ships full of grain were moored in the harbour, and discharged their freight.

Then Alfonso of Arragon perceived that he could not reduce the town of Bonifazio, and accordingly he raised the siege, taking the hostages with him; and, deeply ashamed and vexed at heart, he set sail for Italy in January 1421.

CHAPTER VIII
OTHER REMINISCENCES OF BONIFAZIO, AND A FESTIVAL

My locanda stood opposite an old and gloomy house, the marble entablature of whose door attracted my attention. There were old sculptures on it—the arms of Genoa, and Gothic initials. It gave me great pleasure to learn that the Emperor Charles V. had spent two days and a night in this house. It affected me as deeply as if I had suddenly met a countryman and friend on this foreign rock. The house speaks German to me; and when I look at the window where Charles V. stood, there crowd upon my mind many epochs of German history, and many great names rise before me—Luther, Worms, Augsburg, Wittenberg, Maurice of Saxony, Philip of Hesse, Schiller and *Don Carlos*, Goethe and *Egmont*. Charles V. was a striking phenomenon. He was the last Emperor in the full sense of the word; for there arose against the Emperor, on whose dominions the sun never set, a little man, in a gray capote and cowl, and let fall a word which, like a bomb, shattered all the magnificence of the empire of the Cæsars. Yet are those men foolish who abuse Charles V. because he did not comprehend the Reformation, and put himself at the head of that movement. He was Emperor, and nothing else. He grew weary; and the man whose stormy life had been a perpetual struggle with powers which ruined Germany—with France, and with the Reformation—gave his kingdoms away, and, recognising the all-changing hand of time, became an anchorite, and laid himself in a coffin. I am much pleased that I have seen Titian's splendid portrait of Charles V. My neighbour at the window there is now no image of my fancy, but a creature of flesh and blood.

It was an accident which brought Charles to Bonifazio. My friend Lorenzo gave me the following account of it. Charles was on his way home from his unsuccessful expedition against Algiers; a storm forced him to take refuge in the Gulf of Santa Manza, in the vicinity of Bonifazio. He stepped ashore with his retinue, and, curious to learn what kind of land this Corsica was, which, in those times as well as now, had the character of being barbarous and warlike, he entered a vineyard. Filippo Cataccíolo, the proprietor, happened just at that moment to be there. He offered grapes to the Emperor; and in the course of conversation awoke in him a desire to see the wonderful town of Bonifazio, which Alfonso of Arragon had been unable to take. The Corsican then offered to be his guide, and put his house in the town at the Emperor's service, promising at the same time to preserve his incognito. He gave him his horse, the Emperor mounted, and the little procession set itself in motion. Catacciolo in the meantime despatched a messenger to the magistrates with this announcement—"Charles, King of Spain and Emperor of the Holy Roman Empire, will this day be Bonifazio's guest." As Charles was approaching the town, suddenly the cannon thundered, and the people rushing out of the town shouted, *Evviva Carlo di Spagna!* He turned with surprise to Catacciolo, and said, "Friend, you have betrayed me!" "No," replied the Corsican; "for this is the nature of the cannons of Bonifazio—the sunbeams discharge them of their own accord when a prince such as you approaches."

Charles then entered Catacciolo's house, and was well entertained there. On his departure, he called his host, and said to him, "My friend, since you have entertained your guest so well, you are at liberty to ask three favours." Catacciolo begged three privileges for the town of Bonifazio; and these being granted, the Emperor gave him permission to ask still one favour for himself. After some reflection, the Corsican at last said, "The boon I ask is that your Highness command that when I am dead, my body be laid under the high altar of the Cathedral; for as that privilege is never accorded to a layman, the honour and distinction will be the greatest which has ever been conferred on a citizen of Bonifazio."

The Emperor granted this also. Catacciolo then conducted him back to the harbour, and, when his guest had embarked, took the horse on which he had ridden, and killed it on the spot.

Catacciolo's house is incomplete. A few gaps are visible in the wall. The reason of this is that the magistrates, out of consideration for the fortress, prohibited his erecting a house on that spot. Catacciolo then promised to construct a beacon for them at his own cost, if they gave him permission to build. The chief magistrate thereupon consented; but it was stipulated that Catacciolo should not be allowed to finish his house until he had completed the beacon. Accordingly, he carried on both buildings at the same time; but although he never did more than lay the foundation of the beacon, he completed his house, only leaving a few gaps in the wall to evade the contract.

Catacciolo was tall and handsome, and on that account went by the name of Alto Bello. His family was one of the wealthiest and oldest in the town, and is frequently mentioned in its history.

Looking past Charles V.'s house, the eye falls upon the island of Santa Maddalena, on the Sardinian coast. I distinctly perceive the tower, and see the young artillery officer, Napoleon, leap out of the ship to take it. Napoleon dwelt eight months in Bonifazio, opposite Charles V.'s house. The meeting of these two great imperial names on this spot is a remarkable coincidence, for it was Napoleon who overturned the old and far-famed imperial throne of Charles V.

Bonifazio, in the days of its prosperity, had some twenty churches and cloisters. The cloisters were abolished, and only three churches remain—the Cathedral of Santa Maria of the Fig-tree, San Domenico, and San Francesco. Santa Maria is of Pisan architecture—a large, heavy church, lost among narrow streets. Its spacious porch is the resort and promenade of the citizens, who walk about there as the Venetians do in the square of San Marco. In olden times, the Senate of Bonifazio used to assemble in this cathedral, to deliberate on civic affairs.

Farther on, towards the edge of the rock, lies San Domenico—a beautiful church of the Templars, whose emblematic triangle is still visible on the walls. It is a graceful structure, of the purest Gothic proportions, and only wants the overlaid façade to have a pleasing effect outside as well as in the interior. Unquestionably it is the finest church in Corsica, next to the ruins of the Canonica at Mariana. Its snow-white octangular tower, which the Pisans began, resembles an indented fortress-turret; it is incomplete. In the church, I found many monumental tablets of Knights-Templar and of Genoese nobles—among others, that of a Doria. Cardinal Fesch sent a few pictures to it, but they are of little value. Far more interesting are the little *ex votos*—the votive pictures on wood, which Bonifazian citizens who have been delivered from some impending danger have dedicated to the Madonna and St. Dominic. There are many pirate-scenes among them, right vividly delineated. The third church—San Francesco—is small; but it possesses great interest as containing the only spring in Bonifazio. Elsewhere, the Bonifazians content themselves with the rain-water collected in cisterns, drawing their main supply from the large, deep reservoirs into which one may descend by stone steps—a meritorious work of the Genoese.

Most of the old cloisters in Corsica belonged to the monks of the order of St. Francis. These gentlemen had settled in great numbers on the island, and their saint himself, they say, was once in Corsica. He visited Bonifazio; and as the citizens of this town are accounted the most religious in the whole island, I shall relate the legend in the words of my friend Lorenzo.

You may see, lying on the other side of the gulf, the deserted monastery of San Giuliano; the holy Francis himself gave the following occasion for its erection: One day, on what voyage I cannot tell, he put in to the harbour of Bonifazio and stepped ashore. When night came, he knocked at the door of a house, and begged admission and shelter. But he was not so fortunate as Charles V., for they shut the door upon him—and no wonder, for he looked wild and shaggy, like a Corsican bandit. The holy Francis turned away with a troubled heart, and laid himself down in a cave near the house; and, after commending himself to God, fell asleep, In the meantime there came a maid-servant out of the house, to throw foul water into the cave, as she had been wont to do. As she entered, she saw therein something shining, and was so frightened, that she had almost poured the unclean water over the holy Francis—for it was the good man himself that shone. I am told that the holy Francis thereupon raised himself from the ground, and with his gentle smile said to the maid: "My friend, do as you have been wont to do; I lived a whole year in a pig-stye, as all the world knows." The stupid maid, notwithstanding, ran towards the house with loud cries of alarm, and told how she had found a man in the cave, who had the strange property of giving out light from some parts of his body. The news of this spread like wildfire through Bonifazio; the Bonifazians hastened to the spot, and when they had found the holy man, they raised him up in their arms, made much of him, and besought him to leave behind a memorial of his having been there. The holy Francis said: "My friends, let us then build a little convent here, as a perpetual remembrance." On the instant, the Bonifazians set about carrying stones to the spot, and Francis laid the foundation-stone with his own hands; and after having done this, he took leave of them, and again went on board his ship. Now the convent was not named after his name, because he was not yet canonized, but after the name of St. Julian. At a later period, the Bonifazians built the Church of San Francesco in honour of the saint. Hard by, there stood on the rock in olden times a grove of pines, myrtle, and box-wood—a truly miraculous growth, as it rested on the bare limestone rock. It was forbidden to fell a tree there on pain of losing the right hand. Holy men of the bush, anchorites, sat there in a mountain hermitage, worshipping God and singing pious hymns, high above the strait, near to heaven. The wood and the hermitage are now both gone; and where they once stood, the sentinel in his red hose now paces up and down, whistling some merry soldier's air.

On the 15th of August, I was awoke by the thunder of cannon under my window. In my sleep I thought it was the Spaniards and Alfonso of Arragon, with their bombs, making a desperate assault on the rock; but I soon remembered that the Bonifazians were celebrating the anniversary of the birthday of the old Emperor Napoleon, and the Assumption of the Virgin Mary. For it was on the holiday of the Assumption of the Mother of

God that Napoleon was born, and both these events have now the honour of being commemorated throughout the whole of France on the same day. The reports of the guns rolled and boomed over the strait, and awoke Sardinia from its sleep. What a beautiful festal morning!—the sky and the sea so blue, the air so calm and cool, rose-red banners waving everywhere!

The people of Bonifazio literally revelled in a sea of rapture that day. The streets were crowded in every part, and adorned with national flags, whereon one might still read the proud inscriptions: *République Française, liberté, égalité, fraternité.* "You may believe me when I tell you," said a Bonifazian to me, "that we were genuine republicans in those days." I saw many groups playing draughts in the street; and beside the great gates, too, they sat at this old, knightly game. Others walked about the piazza, dressed in their best clothes, and all were very merry.

I love to look on a multitude keeping holiday. One feels on such occasions that he lives on a good earth and fair; it was very pleasing to see this little world-forgotten people resting a while on its solitary rock, and out of its poverty preparing for itself a simple, childlike festival. These poor people have so little of all that makes life varied and agreeable—no drama, no society, no horses, carriages, or music—not even a newspaper, except at wide intervals. Many here, are born and step into their limy graves, without having seen even Ajaccio. They live here perched high up in the air on their dry rock, and have nothing but the air and the light, and that one grand view over the strait to the Sardinian hills. One may guess, therefore, what a holiday is likely to be in Bonifazio.

The people of the surrounding country added to the multitude; they had come to see the great procession. It was strange to see so many well-dressed people filling the usually desolate streets. The young girls laughed sweetly from the windows of their houses, all clad in white, with flowers in their hair: I believe that all the maidens of Bonifazio were angels that day, in virtue of the procession.

The firing of cannon announced that the procession had begun. It issued from the Church of Santa Maria of the Fig-tree, which was all ablaze with lights, and marched towards that of San Domenico. The crucifix and some old church banners, which seemed to be Genoese, led the way; then came men, women, and maidens, with waxen tapers in their hands, and, last of all, the heavenly Virgin herself. Four strong men bore her on a bier; on each corner of which stood a motley-coloured little angel made of wood, and carrying a nosegay in his hand. In the centre, a wooden image of Mary floated on blue wooden clouds. There was a silver glory above her head, and round her neck was hung a costly chain of coral, found near Bonifazio and presented by the fishermen to the Virgin. Half the inhabitants of Bonifazio walked in the procession, and many pretty girls among them, with white dresses and pale faces, as if they had been sculptured out of Bonifazian gypsum. All bore tapers, but the sea-breeze insisted on walking in the procession too,—a huge long fellow made of white lime, and all enveloped in a white cloak of lime-dust. He blew out the wax-light of one pretty gypsum figure after the other, and ere the procession had reached San Domenico, he had won the moccoli-game, and extinguished them all. I also accompanied the procession. When one asked me how I liked it, I saw from his eyes, which were beaming with a heartfelt pleasure, what I ought to say; and I replied, "*Signore mio, ella è maravigliosa.*" The childlike simplicity and joy of this festival-day were very touching. In the evening they illuminated the streets with a large bonfire, which had been piled up in front of the town-hall. When I inquired why they did so, I received for answer, "This fire is kindled in honour of Napoleon." So did Bonifazio celebrate the great festival, and was joyful and light-hearted; and when it was night, I heard in the streets the cheerful sound of song, and the jingling of the mandoline.

CHAPTER IX
THE STRAIT

In the evening, a little before twilight, I love to go through the old fortress-gate, and sit down on some point of the high coast. Here I have around me no common picture,—Bonifazio on its beetling cliff hard by, at a giddy height above the sea; the beautiful strait, and the near Sardinia. There is an old book which reckons this rock of Bonifazio as the seventy-second wonder of the world. My good friend Lorenzo has read it. If I look down upon the sea-border from my little bench of stone, I have a complete view of the path of steps which leads down to the Marina. There I see people continually passing out and in through the gate; and from below they ride up the declivity mounted on their little asses, or drive them before them laden with melons, crossing and recrossing the path to make the ascent easier. I do not remember having seen such small donkeys as those of Bonifazio, and it was incomprehensible to me how a man could ride on so diminutive a creature. I saw no one with the fucile; fire-arms are here, comparatively speaking, unknown.

When at any time I sat down on the bench by the little Chapel of San Rocco, I was soon surrounded by the curious, who would frequently take a place beside me with a kind of simple confidence, and ask me whence I came, what I came for, and whether or not my fatherland was civilized. This last question was very frequently addressed to me when I said that I came from Prussia. A very gentlemanly person sat down beside me one evening, and when we had fallen into a political conversation regarding the present king of Prussia, he suddenly expressed his surprise that Prussians should speak Italian. I have frequently, on other occasions, and in all earnest, been asked whether Italian was spoken in Prussia. My good friend then inquired whether I spoke Latin. When I replied that I understood it, he said that he also was acquainted with it, and immediately began: "*Multos annos jam ierunt, che io non habeo parlato il latinum.*" When on the point of replying to him in the same language, I suddenly made the discovery that my Latin insisted on slipping into Italian, and that I was just about to express myself with greater elegance than even my Bonifazian friend. Two cognate languages are very apt to be mingled on the tongue if we are in the habit of daily expressing ourselves only in one of them.

This gentleman accurately quoted Rousseau's prediction on Corsica, which it is impossible to escape hearing when in conversation with educated Corsicans.

The strait becomes more and more beautiful as the sun-set light begins to fall upon it. Sailing-boats flit past, breasting the waves; they pass into the distance with the golden gleam of the setting sun upon them; isolated rocks tower darkly out of the water, and the mountains of Sardinia are tinged with violet. Directly opposite stand the fair hills of Tempio and Limbara; yonder the heights which conceal Sassari; on the left, a magnificent mountain-cone, the name of which I cannot discover. The evening sun falls brightly on the neighbouring coasts, but with full effulgence on the nearest Sardinian town of Longo Sardo. A tower is visible at its entrance. I clearly discern the houses, and would willingly imagine those flickering lines of shadow to be Sardinians promenading. In a calm night, they tell me that the beating of drums in Longo Sardo may be heard. I counted six towers along the coast; Castello Sando, and Porto Torres, the nearest towns in the direction of Sassari, were invisible. My hospitable Lorenzo had studied three years in Sassari, knew the Sardinian dialect, and could give me much information about the people.

> Long silent sat we on the hill together,
> And gazed upon the foam-fringed coasts the while;
> And on the deep-blue of the narrow waters
> That part Sardinia from her sister isle.

> How passing beautiful art thou, Sardegna!
> Whom the luxuriant myrtles fondly crown,
> And sparkling zones of snowy shell engirdle,
> Corsica's sun-burnt sister, wild and brown.

> Red reefs and craggy islets round thee hanging,
> Rude capes that cleave the sea with zig-zag line,
> —Their crimson cliffs thou wearest in thy beauty,
> Like blood-red necklace of the coral fine.

> My friend Lorenzo, yonder purple mountains
> They beckon in their gracious calm to me—

They stir my bosom with a fiery longing,
And my heart leaps to cross that narrow sea.

Whereto my good Lorenzo thus made answer,
And spoke low to himself, with doubting air:
"Ah! the fair mountains of Limbara yonder—
The pictured lies—only afar are fair.

"They seem like sapphires in the magic distance—
Like wondrous crystal domes they kiss the sky;
But when the weary, spell-drawn wanderer nears them,
They throw the purple and the glitter by.

"They offer you their gray sides, rude and naked,
Save where the tangling briers harsh cov'ring lend;
With tempests threaten you, and with abysses,
—Like life—too like the cheats of life, my friend."

—Yon leaden level stretching to the margin,
Laughs to me, winsome in its hue of gold,
How the Sardinian lives, my friend Lorenzo,
In his fair island, fain would I be told.

"Wooded the highlands as you travel inland,
The little yellow towns in verdure hide,
The Catalonian drives—their bells low tinkling—
His train of mules along the mountain side.

"O'er his swart face he slouches the sombrero,
Pistols and dagger in his belt he wears;
In his old Latin tongue he hums a ballad,
And onwards to its time he slowly fares.

"But if far southward to the strand you wander,
Where Cagliari lies, 'mid rocky bays,
There, in the hamlets, chants the darker Moro,

To castanet and tambourine his lays.
"From Algesiras comes the Moorish pagan,

His falt'ring accent tells the distant land,

He shakes his tabour, dances round the fan-palm,

The brown Sardinian maiden in his hand."

How perceptible in Bonifazio is the vicinity of the third great Romanic nation, Spain! My room is covered with pictures about Columbus, which have long Spanish explanations, and now and then one meets a Sardinian who speaks the Catalonian dialect. Both islands—in former epochs connected, but now torn asunder—are conveniently situated for the smuggling trade. The very favourable position of Bonifazio would undoubtedly have raised it to early prosperity had trade been free. The surveillance is extremely strict, as even the bandits of both islands maintain communication with each other, although it seldom happens that Sardinians seek an asylum in the little Corsica, as it does not afford means of support. Many Corsican avengers, on the contrary, take refuge among the Sardinian hills. The police in Bonifazio are very vigilant. My pass was never asked throughout the whole of Corsica, except in the southerly-lying Sartene, and in Bonifazio. A land-owner had been my fellow-traveller from Cape Corso to Bonifazio; and as he very kindly offered me his boat, which lay at Propriano, in which to return to Bastia, and also put his house at Cape Corso at my service, I invited him to share my spacious room, which was much superior to his own miserable lodging. This man had now the honour to pass for a bandit, who, under some good pretext, was desirous to pass over to Sardinia.

When the evening sets in, the lighthouse of Bonifazio shows its light. The Sardinian coast is wrapt in darkness; but soon, from Longo Sardo, a red light replies, and so these two sister islands, as well by night as by day, maintain a friendly intercourse with their beacons. The warders on either side lead a lonely life. Each is the first or last inhabitant of his island. He of Bonifazio is the most southerly Corsican I have ever met with; and he of the cape opposite the most northerly Sardinian. They have never seen each other or conversed; but daily they interchange a beautiful good-evening—*felicissima notte*, as they say in Italy when the mistress brings in the light. The warder of Corsica is the first to bring out his light into the darkening night, and to say *felicissima notte*; then his brother warder of Sardinia comes to meet him, and also says his *felicissima notte*; and so they go on night after night, and will go on while life lasts, till some evening the beacon shall remain for a time unlighted. Then will the warder on this side know that his old friend on the other is dead; and with a tear perchance that night, he will say *felicissima notte!*

I visited this most southerly of Corsicans in his turret. It lies a league from Bonifazio, on the low Cape Pertusato. The south of Corsica runs out here into an obtuse triangle, at whose western extremity Cape Pertusato, and at whose eastern Cape Sprono lies—the latter a small rocky point, standing nearer to Sardinia than any other part of Corsica. With a favourable wind, one could be in Sardinia in half an hour. The little lighthouse is surrounded by a white wall, and resembles a fort. The keeper received me kindly, and set before me a glass of goat's milk. He lives like Æolus, in the wind. There is something strange in the thought, that the long years of a man's life all turn round an oil-lamp, and that it is a human being's sole destiny to burn a lamp-wick on a lonely cliff by night. There can be nothing apparently more unsatisfactory, and nothing more unpretending than such an existence.

The warder led me to the parapet of the lighthouse, where the violence of the wind compelled me to hold fast by the railing. From his roof-top he pointed out all his island domain and sovereignty, which consisted of thirty head of goats and a vineyard; and as I perceived that he was contented and possessed sufficient of the goods of the earth, I at once esteemed him happy, even before his death. He directed my attention to the majestic beauty of Sardinia, the islands and islets which swarm round it, Santa Maria and Santa Maddalena, the island Caprara, Reparata, and many more. The western mouth of the strait is strewn with insular rocks; the eastern is broader; and over against the Sardinian Cape Falcone lies the island Asènara, a picturesque ridge of hill.

To Corsica belong a few little island-reefs of the most irregular form, which lie scattered in the strait quite near, and are called San Bainzo, Cavallo, and Lavezzi. They consist of granite. The Romans had worked quarries on them, to procure pillars for their temples and palaces. The positions occupied by their workshops are still easily discernible; even the coals in the old Roman smithies have left their traces. Enormous, half-hewn pillars still lie on these rocks—two of them on San Bainzo—and other blocks of stone shaped by Roman chisels. It is impossible now to say for what building in Rome they may have been destined; no one can tell what terrible panic it was which suddenly drove the quarrymen and masons from their solitary workshop on the sea, leaving the labour of their hands unfinished. It may be that the sea overwhelmed them; it may be that they were massacred by the wild Corsican, or the fierce Sardinian. It surprises me that there is no legend current of a ghostly Roman workshop; for I myself have seen in the moonlight the dead workmen rise out of the sea, clad in Roman togas—grave men, broad-browed, with aquiline noses, and deep-set eyes. Silently they applied themselves to the two pillars, and after a ghostly fashion began to beat and chisel them. One stood erect among them, and, with outstretched finger, gave directions. I heard him say in Latin—"This pillar will be one of the fairest in the golden palace of Nero. Quick, comrades, make haste; for if you are not ready within forty days, we shall all be cast to the wild beasts." Fain would I have called out to him, "O Artemion, and you other dead men! the palace of Nero has long since vanished from the face of the earth—why hew pillars for it still? Go, sleep in your graves!" But just as I was about to utter this, the Latin words became Italian, and I could not. And it is owing to this circumstance alone, that the spirits of those old Romans still busy themselves unceasingly with the pillars in that ghostly workshop; and night after night they rise up out of the water, and strike and chisel with restless haste; but as soon as the cocks crow in Bonifazio, the pale and shadowy forms spring back into the sea.

I threw again one long last look on the wide-extended Sardinian coast, on the land of Gallura, and thought of the beautiful Enzius, the Emperor Frederick's son. He, too, once was, and was moreover a king. A few months ago, I stood one evening in his prison at Bologna. A puppet theatre was erected near it, and across the still, large square sounded loudly the voice of Pulcinella.

The world is round, and history a circle like the individual life of men.

CHAPTER X
THE CAVES OF BONIFAZIO

One beautiful morning, going out of the town by the old Genoese gate, on whose wall are carved a lion-rampant and the sainted dragon-queller George—the arms of the Bank of Genoa, I descended to the Marina and called the boatman and his boat. The calmness of the day allowed me to explore with safety the caverns of the coast, although the water was still stirred by the maestrale and played rather roughly with our little skiff.

In the deep, narrow haven, however, the securest in the world, it is a perfect calm, and there the few sailing boats, and the two merchant-brigs of Bonifazio—the *Jesus-Maria* and the *Fantasia*—rest peacefully, as if in Abraham's bosom. Fantasia is the most charming name a ship has ever borne; and this all will grant, whose fantasy-ship has ever sailed upon the sea and come to port with its treasures, or been stranded on some inhospitable shore. Jesus-Maria, too, is a beautiful name on the sea.

The limestone rocks so entirely enclose the haven on either side, that its opening long remains concealed to those approaching it from the sea. The narrowness of the channel makes it possible to draw a chain barrier across it, as in fact Alfonso of Arragon did. A strong iron ring was pointed out to me, driven into the rock. To the right and the left, both in this vicinity and farther along the coast, the water has formed large and small caverns, which are in the highest degree worthy of a visit, and which would be famous all the world over, did not Corsica, so to speak, lie out of the world.

Close to Bonifazio there are three particularly beautiful grottos. We reach first that of San Bartolomeo. A narrow excavated channel just admits of the entrance of the boat. It resembles a cool Gothic apartment. The sea forces its way almost quite to its farther extremity—farther than the eye can penetrate, and covers its floor with still, clear water. It is a rendezvous for the fishes, which frequent it, being secure from sharks. I found in it a most amiable and happy family of fishes, Muggini and Loazzi. They were not at all alarmed by our entrance, but swam playfully round the boat. The cavern recedes far under the rock of Bonifazio.

We steer out of this grotto, in a short time reach the open strait, and have the wonderfully grand sea-view of the rock, rising majestically with its broad, double breast to meet the advancing waves. This gigantic façade is a glorious piece of Nature's architecture. On both sides she has thrown up pillars—powerful buttresses of lime and sandstone, deeply channelled by the waves. One of them is named Timone. A colossal arch is thrown from one to the other, on which, high above, stand the white walls of Bonifazio; and in the centre a magnificent grotto forms a natural portal. I was astonished as I gazed on this huge and unparalleled structure—the prototype of human handiwork, of the temple and the palace. The tumultuous sea dashed its waves against the walls of the grotto; but within, all was calm. It does not recede far into the cliff. It is only a grand rock-niche—a rostrum, hung round in semicircles with clustering garlands if stalactites—a niche in which one might fitly erect a colossal statue of Poseidon. *Sotto al Francesco* is its name.

If we steer eastwards to the right, we find a long extent of coast undermined by curiously-shaped vaults into which he sea forces its way. I entered one of these—the fisherman called them *camere*. Hard by is one of the grandest grottos of Bonifazio—that of Sdragonato; I lack words to describe this miraculous structure. I never saw anything resembling it, and perhaps this cavern stands alone in Europe. The entrance, like that of Francesco, is a gigantic stalactitic arch, but it opens into the hill, and a little porch admits you into an inner cave completely enclosed. It was at once a fine and somewhat alarming sensation to steer through the little gorge; the water boiled tumultuously against it, spraying its white foam on the stone walls, then fell back into itself, and again threw up its seething tide. To listen to such wild commotion of the waters is truly an elemental pleasure; the Italian language alone furnishes a name which indicates the sound— *rimbomba*. The boat having been safely washed through the gorge, glided at once into a lordly, vaulted temple of immense circumference, moving over a mirror of water, here green, there deep black, here azure, and yonder again of a roseate hue. It is a wonderful natural Pantheon. Above, the cupola parts, and the clear heaven shines through; a tree bends, waving its long branches over the edge; green bushes and herbs creep further down into the fissure, and wild doves come fluttering in. The walls of this beautiful cave are almost regularly vaulted, the water trickles down their sides, and hangs them with stalactites, which, however, have not the strikingly bizarre forms of those in the cavern of Brando at Cape Corso, or in the caves of the Hartz. It either hangs round in masses, or has overspread the stone, like a coating of *lapis lazuli*. One may ply about through the grotto, or disembark at pleasure; for, all round, Nature has thrown up seats and stone steps which are high and dry, except in stormy weather. Hither come the sea-dogs of Proteus, and lie down in the magic hall. Alas! I saw none of them, they had gone out on a water-excursion; I alarmed nothing but wild doves and dippers. The bottom is deep and clear; shells, fishes, and sea-weeds may be seen. It might be worth one's while to erect a summer-house here occasionally, in which to read the *Odyssey*, and keep silent watch as the creatures of the mysterious ocean-depths come in. Man understands neither the plant nor the beast which live on the dry land like himself, and are his daily companions, still less those dumb, strangely-formed creatures of the great element. They live and have their own laws and understanding, their own joys and sorrows, their own love and hate. Unlike terrestrial animals, bound to the clod, they rove through the boundless element, and dwell in the ever clear, crystalline deeps; form mighty republics, have their revolutions, their migrations, and piratical excursions, and the most charming water-parties, too, when they will.

The coast from Cape Pertusato to Bonifazio is much broken by the sea, and torn up into singular shapes. Many organic remains may be found there; and, among other things, a remarkable species of architectural spider. This spider constructs for itself, in the sand of the coast, a complete little sand-house; and in the sand-house a little door, which it can open or shut at pleasure. If it wishes to be alone, it shuts the door; if it wishes to go abroad, it opens it and goes out, taking its daughters with it, to enjoy a promenade by the beautiful strait, if only they have been industrious and have spun enough of their marriage outfit for one day. This excellent little building-spider is called the *Mygal pionnière*, or the Araignée Maçonne of Corsica.

I saw likewise the *Scalina di Alfonso*, the steps of the King of Arragon; hewn by him, says tradition, out of the rock, close under the walls of the town. Because Alfonso, they say, was unable to reduce the city, he fell on the bold plan of hewing a secret approach up the perpendicular cliff. Accordingly, by night the Spanish were in the habit of landing at a spot, invisible from the walls, where a grotto is formed in the side of the hill, containing fresh water, and capable of concealing three hundred men. There the Spanish cut out the steps, and, in fact, had succeeded in reaching the fortress-walls, when a woman perceived them, gave the alarm, and the citizens, hastening to the spot, hurled them back. Such is the legend; so we must call it, for it seems to me incredible that the Spanish should have hewn out these obliquely-ascending small steps without being seen by the Bonifazians. The monks of San Francesco cut out for themselves a stair of a similar kind, by which to descend to bathe; but it too is for the most part worn away.

I am unlucky—the tunny is not caught at this season, and the coral-fishers are not on the water, on account of the maestrale. The strait is rich in corals, but the Corsicans leave the fishing to the Genoese, the Tuscans, and the Neapolitans. These come in April, and remain till September. I saw beautiful red corals in the shop of a Genoese. They are sold by the weight, at three francs per ounce. The greater part of the corals, which are worked in the manufactories of Leghorn, comes from the Strait of Bonifazio. But ever since the French discovered richer and better corals on the coast of Africa, the fishery in the strait has declined. At the present day it is chiefly confined to the shores of Propriano, Figari, and Ventilegne, where the tunny also is particularly abundant.

After I had made myself well acquainted with the country and coasts of Bonifazio, I prepared for my departure from this remarkable spot. I had found the people of Bonifazio as Lorenzo had told me I should. They are, properly speaking, no longer Corsicans. "We are poor," said Lorenzo to me, "but we are industrious, and possess sufficient to supply our wants. The olive grows in abundance on our limestone soil, the vine yields enough for family use, and the air is salubrious. We are merry and contented, and receive with grateful hearts the days God gives us on our rock. When the poor man returns at sunset to his home, he always finds wine to mix with his water, and oil with his fish, perhaps even a bit of meat, and in summer always his melon."

I shall remember the hospitality of the Bonifazians with as much gratitude as that of the Sartenese. In the morning before sunrise, when I was about to start for Aleria, I found Lorenzo at the Gate, waiting to wish me once more a good journey, and accompany me to the Marina. Descending the rock in the light of the rising sun, I took leave of this singular town with one of those scenes which, trifling though they appear, are for ever imprinted on the memory. Under the gate, on the edge of the rocky coast, there lies the little, unobtrusive chapel of San Rocco, erected on the spot where the last victim of the plague of 1528 died. Descending the cliff, I looked right down upon this chapel. The doors stood wide open, the priest officiated at the altar, on which the waxen tapers were burning: before him, two rows of women were on their knees worshipping; and before the door kneeled men and women on the rock. The view from above, down into this calm, pious assemblage, raised high above the strait, kneeling with the ruddy light of the rising sun upon them, impressed me deeply; it seemed to me that I beheld a picture of true devotion.

BOOK X
WANDERINGS IN CORSICA

CHAPTER I
THE EAST COAST

The localities from Bonifazio upwards, along the east coast, are lonely and desolate. The road runs past the beautiful Gulf of San Manza to Porto Vecchio, a distance of three leagues. By the way-side, at the little village of Sotta, there lie the ruins of the old baronial castle Campara, which tell a singular tale. In olden times dwelt here one who was known as Orso Alemanno, or the German Bear. He had compelled his vassals to yield him the horrible *jus primæ noctis*. When any one married a wife, he had to lead his bride to the castle, and leave her with the German Bear for a night; and, besides, he had to take to the Bear the finest horse in his stable for him to ride upon. As the years came and went, the chamber of the Baron was never empty, and his stable was always full. A young man, by name Probetta, wished to marry a beautiful maiden. Probetta was a daring horseman, and could skilfully throw the lasso. He concealed the sling under his coat, and, mounting a fine horse, rode in front of the Baron's castle—for he wished, he said, to ride the beast up and down before Orso, to show him what a splendid animal it was. The German Bear came out of his gate, and laughed with joy, because he was to kiss the fairest of maidens and ride the best of horses. As he stood there laughing and looking at Probetta, the youth suddenly dashed past, threw the lasso round Orso, and rushed like a storm down the hill, dragging Orso over the stones. And they pulled down the baronial castle, and buried the German Bear in a dark spot. But after a fear had passed away, some one thought to himself, What has become of the dead Orso? and the people ran in haste to the spot where they had buried him, and dug him up. And there flew out from the grave a fly. And the fly flew into all the houses, and stung all the women; and it became always bigger and bigger, and in the end became as big as an ox, and stung everything in the whole country-side. Then no one knew how they were to get rid of the ox-fly. But some one said that in Pisa were miracle-doctors, who could cure all sorts of things. Then went they to Pisa and fetched a miracle-doctor who could cure all sorts of things.

As soon as the doctor saw the great fly, he began to spread a plaster, and spread 6000 Spanish fly-plasters, and rolled 100,000 pills. And the 6000 fly-plasters he laid on the fly, and the 100,000 pills he gave it to swallow. Thereupon the fly became always smaller and smaller, and when it had become as small as a right fly, it died. Then took they a great bier and covered it with a snow-white cloth, and on the cloth they laid the corpse of the fly. And all the women came together and tore their hair and wept bitterly, because so proper a fly was dead; and twelve men carried the fly on the bier to the churchyard, and gave it a Christian burial. Thereafter they were delivered from the evil.—This fine legend I have related in the words of the Corsican chronicler, up to the appearance of the miracle-doctor on the scene, who is brought from Pisa, and who simply kills the fly. The rest I have added.

Porto Vecchio is a little unwalled town, of about two thousand inhabitants, lying on a gulf of the same name, the last which occurs on the east coast. It is large and beautiful, and, as it lies opposite the mainland of Italy, might be made of the highest importance. The Genoese founded Porto Vecchio in order to ward off the piratical attacks of the Saracens. They granted many privileges to colonists, to induce people to settle there; but as the numerous marshes made the locality unhealthy, fever began to rage, and Porto Vecchio was three times forsaken and left desolate. Even at the present day, the whole of this large district is one of the most uncultivated and most thinly peopled in all Corsica, and is chiefly inhabited by deer and wild swine. Yet the soil is uncommonly fertile. The surrounding country is rich in olives and vines. Porto Vecchio itself is built on porphyritic rocks, which are visible on the surface. I found it almost deserted, as it was August and half of the inhabitants had fled to the hills.

Northward from this beautiful gulf, the coast runs in straight lines; the mountain-chain is still visible on the left, till it recedes into the interior in the district of Salenzara, and leaves behind it those extensive plains which give to the east coast of Corsica an aspect so different from that of the west. The whole west of the island is an uninterrupted series of parallel valleys; the mountain-chains run into the sea, terminating in promontories and enclosing splendid gulfs. The east has none of this protending valley-structure; the land loses itself in flats. The west of Corsica is romantic, picturesque, grand; the east smooth, monotonous, melancholy. The eye here sweeps over leagues of level country, seeking for villages, men, life, and discovers nothing but heaths, dotted here and there with clumps of wild bushes, and covered with morasses and ponds, extending far along the shore and the land with gloom.

The good and always level road leads us next from Porto Vecchio to the ancient Aleria—a day's journey. The grass grows on it a foot high. In summer, the people fear to travel over it. Along the whole road I met not a living soul. No village is to be met with along this dreary route, only here and there a hamlet may be descried in the distance, far among the hills. On the sea-coast, in such places as possess a little harbour, a cala or landing-place, a few isolated and deserted houses may be seen—as Porto Favone, to which the old Roman road ran, Fautea, Cala di Tarco, Cala de Canelle, Cala de Coro, which also goes by the name of Cala Moro or Moorish landing-place. Here, too, stand a few isolated Genoese watch-towers.

All those houses were forsaken, and their windows and doors shut, for the air is pestilential along the whole coast. The poor Lucchese perform the little field-work there is to do. The Corsicans do not venture down from the mountains. I am happy to say that I did not suffer from the unwholesome atmosphere, but perhaps I may ascribe my escape to my prudently following the example of my travelling companion, who snuffed camphor—said to be a good antidote.

Furnished with a very meagre travelling-wallet, we soon ran short, and hunger caused us considerable annoyance during this and half the following day. Neither open house nor hostelry was anywhere to be found. The pedestrian would here inevitably die of want, or be compelled to take refuge in the hills, and wander about there for hours till the fortunate discovery of some footpath led him to a herd's cabin. It is a *strada morta*.

We cross the Taravo. From that point the series of ponds begins with the long narrow Stagno di Palo. Then come the Stagno di Graduggine, the ponds of Urbino and Siglione, the Stagno del Sale, and the beautiful pond of Diana, which has retained its name since the time of the Romans. Tongues of land separate these fish-abounding ponds from the sea, but the most of them have an inlet. The fish found in them are famous—large fat eels and huge ragnole. The fishermen catch them with rush nets.

From Taravo stretches far to the north a magnificent plain—the Fiumorbo or the Canton Prunelli. Watered by rivers and bordered by numerous ponds and by the sea, it resembles, when beheld from a distance, a boundless, luxuriant garden lying by the sea-shore. But scarcely a rood of arable land is visible; the fern covers an immeasurable extent of flat country. It is very depressing to travel through so beautiful a plain, and see no sign of life or cultivation. One cannot understand how the French should have overlooked the colonization of these parts. Here the prosperity of colonies would be more certain than in the life and money devouring sands of Africa. There is room here for two populous towns of at least 50,000 inhabitants each. Colonies of industrious peasants and citizens would soon convert the whole plain into a garden. Good drainage would soon cause the morasses to disappear, and make the air wholesome. There is not a finer strip of land in all Corsica, and none whose soil would be more productive. The climate is milder and sunnier than that of southern Tuscany; it might grow the sugar-cane, and grain would certainly yield a hundred-fold. Only through colonization and industry, which create demand and increase competition, could those Corsican mountaineers be induced to leave their black mountain villages for the plains, and cultivate the soil. Nature here, with the most lavish hand, offers everything which can give birth to a great industrial life; the hills are literally treasure-chambers of precious stones; the forests yield pine, larch, and oak; there is no lack of medicinal springs also, which might be conveyed to any part of the country. There is abundant pasture for the most populous herds; and the unbroken succession of mountain, plain, and the Italian sea, which swarms with fish, leaves nothing to be desired.

To the coast, as it appears at the present day, the description which Homer gives of the Cyclops Isle is strikingly appropriate; its soil is represented by him as in the highest degree adapted for the cultivation which it does not receive: —

> "For stretch'd beside the hoary ocean lie
> Green meadows moist, where vines would never fail;
> Light is the land, and they might yearly reap
> The tallest crops, so unctuous is the glebe;
> Safe is its haven also, where no need
> Of cable is, or anchor, or to lash
> The halser fast ashore: but, pushing in
> His bark, the mariner might there abide,
> Till rising gales should tempt him forth again."

As I gaze on these glorious plains, I cannot but admire the discernment of the old Romans who planted the only colonies they had in Corsica just on this spot.

CHAPTER II
SULLA'S COLONY

As the traveller approaches the Fiumorbo river, he sees isolated palatial mansions; some of them are the seats of French capitalists who began imprudently, and became bankrupt. Others are mansions belonging to rich domains, true earldoms in extent, as Migliacciaro in the Canton Prunelli, which belongs to a French company, and was formerly a source of revenue to the Genoese family of Fiesco.

The Fiumorbo, which takes its rise in the highest mountain range of Corsica, disembogues above the Stagno di Graduggine. It takes the name of "Blind River" from its course, for it moves like a blind man circuitously through the plain, feeling out its way to the sea. The country between it and the Tavignano is said to be the most fertile in Corsica.

As the evening approached, the temperature changed with striking rapidity, from the most sultry heat to a moist and foggy chillness. In many parts the atmosphere was laden with miasma. I stumbled on a gravestone by the roadside. It seemed erected in this solitude to indicate a memorable spot. It was the monument of a road-contractor whom a paesane shot, because he had an amour with a maiden whose suitor the latter was. Nothing enchains the interest of men so powerfully as the romance of the heart. A simple love-tragedy exercises the same power over the fancy of the many, as a heroic deed, and its memory is often preserved for centuries. It is a beautiful thing that the heart too has its chronicle. The Corsicans are perfect devils of jealousy; they avenge insulted love as they do blood. My fellow-traveller related to me the following incidents:—"A young man had forsaken his betrothed, and attached himself to another girl. One day he was sitting in the open square of his village at a game of draughts. His rejected sweet-heart approached, and after overwhelming him with a torrent of imprecations, drew a pistol from her bosom and blew his brains out. Another forsaken maiden had, on one occasion, said to her lover, 'If you ever desert me for another, she will never be yours.' Two years passed away. The young man led another maiden to the altar. As he left the church-door with her, the girl whom he had forsaken shot him; and the people exclaimed, 'Evviva, may your countenance live!' The judge sentenced the maiden to three months' imprisonment. Many youths sued for her hand, but none desired the young widow of the murdered bridegroom."

The Corsican women, who sing such bloody songs of revenge, are capable of carrying pistol and fucile, and fighting with them too, when there is need. How often have they fought in the battles of their country, spite of their husbands! They say that the victory of the Corsicans over the French at Borgo, was, in a very great measure, owing to the heroic daring of the women. They fought also in the battle of Ponte Nuovo; and the bold wife of Giulio Francesco di Pastoreccia, who fought by her husband's side during the battle, still lives in every mouth. She had a hand-to-hand encounter with a French officer, conquered him, and took him prisoner; but when she saw that the Corsicans were scattered in flight, she gave him his freedom, saying, "Remember that a Corsican woman overcame you, and restored to you your sword and your freedom." These Corsican women are the heroines of Ariosto and Tasso realized.

Behind the Fiumorbo begins the river district of the Tavignano, which disembogues at Aleria, under the pond of Diana. I was going to leave the Vettura there, as I had a letter of introduction from a citizen of Sartene, for *Casajanda*, a rich manor near Aleria, the property of Captain Franceschetti, the son of the general who became so famous in Murat's last days. Alas, Signor Franceschetti had gone to the mainland, and I lost the pleasure of making the acquaintance of this energetic man, and gaining information from him on many points. Meanwhile night had set in, and we were near Aleria—Sulla's colony. From the road we distinguished the dark rows of houses, and the fort on the hill by the wayside; and in the hope of finding a locanda in the little town, but with many misgivings, we ordered the vettura to wait, and walked towards the entrance.

The scenery all round seemed to me to be truly *Sullanian*; a night as still as the grave, a desolate plain under our feet reeking with pestilential vapours, night-wrapt hills behind the fort, and the horizon red as if with the firelight of burning towns, for the copsewoods all round were blazing;—the little town itself dead and dark. At last a dog began to bark and gave us hope, and soon the whole population of Aleria came to meet us—two *doganieri* namely, who were the only inhabitants of the town. The people had fled to the hills to escape the malaria, and every door was shut except that of the fort, in which the coast-guard lay. We begged hospitality for the night, as the horses were unable to proceed farther and there was no place in the vicinity which could receive us. But these brave Sullanians refused our request, afraid of incurring their captain's displeasure, and having to begin their night-watch in an hour. We conjured them by the heavenly Virgin not to drive us away and expose us to the night miasma, but to grant us shelter in the fort. They were inexorable, however; and we turned back, at our wit's end what to do—my companion very much annoyed, and I far from pleased to think that I had been thus turned out of the first Roman colony which my feet had trodden, and this spite of the two Cæsars[O] who are my most particular friends. At length, the Sullanians were visited by a touch of human pity, and came running after us, calling out, *Entrate pure!* With great satisfaction we entered the little fort, a square building undefended by battery, rampart, or fosse, and groped up the stone steps into the guardroom.

Not long after we had established ourselves here, the poor coast-guardsmen flung their fuciles over their shoulders, and took their way, accompanied by their dogs, to the pond of Diana, to lie in wait for smugglers. Their service is a dangerous one; were they not relieved every fifteen days, they would fall victims to the fever. I lay down on the floor of the room and attempted to sleep, but the stifling sultriness of the atmosphere was intolerable. I preferred returning to the vettura and breathing the noxious air of the plains—it was at least cooling. I spent a truly Sullanian night in this Aleria, in front of the church in which Father Cyrnæus had been deacon, meditating on the greatness of the Romans and their fall, and on those splendid Sullanian banquets, at which there were pasties of fish-livers, and fountains of costly sauces. It was a diabolical night, and more than once I sighed, "*Aleria, Aleria, chi non ammazza vituperia*"—Aleria, Aleria, who but a murderer would not curse thee!—for this is the verse with which the Corsicans have stigmatized the place; and it seems to me highly appropriate to a colony of Sulla.

The morning dawned. I jumped out of the vettura, and set about making myself acquainted with the position of Aleria. The site is well selected. The plain is commanded by a hill, from which there is a splendid view of Diana's pond, the Stagno del Sale, the sea, and the neighbouring islands. Fine mountain-cones enclose the panorama on the land side. The morning was deliciously refreshing, the air full of the transitory radiance of the early dawn, the view unlimited and comprehensive, and the ground on which I stood, Roman—nay, more still, Phœnician.

The Aleria of the present day consists of only two houses, which lie close to the Genoese fort. The ancient Aleria included several hills, and extended down towards the bed of the Tavignano, as far as the plain; at Diana's pond old iron rings still indicate the position of the town harbour. I stroll towards the ruins hard by. All round, the hills are strewn with stones—the ruins of walls and houses, but I find no remains of ornamental architecture, neither capital nor frieze, nothing but rude materials of a small size. Here and there may be seen remains of arches, also a few steps belonging to what was once a circus, and a ruin which the people call *casa reale*, and which is said to have been the Prætor's house; but I do not know on what grounds, for the remains tell nothing—there is nothing to indicate even the epoch. If one might infer from the extent of ground which it seems to have covered, Aleria must have been a town of about 20,000 inhabitants. Vases and Roman coins have been found on the soil; some goat-herds informed me, that three days before, some one had picked up a gold coin. One of the coast-guard, returning to the fort, roused my curiosity to the utmost by telling me that he had found two marble tablets, with inscriptions on them which nobody could decypher. The tablets, he said, were shut up in a house, but he had taken a copy of the inscription. He then drew out his pocket-book; the inscriptions were in Latin, and copied by this excellent archæologist in a style so truly Phœnician, that it was with difficulty I could make out that the one was a votive-writing of the time of Augustus, the other a monumental inscription.

That was all I found of the ancient Aleria.

CHAPTER III
THEODORE VON NEUHOFF

"Abenamar, Abenamar,

Moro de la Moreria,

El dia que tu naciste,

Grandes senales avia." —*Moorish Romance.*

It was at Aleria that, on the 12th of March 1736, Theodore von Neuhoff disembarked, who was the first of a succession of Corsican *parvenus*, who give a mediæval and romantic character to modern European history.

That morning in Aleria, I had a vision of that strange knight-adventurer, as I had seen him represented in a still unedited Genoese manuscript of the year 1739: "Accinelli, Historico-geographico-political Memorials of the Kingdom of Corsica." This MS. is in the possession of Mr. Santelli of Bastia, who willingly permitted me to examine it, but refused to let me copy some original letters, which, however, I procured elsewhere at a later period. The spirit in which the Genoese has written his history may be gathered from its motto, which describes the Corsicans thus: *Generatio prava et exorbitans: Bestiae et universa pecora*—a wicked and depraved generation—beasts and cattle all. The Genoese has stolen his motto from the Bible. In his MS. he has painted Theodore in water-colours after life, in Moorish dress, peruke, and small hat, heavy sabre and cane. He stands gravely on the sea, and out of it an island is seen to project.

The portrait of Theodore of Corsica may also be found exquisitely drawn in an old German book of the year 1736, which was published in Frankfort under the following title: "An Account of the Life and Deeds of Baron Theodore von Neuhoff, and of the Republic of Genoa so injured by him, edited by Giovanni di S. Fiorenzo."

The vignette gives a full-length portrait of Theodore in Spanish costume, with a very white beard. In the background may be seen an unwalled town, probably Bastia, before which are represented in the most satisfactory style three men, one of whom hangs on a gallows, another is impaled, and a third is in the act of being quartered.

The appearance of Theodore in Corsica, and his romantic election to the sovereignty of the island, attracted the attention of all Europe at the time. This may be gathered from the German book which I have just referred to, and which made its appearance in the very year in which that singular event occurred, 1736. As this volume is the only German book which I have made use of in my Corsican studies, I shall transfer some of it to these pages.

The following is the description it gives of the island of Corsica: "Corsica is one of the largest islands of the Mediterranean sea, lying above Sardinia. It is about twenty-five German miles long, and twelve broad. On account of its atmosphere, it is not considered very healthy; yet the land is pretty fertile, although varied by much hill-country, and having many barren places. The inhabitants are famed for their bravery and hardihood in war; but they are at the same time said to be wicked, revengeful, cruel, and rapacious. Moreover, they go by the name of coarse Corsicans—a character whose fitness I shall not here dispute."

The news of the landing of Theodore was, according to this little book, communicated in letters from a correspondent in Bastia, dated the 5th April. We shall quote from these letters.

"In the harbour of Aleria an English ship lately arrived, which is said to belong to the consul of that nation at Tunis; and in it there came a person, in outward appearance of high distinction, whom some took to be a royal prince, others an English nobleman, and whom a few supposed to be the Prince Ragotzy. This much is known, that he professes the Romish religion and bears the name of Theodore. His dress is in the fashion of the Christians who travel in Turkey, and consists of a long scarlet furred coat, peruke and hat, with a cane and sword. He has a retinue consisting of two officers, a secretary, a chaplain, a lord high steward, a steward, cook, three slaves, and four lackeys: in addition, he has brought with him out of Barbary ten cannons, above 7000 muskets, 2000 pairs of shoes, and a great quantity of provisions of all kinds—among them 7000 sacks of grain, as well as several chests full of gold and silver coins—among them a strong plate-chest with silver handles, and full of whole and half zechins. The whole treasure is reckoned to amount to two million pieces of eight. The leading men among the Corsicans received him with great marks of honour, and addressed him as Your Excellency, and gave him the titles of a viceroy. He immediately made four of the Corsicans colonels, and assigned to each a hundred pieces of eight per month; then he raised and equipped four companies, and presented a musket, a pair of shoes, and a zechin to every common soldier: a captain receives eleven pieces of eight per month, but, when the companies shall be in a state of full efficiency, he is to receive twenty-five. He has taken up his residence in the episcopal palace at Campo Loro, before which four hundred men with two cannons keep guard. It is rumoured that he means to go to Casinca, not far from St. Pelegrino, and that he only waits for some large war-ships, which, it is said, will arrive about the 15th of this month, in order to attack the Genoese with all his forces by land and sea, and for this purpose he means to raise many additional companies. It is confidently affirmed that he has been sent by a Catholic potentate in Europe, who means to support him in every way in all his undertakings; consequently, at Genoa, they are in the greatest alarm, and look upon the supremacy of the Genoese in this island to be as good as lost. We have just received here some later intelligence, to the effect that the afore-mentioned stranger regulates his household in a more and more regal style, and is always accompanied to church by a body-guard; that he has appointed one Hyacinth Paoli his treasurer, and has raised one of the most distinguished men of Aleria to the rank of knight."

People were now naturally very eager to learn something about the life and family of Theodore. His adventures and his connexions pointed chiefly to romantic Spain and to Paris. The following letter, written to a friend in Holland by a Westphalian nobleman, and quoted in the little German book which we have referred to, will give us some information on this point.

YOUTH-ROMANCE OUT OF THE LIFE OF THEODORE OF CORSICA.

IN THE FORM OF A LETTER.

"Sir, — I have too great a pleasure in giving you satisfaction, as far as it is in my power, not to be willing to impart to you all that is known to me of the life of a man who now begins to make an appearance in the world.

"You have no doubt read in the newspapers that Theodore von Neuhoff, on whom the Corsicans have conferred the crown, was born in Westphalia, in a district belonging to the King of Prussia. This is true; and I can the more easily confirm it, because he and I studied together, and for some years lived in intimate friendship. The memory of those instances which antiquity affords us of persons of moderate rank who have mounted a throne has been almost entirely lost; but Kuli Cham in Persia, and Neuhoff in Corsica revive such things in our own times. The latter was born in Altena, a little town in Westphalia, whither his mother had gone to pay a friendly visit to a nobleman, after she had prematurely lost her husband, who died, leaving her a widow and pregnant with Theodore.

"His father was captain of the Bishop of Münster's body-guard; and his grandfather, who had grown gray in arms, had commanded a regiment under the great Bernhard von Galen. At the death of the father, the affairs of the family were in great confusion; and had it not been for the activity of a cousin, on whom their management devolved, they would have been in a lamentable condition. When ten years old, he was put to the Jesuits' College at Münster to prosecute his studies, and there he in a short time made good progress. I entered the same college a year afterwards. His father's estate bordered on ours, and we had from our earliest childhood formed a friendship which became closer and stronger as we grew older. He was of a size beyond his years, and his lively and fiery eyes already indicated spirit and courage. He was very industrious, and our teachers continually held him up to us as an example. This, which in the other scholars gave rise to envy, gave me, on the contrary, pleasure, and awoke in me a desire to emulate his industry. We remained together six years at Münster. When my father heard of our intimacy, he proposed not to separate us, but to make him my travelling companion and give him the means of maintaining himself respectably.

"We were sent to Cologne to continue our studies. We seemed to have been transported to a new world, for we were now freed from the limited existence to which school tyranny had confined us, and began to taste the sweetness of freedom. Perhaps, indeed, I should have misused it, had not the good sense of my companion withheld me from every kind of dissipation. We were boarded in the house of a professor, whose wife, though somewhat in years, was of a cheerful disposition, and whose two daughters, as lively as they were beautiful, united these two qualities with a very prudent demeanour. After the evening meal, we generally amused ourselves with games or walked in a garden which belonged to the family, and which lay near the city gate.

This agreeable mode of life had lasted for about two years, when it was disturbed by the arrival of the Count von M— —, whom his father had placed in the same house in which we lodged. He had a tutor, who was a native of Cologne, a man who had for many years had private haunts of his own, not perhaps of the most reputable kind, to which he was so addicted that he neglected his pupil. As we saw that the young Count's time frequently hung heavy on his hands, we were the first to make a proposal to him to join our little society—an offer which he accepted with pleasure.

"Theodore had always occupied a seat between the two sisters, and I one between the younger and her mother. It was now necessary to make another arrangement, and out of respect for the Count's rank, we yielded to him the place hitherto occupied by the Baron von Neuhoff. I had often observed that my companion looked with favour on the elder sister, and that when their eyes chanced to meet, the fair one would change colour. She was a noble-looking girl, with black eyes and an uncommonly fair complexion. The count soon fell desperately in love with her, and as the eyes of a lover are much keener than those of anybody else, Theodore soon became conscious that he was doing all he could to ingratiate himself with Mariana—such was the attractive maiden's name—and thereupon he fell into deep and anxious reflection.

"'What is the matter with you, my dear friend?' I asked one evening when we had retired. 'I have found you for some days quite wrapt up in your own thoughts; you have no longer that vivacity which made your conversation so agreeable; you must surely be the victim of some great anxiety.' 'Ah, my dearest friend!' he replied, 'I was born under an unlucky star; I have never known my father, and there is no one but you to lighten the burden of my life, which, without you, would be still more miserable than it is.'

"'But why these melancholy thoughts now more than at any other time?' I rejoined. 'My father will care for your happiness, and you yourself are able to win by your own talents whatever fortune has denied you. Confess it, Theodore, it is something else which so disquiets you, and, unless I am much mistaken, I fear that the beautiful eyes of Mariana have already too deeply imprinted their image on your heart.'

"'I cannot deny it,' was his reply; 'and I have resolved to make a full confession to you of all my weakness. You know how pleasantly we have spent the last two years in the society of these amiable girls. From the first day, I was conscious of Mariana's power over me; and while I imagined that I entertained towards her nothing more than a tender respect—I certainly intended nothing more—I now find that she has inspired me with feelings of the warmest kind. The arrival of the young Count has opened my eyes; I am too painfully aware of the attention which he pays her, and the superiority of his birth over mine makes me fear that he may find preference in the affections of the beautiful Mariana. In the jealousy which I feel, I perceive how deeply I love her; I forget to eat and drink; I spend the night sleeplessly; and this, in addition to the passion which consumes me, is more than I can bear.'

"'But, my dear Theodore,' I said, 'how can you, so prudent in everything else, let yourself be mastered by a feeling which can have no other than melancholy consequences for you? Mariana is not of a rank to admit of your marrying her, and she has too much virtue to be yours in any other way. Let us change our residence; at a distance from the object which inflames you, you will gradually lose the memory of it.' 'What you say may be all very rational,' replied Theodore; 'but have you ever heard that love reasons? And do you not know that in love, as in honour, one takes nothing but his heart to counsel? It is as impossible that I should tear myself from Mariana, as that I should forget myself; the wound is already so deep that it can never be healed.' 'But what will your friends say,' I continued, 'if you form so intimate a connexion with this girl that no way is left to break it? Your fortunes depend on them; they will not fail to withdraw their protection from you, and deprive you of that inheritance which you may one day expect from them.'

"'They may do,' he said, 'what they please with me; I will never cease to love the adorable Mariana!'

"We then wished each other good-night; I slept, but Theodore did not spend the night so calmly. I found him in the morning so altered in appearance by the sufferings of the past night, that I did not venture to resume our conversation of the preceding evening. We turned to our studies and exercises; and in the evening we found ourselves as usual in the midst of our little society. He was bantered a little on account of his wandering thoughts; he pleaded headache, and begged that they would be so good as to excuse his not taking a part in the amusements. During the evening, he watched the eyes of Mariana and the Count; he imagined that he discovered a certain love-understanding between them, and this drove him to utter despair. We retired; and as we entered our room, he said, 'Well, do you still doubt the love which Mariana and the Count cherish for each other? They have interchanged a hundred loving looks; he whispered in her ear, too, as we came away; my misery is too certain.' 'I have not observed all this,' I replied; 'jealousy has perhaps exaggerated and distorted the most trivial occurrences.'

"Two or three days passed, during which our conversation frequently turned to the same subject. Our professor gave us and some others a party in his garden on the anniversary of Mariana's christening-day. The Count, having been informed of the occasion of the party, had presented Mariana in the morning with a bouquet and a costly diamond pin. It needed nothing more to put Theodore beside himself; he fell into a melancholy silence, and ate hardly anything; the headache had again to come to his help; we rose from the table, and, after some promenading, the ball began. The Count opened it with Mariana, who of course was the queen of the ball. Theodore would not dance, but walked about the garden the whole night. The ball lasted till morning, when we returned home.

"I went straight to my room; my comrade had remained in the court below, and when he met his rival had compelled him to draw. I heard the clash of swords, and ran down with all speed, but came too late; he had already given his adversary a mortal wound, and escaped through the back-door. You may conceive the grief and confusion which this deed occasioned in the whole house. The poor Count was carried to his bed, where he expired two hours after. Neither I nor any of his friends could learn whither Theodore had gone; and we should never have discovered it but for the letter which he wrote us from Corsica a few months ago."

What has come to our ears regarding the life of Theodore previously to his arrival in Corsica, which, as we might expect from the nature of the man, is uncertain and contradictory, shows him to have been one of the most prominent and fortunate of the succession of adventurers who figured in the eighteenth century. The appearance of such men as Cagliostro, Saint Germain, Law, Theodore, Casanova, Königsmark is a counterpoise to these genuinely great contemporaries, Washington, Franklin, Paoli, Pitt, Frederick the Great, highly characteristic of the epoch. While these are busy laying the foundations of a new order of government and society, those, like fluttering storm-birds, give indications of the mighty elemental commotions which were secretly agitating the minds of that period.

It is said that Theodore von Neuhoff became a page in the family of the famous Duchess of Orleans, and there formed himself to the complete and adroit courtier. His Proteus-nature hurried him into the most opposite extremes. In Paris, the Marquis of Courcillon procured him an officer's commission. He became a passionate gambler; he then fled from his creditors to Sweden, where he resided under the protection of Baron von Görtz, and formed connexions successively with the intriguing and adventurously ingenious ministers of that period—with Ripperda, Alberoni, and, finally, with Law;—men who, more or less, transferred into politics the same character of adventurer which distinguished our hero in private life. Theodore became Alberoni's confidant, and gained such great influence in Spain that he accumulated considerable property, till Alberoni was overthrown, when he again came to the ground. He now attached himself to Ripperda, and married one of the maids of honour in the Spanish court. Elizabeth Farnese of Spain, an accomplished mistress of every intrigue, had played a high game with a view to procure for her son, Don Carlos, an Italian kingdom; all this was gone about in a speculative and adventurous way. The world was then a great field for adventurers, and full of *parvenus*, aspiring pretenders, visionaries, and fortune-hunters. One may string together a whole list of them, and this in the field of politics alone. Don Carlos of Spain, Charles Stuart, Rakotzy, Stanislaus Leszcinski the creature of the great adventurer Charles XII. of Sweden; and, in addition to the statesmen already named, the *parvenus* of Russia—a Menezikof, a Münnich, a Biron; Mazeppa and Patkul, too, stand at the head of the long line. It was also the epoch of female supremacy in Europe. We thus see on what ground our Theodore von Neuhoff stood.

His wife was a Spaniard, but of Irish or English extraction, and a relation of the Duke of Ormond. She does not seem to have been a paragon of beauty. Theodore forsook her, and, one may suppose, not without carrying off her jewels and other articles of value.

He went to Paris, where he had the skill to ingratiate himself with Law; and, aided by the Mississippi bond-swindle, he managed to get hold of a good deal of money. A *lettre de cachet* again helped him to recommence his wanderings; and so he dashed about every country in the world, attempting everything; he made his appearance in England and Holland among other places. In the last-mentioned place, he got up a 'speculation,' swindled, and ran into debt. How he came to Genoa, has been related in the history of the Corsicans; perhaps his immense debts made a crown very desirable. And so we have the exciting drama of a man being suddenly elevated to a throne, who, a short time before, counted his very tailor among his creditors. Such things are possible at a period in which the foundations of political and social order are deeply shaken; in such times romantic breezes are continually blowing through the world, and the apparently impossible may any day become the real.

We know that Theodore came to Genoa, formed connexions with the exiled Corsicans there and in Leghorn, conceived the idea of becoming King of Corsica, and went to Tunis. In Barbary he was imprisoned; and in memory of this, he at a later period assumed a chain in his royal arms. His inventive genius not only freed him from his prison, but helped him to procure all the necessaries requisite for the descent upon Corsica. Scarcely out of a prison he became a king.

From Corsica, he wrote the following letter to his Westphalian cousin, Herr von Drost. This letter I found printed as an authentic state-paper in the third volume of Cambiaggi, and read it, as well as all the other documents I give here, in the MS. of the Genoese Accinelli. The little German book, to which I have more than once referred, likewise quotes it; and I will repeat it here, following the German text instead of translating it from the Italian, as it may possibly be the composition of Theodore himself.

"My respected Cousin,—The regard and kindness which you continually showed me, from my tenderest youth up, make me hope that you still honour me with a place in your memory and heart. Although I—on account of the confusion and derangement of my affairs caused by certain enemies, and perhaps, too, on account of my own natural inclination and desire to travel about without maintaining any communication with my former friends, with the view, as I hoped, of being one day useful to my fellow-men—have let slip so many years without informing you of my condition; yet I pray you to believe that you have been always present in my memory, and that I have had no other ambition but to return to my fatherland, as soon as I could do so in a position to show my gratitude towards my benefactors and friends, and to crush the unjust calumnies which have been spread abroad regarding me. Now, however, I cannot, as a sincere friend and good relation, omit this opportunity of letting you know that it has been my fortune, after many persecutions and adversities, to come personally to this kingdom of Corsica, and to accept the offer of the faithful inhabitants here, who have elected and proclaimed me their captain and king. For, inasmuch as I, after having for two years been at great expense on their account and having suffered imprisonment and persecution, was no longer in a position to prosecute further travels, with the view of freeing them from the tyrannous rule of the Genoese; I at last betook myself hither in accordance with their desire, and became recognised and proclaimed as their king: and I hope, by God's help, to maintain myself as such. I would consider myself happy, my worthy cousin, if you would do me the pleasure and consolation of sending to me some of my friends, in order that I might give them such employment as they might desire, and share my good fortune with them— which good fortune I, through the advantages which I have obtained in my travels and through God's help, hope to use still more triumphantly than hitherto to the honour of God and the great good of my fellow-men. It will not be known to you, that a year ago I had the misfortune to be captured on the sea, and taken to Algiers as a slave. I was able, however, to deliver myself from bondage, having suffered nevertheless great loss, &c. I must postpone to another time informing you of what I have, by the grace of God, accomplished; and for the present only beg that you will count upon me as confidently as upon yourself, and be assured that I retain deeply engraven on my heart the sincere tokens of friendship shown to me by you in such large measure from my youth up; and that I will exert myself in every way to give you substantial marks of the grateful attachment wherewith I shall be always devoted to you—whilst I remain yours, with my whole heart, and a true friend and cousin,

"The Baron von Neuhoff,

"King of Corsica by election, under the title of Theodore I.

"*March 18, 1736.*"

"*P.S.*—I beg you will give me information of your condition, and greet all worthy families and friends from me; and inasmuch as my exaltation tends to their honour, I hope they will all together help to advance my interests, and come hither to aid me with their counsel and their deeds. Whereas, too, no letters have for many years been received by my friends of Brandenburg, allow me to send to you the accompanying letter, with the request that you will forward it to Bungelschild; and send me word whether my uncle is still alive, and what my cousins at Rauschenberg are about."

CHAPTER IV
THEODORE THE FIRST, BY THE GRACE OF GOD AND THROUGH THE HOLY TRINITY, KING OF CORSICA BY ELECTION

Scarcely had Theodore set foot in Corsica, and become famous in the world, than the Republic of Genoa issued a manifesto, wherein they animadverted on him very severely; "and the Genoese," says the little German book, "in an edict, describe Theodore very severely."

They describe him very severely indeed, as witness what follows:—

"We, the Doge, the Governors, and Procurators of the Republic of Genoa—

"Whereas we have been informed that a small merchantman, belonging to the English Captain Dick, has disembarked in the port of Aleria in our kingdom of Corsica munitions of war, and a certain notorious, orientally-clad person, who, in an inconceivable manner, was successful in making himself acceptable to the chiefs and the people; whereas this stranger distributed among them arms, powder, and some gold pieces, as well as other things; and whereas also, he, with the promise of more than adequate help, gives them various counsels that disturb the peace, which we are anxious to restore for the sake of the well-being of our subjects in the said kingdom: we have taken means to gain information from trustworthy sources regarding the real character and life of this man. Accordingly, it has become known to us that he is from the province of Westphalia; that he gives himself out as the Baron von Neuhoff; that he pretends to a knowledge of alchymy, of the Kabbala, and of astrology, by whose help he has discovered, he says, many important secrets; further, that he has become notorious as a wandering and vagabond person of little fortune.

"In Corsica he goes by the name of Theodore. In 1729 he went under this name to Paris, where he deserted his child and wife, a lady of Irish extraction whom he married in Spain.

"While travelling through various parts of the world, he has assumed a false name, and denied his birthplace. In London he gave himself out for a German, in Leghorn for an Englishman, in Genoa for a Swede, and he has assumed successively the names of Baron von Naxaer, von Smihmer, von Nissen, and von Smitberg, as appears, along with much beside, from his passes and other authentic writings, dated from various cities and still preserved.

"By so changing his name and residence, he succeeded, by his fraudulent practices, in living at the cost of others; and it is well known that in Spain, about the year 1727, he embezzled the money advanced to him for the purpose of levying a German regiment, and then absconded; and that he also in other ways and in many places has cheated English, French, Germans, and men of other nations.

"Wherever he has practised such tricks, he has laboured to remain concealed. But after his departure he has become notorious on account of his various impositions, as is more especially shown by a letter written by a German cavalier on the 20th day of February of this year.

"That such has been his habitual mode of life, is apparent from the fact that some years ago he borrowed five hundred and fifteen gold pieces from the banker Jaback in Leghorn, with a promise to repay them in Cologne. After the latter saw that he had been deceived, he had him arrested. In order to regain his liberty, he made use of the captain of a vessel whom he entrapped into being surety for him; and after his liberation through the deed drawn up at Leghorn by the notary Gumano, dated Sept. 6. 1735, had become known, he was received into the hospital of the aforesaid town to receive medical aid as a pauper, as he had been very ill during the period of his imprisonment.

"About three months ago he left Leghorn and betook himself to Tunis with letters of introduction, and there he acted the physician and held several secret conferences with the leading men of that infidel land. There, too, he afterwards procured arms and munitions of war with which he next went to Corsica, in company with Christophorus the brother of Bonngiorno a physician of Tunis, three Turks among whom was one Mahomet who had been a slave in the Tuscan galleys, two runaway Livornese—Johann Attimann and Giovanni Bondelli by name, and a Portuguese priest who, at the instance of the mission-fathers in Tunis, and on good grounds, had been compelled to quit that town.

"In such circumstances, and with such indubitable testimonies, and whereas this man has usurped the sovereignty of Corsica, and consequently attempts wickedly to turn aside our subjects from the obedience due to their natural princes; and whereas likewise it is to be feared that a person of such infamous designs is likely to contrive still more confusions and disturbances amongst our people, we have resolved to make everything open and public, and to proclaim, as we now do in the present edict, that this so-called Baron Theodore von Neuhoff, as being an undoubted originator of insurrections, a seducer of the people, and a disturber of the common peace, is guilty of the crime of high treason, and has consequently incurred all the penalties ordained by our laws for that offence.

"Therefore, we forbid all to maintain intercourse or communication with the said person, and we declare all those who give him assistance or in any other way join the party of this man in order still more to disturb our people and incite them to revolt, to be in like manner guilty of high treason, and disturbers of the public peace, and to have incurred the same penalties.

"Given at our Royal Palace on the 9th May 1736.

(Signed)   "Joseph Maria."

This manifesto of the Genoese Republic had no effect. Even in their own town of Bastia the people wrote under it—*Evviva Teodoro I. Re di Corsica*; and Theodore, so far from being ashamed of his *parvenu* character, said with manly humour: "Since the Genoese stigmatize me as an adventurer and charlatan, I shall lose no time in erecting my theatre in Bastia."

He meanwhile issued a manifesto in reply to the Genoese, a very charming production.

"Theodorus, King of Corsica,—To the Doge and Senate at Genoa his greeting and much patience.

"It has not till now occurred to me that I have committed a sin of omission in not having made known to your Highnesses my intention of removing to Corsica: to speak the truth, I considered such formality unnecessary, thinking that rumour would quickly inform you thereof. I indeed considered it quite superfluous to acquaint you with a trifle like this, as I felt persuaded that your Corsican Commissioner had already told you all about it in a pompous enough narrative.

"Since, however, I now discover that you have been complaining that I kept silence about my intentions, I feel myself constrained, as a dutiful citizen, to announce to you, as one friendly neighbour is in the habit of doing to another, that I have changed my residence. I must therefore take the liberty to observe that I—disgusted with the long and many wanderings which, as you are aware, have occupied my past life—have at last come to the conclusion to select for myself a little place in Corsica; and since this place happens to lie in your vicinity, I take the liberty now to pay you in writing my first visit of ceremony. Your present delegate at Bastia, if he does not deceive you like his predecessor, will be able to assure you of my particular exertions to send to the said town an adequate number of troops in order to pay my respects to you in a way which may give the fullest publicity to our new neighbourhood.

"Inasmuch as, however, the departure of one neighbour from another often gives rise to criticism, or it may be even disputes, on account of the difficulty of settling boundary lines, I will refrain from further compliments and immediately talk with you about our concerns; and I do so all the more willingly that I have heard from various quarters that our new neighbourhood is very disagreeable to you, that you bitterly inveigh against it, and, indeed, in defiance of every law of etiquette, entirely repudiate it. The declaration made by you that your neighbour is a disturber of the common peace, and a seducer of the people, is a most barefaced lie, promulgated as the truth not only in one or two places, but in the face of the whole world, although everybody knows that peace and quiet have been these seven years entirely banished out of Corsica, and that you yourselves were the first to disturb them by your tyrannous and unjust rule, and then by your cruelty to extinguish them entirely. The state-maxims according to which you have acted have, under the pretence of promoting peace, bathed the poor Corsicans in a sea of blood.

"This has been your conduct, and in this way have you chased peace and quiet out of Corsica after it had been with such great difficulty restored by the Emperor. Your wicked and stubborn Pinelli misled the people, and such is the condition in which I find it after having lived here for only a few days. Why is the guilt of your crimes rolled over upon me? In what law is it written that so simple and innocent a neighbour as I am can be guilty of high treason? Treason supposes a friendship broken by the lowest crimes, and those crimes perpetrated under the pretext of friendship. Grant that you were by me grievously injured, what friendship has ever existed between us two? when was I your friend? Heaven prevent me from sinking so low as to be the friend of a nation which has so few friends!

"Further, you would fain with all your might demonstrate that I have committed the crime of high treason against royalty! The very thought of so horrible an offence at first made me tremble. But after having made earnest inquiries regarding the place from which your Majesty comes, I have at last regained my peace of mind, as I could nowhere discover what I was in search of. Tell me, have you inherited this Majesty from your Doges, or pirated it upon the high seas at the time you gave up your city as a place of resort for the Mahometans, and through greed of gain, drew so many Turks to your country that they almost threatened to overwhelm the whole of Christendom? Perhaps you brought this Majesty out of Spain on your back, or it may be that it found its way to your country in a ship from England, which was consigned by an English merchant to one of your countrymen who had just been elected Doge, and which, as you remember, brought a letter the address of which ran thus: 'To Monsieur N.N., Doge of Genoa, and Dealer in General Wares.'

"Tell me, in Heaven's name, whence you have obtained the dignity of a monarchy and the title of royalty, when the fact is that your Republic has, in bygone times, been nothing but a corporation of gain-greedy pirates? For these many centuries have any had a seat in your councils save such as held civic offices? Is it from them that you have got 'your Majesty?' Is not even the name of Duke, which you give to your Doge, an improper title? I am assured that the laws and fundamental articles of your Republic are so constructed that no one can be prince save the law itself, and you consequently, as the organs and administrators of it, improperly assume to yourselves the name of 'sovereign;' and the people are with as little propriety called subjects, since they must rule conjointly with you, as is in fact the case. Although you still remain in peaceful possession of your country, which is much more than you deserve, yet I am not able to see that it must therefore go equally well with you in Corsica, where the people, having their eyes open, stand by their just demands, and feel themselves constrained to throw the yoke from their neck. I, for my part, am firmly resolved to act as reason and love of justice prompt. And because you have proclaimed me through the whole world as a deceiver of all and every nation, I have now proposed to myself to demonstrate the contrary by deed in the case of one nation at least, and that, the oppressed Corsicans. As often as I can deceive you, by undeceiving you as to the estimate you put on my character, I shall do so with more than ordinary pleasure, and give you permission to do the like to me—when you can.

"Meanwhile, rest assured that my creditors will get your property; because those effects of yours, which the Corsicans have legally presented to me, more than suffice for the payment of my debts. Yet it would grieve me much if I should be unable to give a sufficient equivalent to your Republic, for the severity it has exercised towards this kingdom; because no payment seems to be great enough as a requital for this.

"Let me not forget likewise herewith to inform you—what, however, you will I daresay have heard—that my progress has been so triumphant, that I have now as many troops in pay as will suffice to show that I am not only able to live at the expense of others, but clever enough to support a thousand men at my own cost. Whether these get their full pay and rations let those heroic soldiers testify, who keep themselves shut up within the walls of Bastia, because they have not the courage to come out into the open field, in order that one may look at them a little nearer.

"As to other matters, I assure you that, however much you exert yourselves to asperse my good name in the eyes of the world, I do not fear its having the impression which you imagine on the people here; and I do not doubt but that the ducats which they have got will have a much more powerful effect than all the calumnies which you are perpetually inventing against my person. Still, I must beg you to do me a favour, namely, that in the battles likely to take place between my troops and yours, some of your countrymen may show who it is that commands them, because the heroism which true-hearted citizens must cherish for their fatherland cannot fail to be met with in men such as they are. But I believe that I am not likely to obtain the fulfilment of my request; because, what with their bills of exchange, commercial transactions, and trades, they have so much to do that the spirit of valour can find no place among them. On this account I do not at all expect that you will ever acquire honour with your soldiers; because those who should be at their head possess neither time nor bravery enough to lead them into the field, as the men of other high-souled nations do.

"Given in the camp before Bastia, July 10, 1736.

"Theodorus.
"Sebastiano Corsa,
"Secretary of State and High Chancellor of the Kingdom."

This savagely-satirical document must certainly have deeply wounded the Genoese Republic. But such is the course of events; the proud mistress of the seas was now sunk low—a little nation not far from her gates made her tremble—a foreign adventurer mocked her with impunity.

The conditions of coronation were finally drawn up and signed at Alesani, on the 15th April 1736; Theodore was elected king of Corsica for the period of his natural life; after him the crown was to descend to his male issue, in the order of birth, and, failing male heirs of his body, his daughters were declared capable of succession. If he had no direct heirs, then his nearest relation was to succeed to the throne. But the Corsicans, after all, gave only the title to their king; they preserved their constitution entire.

I have not heard that the new ruler thought of giving the country a queen; perhaps there was no time. He took up his quarters in the Episcopal house at Cervione, and conducted everything in quite a regal style, so far as all outward ceremonies were concerned; surrounded himself with guards and all princely ceremonial, and played the king as well as if he had been born in the purple. We know that he introduced a magnificently sounding court-state, and, as befits a noble king, created counts, marquises, barons, and court officers of the most ostentatious kind. Men and their passions are everywhere the same. One may feel himself a king in the dirty room of a village house, just as well as in the state-rooms of the Louvre, and a Duke of Marmalade or Chocolade, in the court of a negro king, will wear his title with scarcely less pride than a Duke of Alba. In Cervione, as elsewhere, men might be seen pressing eagerly forward to warm themselves in the beams of the new sun, craving title, and desirous of the royal favour. In a dirty mountain-hamlet, in a black and storm-battered house, which was now a royal palace, because so it was called, ambition and intrigue played their part quite as well as in any other court in the world.

One of the acts of Theodore's sovereign prerogative was the institution of a knightly Order—for a king must dispense orders. As I have related elsewhere, it was called the Order of Liberation. The knights looked very magnificent. They wore an azure-blue gown and a cross; in the middle of the cross was a star of enamel and gold, and therein the figure of Justice with a balance in her hand. Under the balance a triangle might be seen, in the middle of which was a T; in the other hand Justice held a sword, under which one could perceive a ball surmounted by a cross. In addition to all this, the arms of the royal family were forced into the corner of the decoration. Every knight of the Order of Liberation had to swear obedience to the king by land and water. Daily, moreover, he had to sing two psalms, the fortieth, "The Lord is our refuge;" and the seventieth, "In thee, O Lord, have I trusted."

The now very rare coins of gold, silver, and copper, issued by Theodore, show on one side his bust with the circumscription: *Theodorus D. G. unanimi consensu electus Rex et Princeps regni Corsici*—on the other side the words: *Prudentia et Industria vincitur Tyrannis*. On other coins a crown upborne by three palm-trees may be seen on one side with the letters T. R., and on the reverse the words *Pro bono publico Corso*.

Theodore gave the necessary amount of court business to the executioner, and had many a man executed because he seemed to him dangerous. He gave particular offence to his subjects by ordering Luccioni de Casacciolo, a distinguished Corsican, to be put to death; and at another time, too, he was reproached with having made an attempt on the virtue of a young Corsican girl, a licence which was not to be found in the conditions of coronation. But for a couple of years the Corsicans clung to him with great fidelity. These poor people had, like the Jews of old, in their despair longed for a king, who should deliver them from the Philistines. On the first occasion of his leaving them, their fidelity continued unshaken; and as a mark of confidence, they issued the following manifesto:—

"We, Don Luis Marchese Giafferi, and Don Giacinto Marchese Paoli, the Prime Minister and the General of his Majesty King Theodore our Sovereign.

"Scarcely had we received the letter of King Theodore I., our Sovereign, when we, in obedience to his commands, summoned to Parliament all the people of the provinces, towns, villages, and forts in the kingdom, in order to hold a General Assembly respecting the regulations and commands of our aforesaid Sovereign. The assembly was general; they came from one side of the hills as well as from the other. All received with satisfaction and submission the commands of his Majesty, towards whom they unanimously renewed the oath of fidelity and obedience, as towards their legitimate and supreme Lord. They have in like manner confirmed his election to be king of Corsica, and have ratified the law which secured it to him and his descendants for ever, as already in the convention of Alesano it was unalterably decreed.

"To the end that all whom it may concern, and, in fine, the world, may know that we will continually preserve an inviolable fidelity to the royal person of Theodore the First, and that we are resolved, as his subjects, to live and die for him, and never to recognise any other Lord except him and his legitimate descendants: we do now again swear on the Holy Evangel to keep the oath of fidelity in every part, in the name of the people here assembled.

"And in order that the present act may have all power and requisite authenticity, we have ordered it to be registered in the Chancery of the kingdom, and have signed it with our own hands, and confirmed it with the seal of the kingdom.—Given in Parliament, Dec. 27, 1737."

Similar declarations were repeated also in the year 1739, when Theodore again landed in Corsica in the midst of great popular rejoicings. On his way back to the island, he narrowly escaped being burnt alive. A German, Captain Wigmanshausen, who commanded his ship, had been bribed by the Genoese to blow it up during the night. Theodore awoke several times with a sensation as if he were being burnt alive. His suspicions were at last roused, and going into the captain's cabin, accompanied by three of his attendants, he found him busy making preparations to set fire to the powder-magazine. King Theodore sentenced him on the spot to be burnt, but afterwards changed the punishment to hanging on the ship's mast; and the sentence was immediately executed. Thus it happened, that Theodore, in his short royal career, among other kingly experiences, nearly fell a victim to an attempt upon his life.

Theodore's further fortunes in Corsica are already known to us. After attempting in vain to regain his island-crown, he returned to England. He left behind him a wonderful life-dream, in which he had once beheld himself on a semi-barbarous island, with a crown upon his head, and a sceptre in his hand—marquises, counts, barons, cavaliers, chancellors, and keepers of the Great Seal, around him:—now, he sat melancholy and a beggar in the London debtor's prison, and, as he thought on the king-romance of his changeful wandering life, complained no less bitterly and with no less suffering, that it should now be his fate to pine away a captive in the hands of English shopkeepers, than Napoleon did at a later period in the English prison of St. Helena. Theodore, too, had been a king; he, too, was fallen greatness, a tragic personage. The Minister Walpole opened a subscription to aid the poor king of the Corsicans, and in this way he was freed from confinement. As a mark of gratitude, Theodore sent him the Great Seal of his kingdom. Like Paoli and Napoleon, he died on the soil of England in the year 1756. He lies buried in Westminster churchyard.

He was a man of wonderful daring, of a singular ingenuity, inexhaustible in plans, more persevering than his singular fortune was steady; and of all bold adventurers we may call him the most praiseworthy, because he employed his head and hand in defence of the freedom of a brave people. The greatest extremes in human life—royalty, and a debtor's prison in which he had scarcely bread to eat, were among his bitter experiences. We Germans will willingly give the poor man a place among the braves of our nation; and I raise this little memorial to my bold countryman, to revive his memory among us.

CHAPTER V
MARIANA, AND RETURN TO BASTIA

Era già l'ora che volge 'l disio,
A' naviganti, e 'ntenerisce il cuore
Lo dì ch' han detto a' dolci amici a Dio.—Dante.

The paese of Cervione lies northward from Aleria, on the slope of the hill. I wish that I had visited it, and this desire is now my punishment for neglecting the opportunity of doing so when it was in my power; for although it contains nothing worth seeing, it was the royal residence of Theodore. It happens at times that one is afflicted with the travelling-sickness to such an extent, that with a sleepy eye he passes heedlessly over many interesting objects. I just got a glimpse of Cervione on the height, and gave it up for the ruins of Mariana.

Northward from Cervione, the Colo River disembogues—the largest stream in the island, watering numerous valleys in its course. The heat of summer had almost dried it up. All around, the stream has at various times overflowed on the extensive flats of Mariana, or Marana as the Corsicans now call it. Here, on the left bank of the river, stood the second Roman colony: Marius founded it. It is remarkable that in this bloody land of the Corsicans the two great avengers and deadly foes, Marius and Sulla, must needs have planted colonies. Their terrible names, which perpetuate the memory of the most horrible cruelties of civil war and intestine revolution, cast a deeper shade of gloom over the already gloomy and oppressive air of Corsica.

I sought for the ruins of Mariana. They lie towards the sea-shore, a league from the highway. As at Aleria, I found here a wide extent of level ground everywhere covered with the debris of walls. It is melancholy to wander over such ground—one cannot but reflect that these stones once constituted a city, in which the life of many centuries dwelt. Fain would one take Amphion's lyre and try, by the magic power of melody, to reconstruct the fragments, and have one peep at the town and the citizens as they were. What kind of people? to what epoch did they belong? The ruins of Mariana tell even less than those of Aleria: they do not afford materials even for fixing the date of the town's existence. It flatters the Corsican if the stranger finds in those stones the remains of Roman buildings; and in pleasing self-delusion, the traveller may sit down on one of these ruinous heaps and think of Marius sitting on the ruins of Carthage, and mourning the fall of that mighty city. The remains of two churches are the only objects which attract attention. They are the most remarkable mediæval remains in Corsica. The first and smaller must have been a handsome chapel—its long nave is still in good preservation. It has a pulpit ornamented on the outside by six semicircular pillars of the Corinthian order. There are sculptures of very simple workmanship on the entablature of the side entrance. A mile farther on, lie the beautiful remains of a larger church, the nave of which is also still standing. It is called the Canonica, a cathedral church, consisting of three naves, with rows of ornamental pillars of the Doric order, and on each side a pulpit of the Gothic chapel-architecture. The central nave is 110 feet long and fifty broad. The façade is very much injured, and of the Pisan style. There are sculptures on the arch of the portal—griffins, dogs hunting a stag, and a lamb—of such wretched execution that it might belong to the eighteenth century. It is said that this Canonica was a Roman temple, which the Mahometans converted into a mosque, and the Christians in their turn into a church, after Hugo Colonna had won Mariana from the Moors. It is easy to see that the building has been at some past time restored, but it does not follow that it was originally Roman. On the contrary, it bears throughout the appearance of a cathedral church erected by the Pisans. Its forms are exquisitely pure, noble and simple, and of the finest symmetry; and this, along with the perfect purity of the Corsican marble with which the church is covered, certainly gives it all the appearance of a piece of ancient architecture.

When I entered the interior of the church, the community of worshippers whom I found there on their knees took me by surprise. They were thriving wild-trees, which stood in rows behind one another across the nave, and quietly flourished in this retired spot. A he-goat with a venerable beard stood right before the altar, and seemed to have forgotten his food and to be lost in religious contemplation. The herds were in the habit of pasturing their goats in the vicinity of the Canonica. I inquired about coins, but without success, although here, as well as in other parts of Corsica, a great many imperial ones have been found—with which, indeed, half the world is blessed. From this old Marian colony, which was planted at an earlier period than Aleria—and which must have been a colony of citizens, and not of soldiers like Sulla's—the only Roman road in Corsica ran by Aleria to Præsidium, and thence to Portus Favoni, terminating in Palæ situated on the strait now called Bonifazio. The island in those times was even more pathless than in the present day, and the Romans never penetrated into the interior of the hill-country.

Bastia is again visible in the distance, and the circle of my wanderings is completed. To the left lie the blood-drenched hills of Borgo, where many a battle has been fought, and where the Corsicans won their last victory over their French oppressors. In the distance shimmers the still, picturesque Stagno di Biguglia, and above stands Biguglia itself, once the head-quarters of the Genoese governors. The old castle now lies level with the ground. The last village before reaching Bastia is Furiani. Its gray keep is in ruins; the ivy and the white wood-vine cover its black walls with the most luxuriant green. Once more the eye turns from this spot to gaze on the lovely Goloebne, and far away towards the misty blue hills, which from out the interior of the island send a farewell greeting from their cloud-capt summits. A beautiful and healthy pilgrimage is now completed. And here the traveller stands still in pleasing retrospect, and thanks the good Powers who have been with him by the way. Yet it is difficult for the heart to tear itself away from this wonderful island. It has now become like a friend to me. The calm valleys, with their olive-groves; the enchanting gulfs; the fresh, breezy hills, with their fountains and their pine-covered summits; towns and villages, and their hospitable inhabitants,—much have they contributed to the mind and heart of the stranger, much that will not soon be forgotten.

Still once more, that Corsican reclining under the old olive-tree yonder, calls up before me the land and its people.

THE STRANGER

Wild mountaineer of Corsica, why laid
In idle dreams beneath the olive shade?
With gun in hand, supinely outstretch'd there,
Gazing half-conscious on the glitt'ring air?
Thy hungry child, in gloomy dwelling pent,
Weeps with his mother o'er her spinning bent;
They weep, their toil unceasing and untold,
Their chamber empty and their hearth-stone cold.
Yet thou can'st falcon-like perch idly there,
And scorn to cultivate that valley fair,
To sow the golden seed in fertile ground,
And train the clust'ring vine thy walls around.
Look, look below thee, where the sunny plain,

Stretches away to yon blue mountain-chain,
And slopes down smiling to the very main:
A Paradise where living streams abound;—
Yet there the rude Albatro chokes the ground,
The myrtle revels in its empire wide,
Tall ferns and heather flourish side by side,
And black-hair'd goats the summer-crop divide.
The Golo creeps along its swampy bed,
Whose tainted vapour thro' the air is spread,
Sapping the fisher's life from day to day,
While amply furnishing his finny prey.
The lonely wand'rer at each onward tread,
Sees heath-birds rise and wheel about his head;
Finds ruin'd fragments of a nobler past—
Traces of Rome, to dust decaying fast.
Up, then, thou Corsican, from dull repose,
Arise and seize thine axe, and deal thy blows;
Take spade and mattock, till the ground, and see
A golden-fruited garden smile on thee!

THE CORSICAN

Stranger, whose fathers I have taught to yield,—
Witness the graves on Calenzana's field—
Why break my rest? Two thousand years of fight
Have seen me struggle for my free-born right:
Have watch'd my desperate, unyielding stand,
'Gainst each invader of my native land.
Those Roman bands, whose traces still you see,
At Col di Tenda were compell'd to flee;
Hasdrubal's force I roll'd back to the strand,
Etruria's army scatter'd as the sand.
The Moor in quest of booty sought my bay,
He seized my children, bore my wife away,
Pillaged my fields, and wrapt my house in flame—
We met, we wrestled, and I overcame!
Again the battle-summons strikes my ear,

Hordes of fresh foes upon our isle appear
Lombards and Turks and Arragon's proud sons,—
Again my hand is raised—my life-blood runs!
Again I see my roof-tree overthrown;
I weep not—Liberty is still my own!
Then Genoa came—be curse on curse up-piled!
'Twas Italy herself that chain'd her child!
Mourn'st thou my country's aspect—waste tho' fair—
Harbours deserted, meadow-lands left bare,
Ivy-clothed buildings falling to decay?
Be sure that Genoa has there held sway!
Hear'st thou the mandoline by yonder sea,
Blend with the solemn Dirge's melody?
Seem the chords struck by sorrow and by pain?
Be sure that Genoa awoke the strain!
Echo the mountains to the rifle's crack,
Lies bathed in blood the victim in thy track;
Dost shudd'ring view the deed by vengeance wrought?
Be sure that Genoa the lesson taught!
Part of our wrongs thou'st heard—now hear with glee,
The grave of Genoa has been dug by me!
Ay, should'st thou e'er behold her, thou may'st boast,
"I've seen thy grave on Corsica's steep coast."
Fierce was the conflict—war unto the knife!
They sold to France our country and our life,
Like some mean chattel gold had power to buy,
And the world look'd on with an unmoved eye!
Hear me, thou Stranger! Ponte Nuovo's height
Frown'd on me wounded in inglorious fight
With French officials trampling on my right.
Weeping, I shrunk off like a wounded deer,
Far from the slaughter-field to hide me here;
Weary at length—by *such* strife weary made—
Grudge not my rest beneath the olive-shade.

THE STRANGER

No bitter word from me hast thou to bear:
I mourn thy doom—thy sense of wrong I share.
Thou ancient warrior, blood-stain'd, weary, wild,
Death and the furies claim thee for their child.
Take now thy rest, since thou alone hast kept
Watch through the slow night-hours when Europe slept;
For freedom striving, when the very word
'Midst other nations had been long unheard.
My heart has thrill'd at thy forefathers' fame—
Leap'd at the mention of Paoli's name—
Felt that such hero-memories could give
A life through which e'en words of mine might live.
What though the shadow of the tomb still broods,
While wand'ring here, o'er all my spirit's moods,
What though grief sadden, or though crime appal?
A hero-spirit breathes throughout it all!
Deep in my heart of hearts I bear away
A sad, sweet echo of thy mourning lay;
And as I sat beneath thy mountain's frown,
And saw thy torrents from the clouds leap down,
New senses woke within, new powers were rife,
Nature baptized me into fuller life!
Thy land of death has own'd me for her guest,
I bear her olive-branch upon my breast;
I turn me homeward with the symbol dear,
Gift of good spirits while I linger'd here.
Thou Corsican, farewell! in yonder bay
Swell my white sails, and summon me away.
May God reward thee for thy roof-tree's shade,
Thy fruits, thy wine, before the stranger laid.
Still may thine olives with their tribute shine,
No subtle blight invade thy clust'ring vine;
O'er golden fields the graceful maize wave high,
Only thy fierce Vendetta droop and die!
Ay, let at last thy sunbeam's burning flood

Dry on thy hero-soil thy hero-blood!
Brave be thy sons, as still thy fathers were—
Pure as thy mountain-streams, thy daughters fair,
High rise thy granite-rocks—a strong defence,
'Twixt foreign manners and their innocence!
Farewell, thou Isle! long live thy ancient fame;
Thy latest sons prove worthy of their name;
That ne'er a future guest have cause to say—
"Sampiero's life and death are but an idle tale to-day."

NOTE

I shall mention here, at the close of my book, the more important of the works which have been of service to me in its composition. The common experience, that every subject, however isolated its nature, drags a whole continent of literature after it, is in this case confirmed. I have already named all the historians—as Filippini, Peter of Corsica, Cambiaggi, Jacobi, Limperani, Renucci, Gregori, &c. I shall add to them, Robiquet's *Recherches Historiques et Statistiques sur la Corse*: Paris, 1835—a book rich in material, and to which I am indebted for valuable information. I have also used Niccolo Tommasco's *Lettere di Pasquale de Paoli*: Firenze, 1846; and the same author's *Canti Popolari Corsi*, in the collection of Corsican, Tuscan, and Greek popular songs. The dirges I have given are extracted from the *Saggio di Versi Italiani e di Canti Popolari Corsi*: Bastia, 1843. I owe the material of the Corsican stories—which are in no case fictitious—to a collection of such narratives by Renucci: Bastia, 1838; the treatment of the material is my own. The English Boswell's book—"Journal of a Tour in Corsica, with Memorabilia of Pasquale Paoli"—is worth reading, because the author was personally acquainted with the great Corsican, and noted down his conversations with him. I am, further, considerably indebted to Valery's *Voyages en Corse, à l'Ile d'Elbe et en Sardaigne*: Bruxelles, 1838. It is unnecessary to mention other works not specially relating to Corsica.

FOOTNOTES

[A] See Browning's Ballad of "The Red Piper of Hameln."

[B] Blackie's translation.

[C] Blackie.

[D] An analogous interjection in English is *tut! tut!* which is an expression of annoyance merely, and not of suffering; in Scotch *hootoot!* — *Tr.*

[E] Cowper's translation.

[F] A specimen of the Roman nænia has already been given, with a view to its being remembered in connexion with the present subject. I refer to Seneca's dirge on Claudius, which is, however, strictly speaking, parodistic.

[G] *Siliqua*, in Latin, the pod or husk of any leguminous plant. — *Tr.*

[H] Of the numerous dirges given by the author, a few of the more characteristic have been selected as likely to furnish an idea of the Corsican Vocero. — *Tr.*

[I] This wild song of vengeance, which is popular in Corsica, is said to have been composed by the mistress of a certain friar (!!) — a friend of Cæsario's. As the ballad predicts, the Paolo therein mentioned — a relative of the fallen men, afterwards avenged them; he then took to the bush, and after living some years as bandit, fell into the hands of justice.

[J] The irony is here so wild as to be at first hardly intelligible. Red is usually a gay and festive colour; when *she* is disposed to be gay — when her absorbing grief leaves her "leisure for laughing," as she says in the original, it will be when she can wear a mandile dyed in her father's blood — that is, never. By the bold figure in the concluding lines of the vocero, she intimates at once the victim's innocence and the cruel circumstances of his death.—*Tr.*

[K] Quarter of the city beyond the Tiber.—*Tr.*

[L] An allusion to the blue flower in the *Henrich von Ofterdingen* of Novalis—*Tr.*

[M] This is incorrect.

[N] An allusion to the fact that Napoleon's wish to be buried on the banks of the Seine was not complied with.—*Tr.*

[O] The author probably here refers to two personal friends.—*Tr.*